STARSTRUCK

ALSO BY CHRISTOPHER McDOUGALL

Born to Run: A Hidden Tribe, Superathletes, and the Greatest Race the World Has Never Seen

Natural Born Heroes: Mastering the Lost Secrets of Strength and Endurance

Running with Sherman: How a Rescue Donkey Inspired a Rag-tag Gang of Runners to Enter the Craziest Race in America

Born to Run 2: The Ultimate Training Guide

STARSTRUCK

A Journalist's Pursuit of a Fugitive Pop Star, Her Diabolical Maestro, and Their Teenage Sex Cult

CHRISTOPHER McDOUGALL

VINTAGE BOOKS
A Division of Penguin Random House LLC
New York

A VINTAGE BOOKS ORIGINAL 2026

Some of the events described in this book pertaining to Gloria Trevi and Sergio Andrade were previously reported in Christopher McDougall's *Girl Trouble. Starstruck* is an entirely new work that incorporates recent events since that publication and new reporting.

Published by Vintage Books, a division of Penguin Random House LLC, 1745 Broadway, New York, NY 10019.

Vintage and colophon are registered trademarks of Penguin Random House LLC.

LCCN 2025045703

Vintage Books Trade Paperback ISBN: 979-8-217-00828-5
eBook ISBN: 979-8-217-00829-2

Author photograph © Luis Escobar
Book design by Christopher M. Zucker

penguinrandomhouse.com | vintagebooks.com

Printed in the United States of America
1st Printing

The authorized representative in the EU for product safety and compliance is Penguin Random House Ireland, Morrison Chambers, 32 Nassau Street, Dublin D02 YH68, Ireland, https://eu-contact.penguin.ie.

To Colleen and John Marsini
Who stepped right up when this book first needed a champion

A WORD BEFORE BEGINNING . . .

One mistake kept bringing me back.

I never stopped wondering about that crucial blunder, the same one that Sergio Andrade and Gloria Trevi must have stewed over each day as they sat in their cells, staring through the bars and realizing that if it wasn't for that single slip—if Sergio hadn't lost his nerve for a beat when it mattered most—they'd probably still be on the outside, living a life of wealth and glamour and sexual excess, free to continue luring dozens of young women into a criminal enterprise. Sergio was such a mastermind that he was able to operate right out in public—literally *on a world stage*—and get away with his crimes for years. He was ahead of his time, perfecting a model of coercion and mental manipulation that could later have been a playbook for abusers like Harvey Weinstein, Jeffrey Epstein, R. Kelly, and Sean Combs.

But awful as those men are, Sergio is in a class of his own. When he began to feel heat from investigators, he didn't lawyer up, dial back, or plead out. Instead, he went international. He gathered his victims and took them with him on the run, sparking a worldwide cat-and-mouse chase as he dodged the police while searching for a safe place to re-establish his sexual abuse kingdom.

That's one reason this story has a hold on me: because Sergio nearly pulled it off. Nothing can teach us more about how to prevent a next time than a near miss the last time. If we're going to stop future Sergios before they get started, we have to get inside the mind of the one we've already captured. And that's the second reason I've stayed with the story so long: because criminal defendants don't talk. That's doubly true for sex offenders, who face an even more immediate risk from their fellow prisoners than from the justice system. But for some reason, Gloria and Sergio opened up to me. I got into their prison lives—and their heads—in a way I never expected.

Thanks to an early tip and some lucky breaks, I was also able to begin reporting on the manhunt before most people even knew it had begun. I spent weeks at a time in Mexico tracking down the families of Sergio's victims, and it was during one of those trips that I became curious about a peculiar photo I saw on a restaurant wall in Chihuahua. It seemed to be an elderly man wearing a dress and sandals, running down a canyon trail. Later that day I spotted a nearly identical picture in a local magazine, this time explaining that the runner was a fifty-five-year-old Tarahumara Indian who'd beaten all challengers in a 100-mile footrace through the Colorado Rockies. Right off the bat, I knew that was wrong. There was no way some random old guy could run four back-to-back marathons in a pair of homemade sandals, let alone defeat America's top ultra athletes. *No way*—or so I thought, until I ventured to the depths of Mexico's Copper Canyons to see for myself. That remarkable adventure catapulted me on a journey that would last more than four years as my book about the experience—*Born to Run*—became a global phenomenon.

But as long as Sergio and Gloria were out there, they were

still on my mind. I published one account of their saga before *Born to Run* even came out, but the story continued to take on fresh twists. I wanted to learn more, dig deeper, and understand it better, so I stuck with the case as it evolved over the years, gathering new information and tracking fresh developments.

I am grateful that so many people who were dealing with their own confusion and fears were gracious enough to share their time, personal experiences, and invaluable background information from the very beginning. I also relied on court records, transcripts, print articles, television and broadcast interviews, and contemporaneous news stories, as well as written and verbal accounts by the individual clan members. Though there may be different opinions about some of the events, I cross-referenced as many versions as possible and re-created the scenes based on the best information I uncovered.

In some instances, the dialogue as presented comes directly from the subjects. In others, it is from people who were present at the moment or briefed afterward. I've also re-created some dialogue based on memory or a plausible reconstruction. It should not be assumed that all the people quoted spoke directly to me. Dialogue in quotation marks indicates passages believed to be reasonably verbatim. Dialogue without marks indicates it is a best-faith approximation based on credible accounts.

With that said, brace yourself. It only gets crazy from here.

STARSTRUCK

1

THE FUGITIVE

The prison warden acted like I wasn't there, keeping his gaze fixed instead on the documents on his desk. That was fine by me. The longer he took to review my appeal, I figured, the better the odds he'd finally buzz open that big steel door and let me through.

Eventually, he glanced up and met my eyes.

"No," he said.

"Respectfully!" The lawyer seated beside me popped to his feet. "Respectfully, sir! Allow me to bring one thing to your attention." The lawyer lunged toward the warden's desk before catching himself and pausing. "May I?" he asked, gesturing toward the scattered papers.

"I've read it all," said the warden. "Everything you sent me. Everything in the arrest file. Everything in the guards' reports."

"Of course!" the lawyer agreed. "Of course you did." He splayed out five fingers of his right hand and the meaty thumb of his left. "But I would like to draw your special attention to six words. Just six words."

It felt desperate, but I was intrigued to see what he had up his sleeve. So was the warden. He nodded, and the two of us leaned closer to the desk as the lawyer began rooting through the papers. He selected a single page and placed it dead center. It was a newspaper clipping.

He jabbed a finger at the logo. "One, two, three, four," he counted:

The New York Times

He skimmed quickly, then forked two fingers above a pair of words in the middle of the page:

"Five, six." He read them out loud:

"Gangster sperm."

I knew exactly the phrase he meant, because I'm the one who wrote it. What I couldn't figure out was why he'd wave it under the nose of the guy who would hate it the most.

For the past year, I'd been on assignment for *The New York Times* to see if I could track down Gloria Trevi, the Mexican superstar being hunted by law enforcement around the world. In the space of a single weekend, Gloria had transformed from a rock sensation who'd sold more than 20 million records worldwide into a fugitive at the center of an international dragnet with her face plastered on Interpol WANTED posters.

The whole saga was bizarre and nearly impossible to believe. In the late '90s dark whispers began to spread that Gloria, who'd fashioned her image as a champion of girl power, was actually a sexual predator who used her fame to entice young women into a brainwashing obedience cult. Wild stories swirled about her involvement in devil worship, torture, kidnapping, and the mysterious disappearance of her own infant daughter.

The rumors were outlandish, of course. Except . . .

Where was she?

When police showed up at her home to investigate, Gloria

was gone. Also missing was Sergio Andrade—her mysterious, domineering manager known as "Mr. Midas"—and her entire entourage of teenage girls. Somehow, one of the most famous performers in Latin America had vanished from the planet along with a dozen of her followers.

For more than a year, Gloria and her band-on-the-run were both nowhere to be seen and everywhere you looked. Sightings poured in from people who swore they'd seen the fugitives on a beach in Miami . . . in a store in Los Angeles . . . at a border crossing in El Paso . . . and in the mountains of Argentina, the backstreets of Madrid, and a commune in Indonesia. Despite a manhunt that spanned dozens of countries, however, none of the leads ever panned out.

Until, one morning in January 2000, a policeman in Brazil became suspicious when two women wearing sunglasses and baseball caps gave him nervous glances and hurried into a store. He questioned them, then demanded their IDs. They led him to a shabby apartment and asked him to wait outside while they ducked in for their passports. He poked his head inside for a look. The room was dark, but in the gloom, he spotted four teenage girls and mounds of clothing and musical equipment.

A pudgy man with stubbly jowls emerged from a back room and tried to take charge. "I can answer any questions you have," he offered, speaking Portuguese in a thick Mexican accent, but by then, the cop was already on his radio calling for backup. Fifteen minutes later, the apartment door opened and the fabulously rich, multi-platinum, once-glamorous "Mexican Madonna" was led out in handcuffs and an old gray T-shirt.

And that's when things *really* got weird.

While Gloria and her crew were being held in Brazil, back in Mexico former members of the clan were emerging with horrifying stories. Gloria's own cousin said Sergio raped her while Gloria stood in the doorway and watched. Others said that when the police were closing in, the clan abandoned a newborn baby in a Spanish church to escape. Several of the girls even swore that Sergio forced them to secretly bury a dead infant. "When I was a nine-year-old girl going to see my favorite music star," one backup singer declared, "I never thought that one day I'd be helping her hide a corpse."

From behind bars, Gloria dismissed the girls as "lying little nobodies." But even as the superstar was denying those crimes, another was unfolding—this time, right inside the walls of the prison hospital I was trying to enter.

2

THE WIZARD

I first got on Gloria and Sergio's trail shortly after returning from Africa, where I'd been searching for a Philadelphia file clerk who had disappeared from his job only to pop up, months later, deep in the jungle as one of the leaders of a rebel band fighting to overthrow Congo's dictator.

"The Clerk Who Would Be King" was one of the strangest stories I'd ever covered and among the toughest to report. I had to track this guy from an apartment in North Philadelphia halfway around the planet and into a part of Africa known as the "Heart of Darkness." I finally located him and got him to tell me his bizarre tale. The second he was done I thanked him, snapped my notebook shut, and headed for the first flight outta there before the country erupted into war again. When I got home and began catching up with the rest of the world, a message was waiting for me from my former college girlfriend, now a reporter in Mexico:

You see Trevi out there? Sort of kidding. Sort of not.

I called her right away. "Is that still going on?" I asked.

"Huge," she replied. "Interpol has a worldwide arrest warrant out for them: *Detain on Sight.*" I heard keys tapping on the other end of the line, and then she said, "Check your email."

I opened it up, and there they were: Gloria and Sergio, staring out from a police advisory. It seemed impossible, like turning on the TV and seeing Jay-Z and Beyoncé featured as fugitives on *America's Most Wanted.* I was stunned to discover that the story was not only alive but wilder than ever. It had escalated into a vanishing act so bizarre that a seasoned Latin America correspondent was asking, at least half seriously, if I'd picked up on any Gloria Trevi sightings in the African outback.

After we got off the phone, I reached out to an El Paso detective I'd met on assignment years ago and he brought me up to speed on the search along the border. "Forget the criminal case," he said. "Why isn't there more urgency to find out if they're even alive? You know how a lot of these cults turn out—in a pile of bodies. It's crazy that for months it wasn't even a priority to check on the safety of those girls. They've been gone so long now, we don't know where to start looking."

That was all I needed to hear. I called an editor I knew at *The New York Times Magazine* and made my pitch: If I could run to earth a missing file clerk in Congo, how hard could finding an attention-hungry celebrity be? The police were hampered by all kinds of jurisdictional restrictions, I argued, but none of that applied to me. I could go anywhere and follow any lead without waiting for anyone's permission. It wouldn't be easy, but if I started right away, I could be in position when the net began to close around them.

One hour later, I was part of the hunt.

"Gangster sperm!" the lawyer repeated.

"I'm aware of the story," the warden said drily, as he pivoted his gaze toward me. "And the source."

That wasn't exactly true. Yes, I'd broken the gangster-sperm story for *The New York Times*. But technically, the source was a confidential police file I'd been given by a contact in Brazil. My scoop spread like crazy, making headlines around the world and forcing Brazilian law enforcement into the humiliating position of grimly repeating "We can neither confirm nor deny." They couldn't deny the story, of course, because one key fact was impossible to hide and growing bigger by the day:

Gloria was pregnant.

Call it a mystery, call it a miracle, but somehow the Mexican Madonna had lived up to her nickname by conceiving a baby behind bars despite being locked for months inside the all-female wing of a maximum security prison.

Gloria refused to reveal the father. Her lawyers implied she'd been raped. Prison guards were swiftly lined up for questioning, but after interrogations and lie detector tests, all of them reportedly were cleared of suspicion. Secretly, investigators were now pursuing a new angle—and that's what made my story so explosive. Gloria, they surmised, had artificially inseminated herself with semen smuggled to her from another prisoner, using a homemade syringe fashioned from a ballpoint pen.

"See? That's what they're saying about Brazil on the front page of the most important newspaper in the world," the lawyer said.

"That's what *he* is saying." The warden tried to fix me with an icy glare, but the dark circles of exhaustion under his eyes just made him look sad. "And that is why I can't allow him access to interview Miss Trevi."

"No," the lawyer said. "That's exactly why you should."

Once again, the warden and I were united in shared confusion. How exactly does letting a writer for *The New York Times* into your prison result in fewer articles for *The New York Times* about your prison? But I knew by now that if anyone was capable of pulling this off, it was attorney Geraldo Magela. I was amazed he'd gotten us this far. I was amazed he was even trying. After all, he wasn't my lawyer.

He was Gloria's.

Geraldo had a reputation as a legal wizard, a guy with a knack for conjuring magical exits from impossible predicaments—or at least, that's what he told me when I first called him late one Sunday on his personal cell in Rio de Janeiro. "How'd you get this number?" he demanded.

I debated how to answer. I wasn't going to lie and he wouldn't like the truth. The fact is, I knew that on Sunday nights the Associated Press offices in foreign countries are staffed by rookies. There's almost never any breaking news on weekends but a million soccer league scores to upload, so new hires always get that grunt-work shift. I waited till about 10 p.m. one Sunday, then called the Rio bureau and told the guy who answered that I was from AP Lisbon (not *with*, so technically true), and needed the personal number for Gloria Trevi's lead attorney, stat. I figured the rookie reporter would be so overworked and frazzled, he'd rather make a senior correspondent happy than ask anyone if he was allowed to.

Minutes later, the entire Gloria file popped up in my inbox.

I didn't know how much of this to tell Geraldo, but before I could open my mouth, he cut me off. "You know what? Good for you," he said. "You have your methods, I have mine. Let's leave it at that."

Geraldo was chatty and charming, and more than happy to share anything about himself but nothing about his imprisoned pop star client. I pushed my credentials—I'm fluent in Spanish and Portuguese after years as a war correspondent for the Associated Press and I write for a magazine with a huge international audience—but Geraldo was a steel fortress.

"We're hoping Brazil will set her free instead of sending her to Mexico in chains," he explained. "So until that is resolved, she's not saying a word."

I thought that was the end of the road. But soon after I published my story about the Gangster Sperm investigation, Geraldo called me out of the blue. It was nearly ten at night, and I wouldn't have picked up if I hadn't recognized the Rio de Janeiro area code on my cell phone.

"Gloria's life is in danger," Geraldo blurted.

Brazilian law enforcement was so scandalized by the rumors surrounding her pregnancy, he claimed, that they'd do anything to make the whole thing disappear. As a safeguard against any "accidents," Geraldo decided it was time to get her story out in the open. I could have the exclusive, but I had to get to Brazil right away. Gloria was due to give birth soon, and she'd just been transferred to a secure hospital ward. No Brazilian prison would ever let a reporter inside its walls, but maybe the hospital would.

"This is our only chance," Geraldo urged.

Buuuuutttt . . . there was a hitch. The prison hospital was deep inland in the hard-to-reach city of Brasilia, and in five days, the whole country would shut down for a full week during the massive street festivals of Carnaval. By the time government offices reopened, Gloria might already have delivered her baby and been returned to prison, or—as Geraldo put it—"been eliminated as a problem."

As soon as I hung up with Geraldo, I started dialing. It was Monday night. Carnaval would begin on Friday. That gave me two days, max, to plane, train, and automobile all 4,230 miles to Brasilia from our farm in Peach Bottom, Pennsylvania. Booking a flight would be rough, I knew, since they'd all be crammed with partiers heading to Rio. This was going to be a nail-biter.

After trying every airline that services Brazil, the best I could manage was standby on a flight leaving at 7 p.m. the next evening out of New York. The sooner I got to the airport the higher I'd be on the waiting list, so I hastily packed a bag, left a message for my editor at *The New York Times*, and set off before dawn on the thirty-mile drive to catch the first train to Manhattan. By 1 p.m., I had made it to JFK airport and hunkered down for six hours of suspense.

Just after five o'clock, I heard my name called. I leaped to my feet and hurried to the United desk.

"Hmmm," the agent said, flipping through my passport. "You've got a *lot* of stamps in here. I'm having trouble finding your visa."

"That's okay," I replied. "I'll get one in the airport when I arrive."

She stopped searching the pages and looked up at me. "You know it doesn't work that way, right?"

"No, I'm sure it does." I was about to list the places where I'd gotten visas on arrival—Angola, Kenya, El Salvador, Mozambique, Burundi, Congo, Uganda—but a sickening realization dawned on me before I opened my mouth. I'd traveled to all those countries on reporting assignments when they were in the midst of extreme upheaval or outright war. In fact, I don't think I'd traveled anywhere in the past seven or eight years that wasn't either visa-free or under fire.

"Besides," the agent continued, "you don't have room left in your passport. The pages are all full."

I continued pleading my case—*I need this for work! I'll go straight to the embassy in Rio for a new passport! And a visa!*—but the agent kept waving forward the people behind me and issuing them the last available seats. "We can put you back on standby for tomorrow night's flight," she offered. "But first you have to sort out your visa and passport."

I left the airport and taxied to a friend's apartment in Manhattan. I had a make-or-break decision and decided on a gamble. There was no way I'd ever navigate the jam-packed New York City passport office for fresh pages in time to reach the Brazilian consulate before it closed at noon, so my only hope was to persuade them to squeeze the visa onto the corner of a page that was nearly full. The next morning, I was outside the consulate at 7 a.m., two hours before opening. Already, a line of Carnaval travelers was stretching down the block. When I finally reached the window, I had my argument rehearsed and ready. They needed to give me a visa, even if it meant overlapping on a couple of other passport stamps, because I wasn't just some tourist: I was a credentialed journalist covering a breaking story.

"Oh, well, that's different," the consulate staffer agreed. "In that case, you'll need a temporary work visa, which requires a letter from your employer to our Department of State. And besides," he added, "you don't have enough space in your passport. We need a completely blank page."

10:27 a.m. I bolted out of the consulate and taxied across town to the Manhattan passport office, the largest and busiest in the country. When I entered, the waiting room looked like a giant gymnasium after a natural disaster, with throngs of dispirited people huddled on seats and long lines that never seemed to move. No way I'd even reach a window before closing.

I took a deep breath and walked all the way across the room, ignoring the hundreds of eyes watching me pass. "Excuse me," I said to the guy at the front of a line I'd chosen at random. I handed my passport through to the clerk. "Gabe said to add new pages to this one."

"Gabe?"

"Yeah, that's what he said. Extra pages. Right away."

The clerk flipped through my passport. "Who'd you say? Gabe?"

"That's right."

"Let me check."

I leaned an elbow on the counter, acting like I nine-to-fived there every day, wondering what the penalty was for Fabricating a Fake Federal Officer Named Gabe. Criminal charges? Passport confiscation? Or just a *get-your-lyin'-ass-outta-here*? Five minutes later, I had my answer.

"Here you go," the clerk said, handing back my newly thickened passport. Gabe, wherever and whoever he was, had just done me a massive favor. I ran out to the street, flagged a cab, and sped back to the Brazilian consulate. Thirty-seven minutes to go. The lines were still crazy long, but I couldn't even attempt to cut this time because there were only two clerks and one of them now knew I was a journalist. No Gabe could help me now. I got to the end of the second line and inched along, angling my body away from the clerk who could out me.

At 11:57, I was the last to reach the window. The clerk skimmed my paperwork. "Tourist?" he asked.

"Yes, sir." I half whispered, afraid the other clerk might recognize my voice.

"Can I see your airline ticket?"

"I'm standby."

"So you have no proof of your return flight?"

"Well . . ." I thought desperately. "Not *proof* proof, but you can see from my passport that I travel a lot. For pleasure! I'm not trying to relocate anywhere. Just Carnaval and then it's right back home."

He glanced at his watch. "You might have to—" He mumbled something I couldn't catch, clearly done with all of us last-minute party planners cutting into his lunch hour so we could dance in Rio while he was stuck in an office. I took a seat next to a raucous gang of vacationers, trying to blend in and remain invisible. It didn't matter because one by one, travelers were called to collect their passports and go, leaving me exposed.

Suddenly, a very large security guard materialized by my side. I hadn't seen him approach because I'd kept my face toward the wall. "Mr. McDougall?" he said. I hesitated, wondering whether the smart move was just to deny it and get out of there before I found myself calling a lawyer from a holding cell for lying on sworn travel documents. The security guard pointed toward the window, where the clerk was waving my passport.

"*Bom viagem*," he called. "Enjoy your trip."

Even though it was nearly 1 p.m. and I hadn't eaten all day, I headed straight for the subway and returned to JFK to get back on the standby list. Six hours later, I was taking off for Brazil, never so happy in my life to be crammed into a middle seat in the back of a plane for a twelve-hour fight. I made it to Brasilia with twenty-four hours to spare, but despite everything it took to get there, I still had one dealbreaker demand:

"The interview has to be just me and Gloria," I told Geraldo. "I can't have you in the room massaging her answers. Even if you keep quiet, it's just not acceptable to have you stage-managing the conversation."

Surprisingly, Geraldo agreed. But he did have a condition of his own. "When we get to the hospital, don't tell anyone you speak Portuguese," he said. "The warden and I both speak English. Keep your ears open and your Portuguese to yourself."

It was a weird request but an easy one to grant. Only later, when things got crazy, would I discover what Geraldo was up to.

"I can't keep having these wild stories flying around about Miss Trevi," the warden was telling us, pushing aside all the documents Geraldo had submitted on my behalf as a sign it was time for us to exit his office. "Maybe we can revisit this after the situation quiets down."

"You'll get slaughtered that way," Geraldo retorted. "How do you put out a fire? Do you feed it one log at a time? Or do you dump on all the logs and let it blaze out for good? Remember what the Bible tells us: *When the wood runs out, the fire dies.*"

Geraldo turned to me. "Proverbs. You can look it up."

To the warden he said, "One last article. We let *The New York Times* weigh in with one big story, then the wood is gone and the rumors die out."

The warden wasn't buying it. He and Geraldo were still arguing when three men in black uniforms with no insignia appeared in the door. One flipped open a federal government ID, then squared his hands on his hips, pushing back his jacket to reveal the pistol holstered on his waist. He barely glanced at me and Geraldo and instead focused all his bristling intensity on the warden.

"We need an extraction of amniotic fluid from Trevi," the Man in Black said. "Don't tell her what it's for. Just get it and give it to us. We need verifiable DNA on the child before it's born."

"*Ay ya!*" Geraldo leaped to his feet again. "Ay ya! Absolutely not! That's unconstitutional! It's an invasion of her privacy."

"You want an invasion?" the officer said. I don't know if he thought Geraldo and I were hospital staff, but he couldn't care less. "I've got a van full of men outside. We'll take this place by force if we have to."

Cell phones appeared all around. Geraldo had several Supreme Court justices on his speed dial. The warden, shaken, called the health minister who oversaw the prison medical unit. I couldn't hear who the Man in Black was talking to because he kept his hand cupped around his mouth.

"Ha!" Geraldo yelled. He handed his phone to the Man in Black. He listened for a moment, grunted a reply, then slapped the phone back into Geraldo's hand and led his two partners out.

The court had granted a stay.

"*Oh! Deus! Meu!*" Geraldo moaned. "Oh. My. God!"

The warden quietly finished his own call, then hung up and slumped back in his chair. He raised both hands in a gesture of surrender. "Okay," he told Geraldo in Portuguese. "We don't need any more scenes while this reporter is around. Go on in, and let's get this over with."

To me, the warden gave a weary smile. He switched back to English. "Enjoy your visit," he said. "Miss Trevi is very—"

He paused, reflecting. "You'll see."

3

THE MURDER CLUB THEORY

"Brace yourself," Geraldo warned me, as we were buzzed through the steel doors into the hospital ward. "I honestly don't know how she's survived this long."

Geraldo hadn't been able to see his famous client in person since she was transferred out of the general prison population, but from their phone calls, he could tell she was in rough shape. "It's appalling," he complained. "They put Mexico's most famous entertainer in the same jail as two of the most dangerous criminals in Brazil. When it comes to incarceration, Brazil unfortunately lives up to its reputation as a Third World country."

Gloria had a target on her back from the moment she was locked up, he added. Not because of her stardom: because of the moms. When she was first being led to her cell, a prisoner down the cellblock shouted, "I HEARD YOU MOLESTED MORE THAN A HUNDRED LITTLE GIRLS. YOU BETTER WATCH OUT. A LOT OF US ARE MOTHERS!" For her own safety, Gloria had to be held in protective custody for the first few weeks with a guard outside her cell and a light constantly burning overhead. When she was moved to another wing, her life only got worse.

"She's endured rats, bedbugs, prison riots . . ." Geraldo ticked the horrors off on his fingers, raising them one at a time as if keeping score. ". . . a cell fire, death threats, and incarceration with an accused murderer. She's spent twenty-three hours a day in a cement cell with a hole in the floor for a toilet and only a cold-water spigot for bathing."

"And sexual assault," I added.

Geraldo paused, his seven splayed fingers still in the air.

"That's the cause of her pregnancy, right?" I asked. Gloria hadn't gone public yet with her secret, but wasn't that why I was there? It seemed strange that Geraldo was still being cagey about it after he'd asked me to travel five thousand miles on twenty-four hours' notice for exactly that reason.

Geraldo curled his fingers back into his fists and lowered his hands. He glanced around uncomfortably, then began walking again. "This isn't the place for that conversation," he muttered over his shoulder.

"Wait," I insisted, hurrying after him. "Just explain this. Why is Gloria still here?"

For more than two years, Gloria and Sergio had battled desperately to remain in Brazil, using one legal maneuver after another to avoid extradition back to Mexico. "She can afford the best lawyers in the world. If it's so terrible here, why doesn't she go home and face the charges? She could be free by now."

Geraldo came to a halt and turned to look me in the eyes. "The charges?" he said. "You think she's worried about the charges?"

Down the hall, two police officers were guarding a door. Geraldo jerked his head toward them, signaling me to keep my voice down. "Everyone says Gloria was running from the law," he whispered. "She was running for her life. Hers, and all those other girls. That's the real secret. She didn't hurt those girls. She saved them."

"Saved them from who . . . Sergio?" I couldn't see how that made any sense, since Sergio was with them the entire time.

"Think," Geraldo urged. "Do you know how many women have been killed in Mexico over the past few years? Hundreds. Do you know how many of the killers have been caught?" He pinched together the tips of his thumb and forefinger in a big 0.

"Zero. Nobody."

That was true. The Juarez Girl Murders remain one of the world's most mysterious—and horrific—open cases. Since the early 1990s, more than five hundred young women have suddenly vanished from the northern Mexican borderlands, only to be found weeks or months later buried in the desert. Making the murders especially baffling are two factors: sunlight, and sheer numbers. Many of the girls were grabbed right off the streets in broad daylight, meaning someone had to have seen *something* . . . yet there's been almost no credible eyewitness testimony.

Second: How could any solo serial killer attack so often? And without ever tripping up, not even once? That's why some detectives are convinced the Juarez Girl Murders have to be the work of a gang, a syndicate of sociopaths working together as a team. The Murder Club theory has its own problem, of course, because the only thing harder to cover up than a crime is a conspiracy. The more people involved, the more likely it is that one of them will blurt the wrong thing to the wrong person or be spotted returning home some night with telltale blood and scratch marks.

But what did any of this have to do with a superstar pop singer?

Yes, many of the girls in Gloria's entourage were around the same age as the murder victims, and several were from nearby hometowns. And yes, Sergio did have a training academy in Chihuahua, not far from the killers' hunting ground. Of course, there was also the matter of Sergio's brother but—

Wait. Sergio's brother! In a flash, I got it.

"Are you saying Sergio's brother is involved in this stuff?"

"What I'm saying is this. Either Mexico has the smartest murderers in the world or—" Geraldo grabbed my arm and leaned close to my ear, lowering his voice. "Or the most protected. The most connected."

I could tell where Geraldo was going with this. The Murder Club theory only makes sense if the killers have some kind of high-level protection. Otherwise, what explains their supernatural ability to elude detection? That's why some investigators believe the killings are the work of religious vigilantes determined to wipe out women they believe are immoral. Mexico's most powerful and corrupt political party—the PRI (Partido Revolucionario Institucional)—is also the most Catholic.

And who's a longtime senator and major PRI powerbroker? Sergio's older brother, Eduardo Andrade Sánchez.

"Now ask me again why Sergio and Gloria won't go back to Mexico," Geraldo said. "They're not in danger for what they did. They're in danger for what they *know*. They ran for their lives and took those young women with them. The world is going to discover that Gloria Trevi isn't a predator. She's a hero."

Before I could point out that Sergio's brother had never been connected to even a hint of any wrongdoing, Geraldo jerked his head again toward the two police officers at Gloria's door. "She's right in there," he said. "Hear it from her own mouth. Then tell me you don't believe her."

4

THE DOPE

The craziest thing about that story, I thought as I left Geraldo and approached the two police officers guarding Gloria's door, is that it's not so crazy.

Geraldo did have some facts on his side, undeniably. But he was also a lawyer, a very good one, a self-described "wizard" with a knack for helping his clients out of impossible situations, and if there was ever a legal equivalent of pulling a rabbit out of a hat, it would be convincing the world that Gloria Trevi wasn't a supervillain but a superhero, a celebrity who rocked stadiums and posed for pinup calendars by day but led a secret second life as the selfless savior of young women being hunted by madmen in the northern Mexican badlands.

My first doubt wasn't about Gloria, though. It was about the villains. As in, who are they? Who, exactly, is out to get her?

The best place to hear about such master criminals, of course, was exactly where I was heading. If you're in the market for a good conspiracy theory, visit a prison. Nearly every criminal I've interviewed over the years could explain, logically and persuasively, exactly how they got caught up in something that totally wasn't their fault. When you're behind bars, you have a lot of time to take apart the facts of your case and reassemble them in a whole new narrative, gently shifting around the pieces of the puzzle until suddenly an entirely new picture emerges—one with you in the center as an innocent victim surrounded by dark forces conspiring to bring you down.

"But it's not your job to be skeptical," I reminded myself as I reached Gloria's door. "It's your job to be dumb."

My tough-as-nails bureau chief in Madrid always used to say that, and it's the best journalism advice I've ever gotten. You're not a professional skeptic, she'd explain; you're a professional dope. The best way to get to the truth of a story is to start by understanding nothing about it. Don't come in armed for bear with both barrels loaded with doubts. Instead, talk to everyone you can and ask them to share everything they know. Keep circling back, drilling down a little deeper each time until their version of the story either holds up or falls apart.

Already that morning, being the dumbest guy in the room had paid off big-time. When the Men in Black burst into the warden's office, everyone ignored the guy on the sofa who kept his mouth shut and his face blank. Nobody paid me a bit of attention as the whole weird showdown played out in front of my eyes.

But compared to Gloria, those guys were amateurs. Gloria had been interviewed more often, and way more aggressively, than any Latin star of her generation. Mexican presidents got less press and easier grillings than Gloria. Playing it clueless with a showbiz veteran like her, I realized, was a gamble that could blow up in my face. If she suspected I was playing games, she could shut herself down and ice me out.

"*A senhora* Trevi?" I said to the two guards, holding up my passport and a bright red AP press pass that looked impressive if you didn't notice it had expired five years ago.

One of the guards led me to a side room. He gestured toward my pockets, which I emptied on a table. I'd been warned that absolutely no electronics were allowed—no phone, no recorder, no cameras—so all I had was a notebook and three pens. The guard examined each page of the notebook, then wanded both covers with a metal detector. He pried the ink straws out of the ballpoint pens and held them up to the overhead light. Then it was on to me: a full pat-down, fingers through my hair, shoes and socks off and toes spread, every inch of clothing squeezed and probed. Maybe Gloria had gotten her hands on smuggled gangster sperm or maybe not, but clearly, these guards were taking no chances of anything like that ever happening again.

Wow, I thought. *If this is how they treat visitors, they must really put prisoners through the wringer.* I could only imagine how they handled a problem case like Gloria. No wonder Geraldo told me to brace myself.

The guard unlocked Gloria's door. I sucked in a breath, steadying myself, determined not to let the once-glamorous beauty see any shock or pity in my eyes at the sight of her transformation after two brutal years behind bars. But nothing could have prepared me for what I saw.

Gloria looked magnificent.

"Well, hello!" she trilled in heavily accented English, scooching higher in her hospital bed and giving me a girlish little wave.

Gloria's eyes were lightly shadowed, her lips were glossed, and the trademark mane that inspired both her No. 1 hit single and her box-office smash movie *Pelo Suelto* (Wild Hair) was fanned forward over her shoulder, the gold strands glimmering in the overhead lights. Except possibly for her very pregnant belly, Gloria could have been ready at any moment to swing her legs out of bed and pose for one of her million-selling pinup calendars.

I was so stunned, I didn't know what to say. I glanced around the room, buying time while I gathered my thoughts. At her feet was a brand-new crib filled with stuffed animals and a photo book titled *Querida Mamãe: Obrigada por Tudo* (Dear Mommy: Thanks for Everything). Her two bedside tables were covered in fresh red roses and Virgin Mary prayer cards. My eyes landed on a big framed photo squeezed between the flowers, tilted just so, like a wedding portrait.

"Who's that?" I asked.

In the photo, Gloria and another woman are wearing prison-issue denim shirts knotted above their navels. The woman has a flirty pout and is running her hands through her long black curls, while Gloria is cozying up against a tall, handsome man, her lips puckering toward the camera in a kiss.

"The man?" Gloria replied. "He's a prison guard. The woman is Mary Raquenel."

María Raquenel Portillo—aka Mary Boquitas, Gloria's bandmate for years and the former wife of Sergio Andrade, whom she secretly married at age fifteen. I kept staring at the photo, trying to make sense of it all. Instead of two women in fear for their lives from vengeful Brazilian prison guards, they look like three best friends out on a bar crawl.

"So," Gloria said, calling my attention back to her. "What would you like to know about me?"

I froze for a beat, still fighting to get my bearings. I felt like I'd wandered on to a movie set and couldn't tell what role Gloria was playing. Was she a brave victim determined to look upbeat? Or was she an icy-cool bandit who could still pull the puppet strings and manipulate everyone around her, even in a notorious hellhole?

I didn't know where to start, so I decided to keep it simple.

"How old are you?" I asked.

"I am thirty-two years old," she said. She smiled brightly. "I will be thirty-three next week. My birthday!"

"That's not what your passport says."

She blinked once, twice, the smile frozen on her face.

"That's a confusion," Gloria finally said. "I lost my original passport and in the copy, they made a mistake with my age."

I paused, my pen hovering over my notebook. Because even this, the very first fact of Gloria Trevi's life, is a mystery.

5

DANCE MOM

I'd walked into Gloria's room with two rare advantages. And from the flash in her eyes when I asked my first question, I could tell she knew it.

Number 1 was time. Lots and lots of luxurious time. I'd begun my career as a foreign correspondent in Portugal, which meant I was responsible around the clock for everything that happened between the Atlantic Ocean and the Spanish border. My coverage area also included the former Portuguese colonies in southern Africa, which wasn't a problem while things were humming along quietly in Cabo Verde, Mozambique, and São Tomé e Príncipe, but every few months life got berserkers whenever a pipeline exploded in Angola or its long-simmering civil war re-ignited. I'd drop everything and fly off on the next flight, staying up all night on the red-eye to read whatever aid-agency reports and UN dispatches I'd snatched on my way out the door, then hop a ride to the hot zone, usually jouncing along in the crammed back of an army pickup truck.

Once, I was returning to Portugal after three weeks covering a turf war between rival diamond-smuggling cartels on the Congolese border when a flight attendant told me an American serial killer was rumored to be on the loose in the Lisbon red-light district. I taxied straight from the airport to the underground brothels on Pink Street and was in the midst of interviewing streetwalkers when the Finance Ministry suddenly announced a press conference on currency rates. I barely made it in time, then raced back to the office to hammer out that piece *plus* a short item whispered to me by a friend in the prime minister's office who was dealing with a woman who'd successfully impersonated an army general for nearly twenty years until her new wife discovered—kind of belatedly—that she wasn't a man. Finally, I wrapped my day covering an FC Porto soccer game alongside a photographer who sipped brandy and smoked Marlboro Lights while editing his film. If I had two hours to research any one of those stories I was lucky, and that mostly came from scribbling interview notes with a phone on one ear while the other rang nonstop from an editor in New York who wanted to know why I hadn't filed already.

But thanks to Gloria's long run from the law, I'd had months and months to track down leads and dig into her past. While police were searching everywhere in the world for her, I was searching Mexico for anyone who knew her. And that gave me advantage #2: the Word Wall.

Usually, sex abuse is devilishly hard to prosecute because it's essentially a crime without clues. There's no weapon, no fingerprints, no corpse or stolen goods or eyewitnesses. The only evidence is one person's memory, and defense attorneys have shown how easy it is to attack painful recollections when survivors have spent years trying to forget them. Of course, incriminating statements would go a long way toward backing up a victim's account, except . . .

Predators keep quiet. Bill Cosby, Harvey Weinstein, Jeffrey Epstein, Michael Jackson, R. Kelly, Gary Glitter, Subway pitchman Jared Fogle, thousands of Roman Catholic priests—they all lived their lives in the public gaze, yet skated along freely for years because as long as they kept their mouths shut, their embarrassed and bewildered victims often would, too. The true horror of #MeToo was discovering how many sex offenders were roaming loose and how many strong, capable women had been intimidated into suffering in silence. One of them, believe it or not, was Shirley Temple. At twelve years old, she was the most famous and beloved actor on the planet. She was due to make a film with MGM Pictures, and while her mother was reviewing the contract with studio head Louis B. Mayer, Shirley waited in a separate office with Arthur Freed, producer of *Singin' in the Rain* and *The Wizard of Oz.*

"I thought he was a producer, but instead he was an 'exhibitor,'" Shirley would relate many years later. "I'd never seen anyone naked before, so I had no clue what was happening." She was so shocked by the sight of this forty-six-year-old man exposing himself that she became hysterical, laughing so manically that Freed quickly pushed her out of the room. She told her mother on the way home what had happened—only to discover that while Shirley was being assaulted by the producer, her mother was being assaulted by the studio chief.

The sheer criminal recklessness was astounding. Unlike other young actresses, Shirley Temple owned the loudest bullhorn in the country. She was the top attraction for celebrity journalists who reached 100 million readers each month, and her mother was a savvy promoter who knew exactly how to attract TV and radio coverage. Shirley and Gertrude Temple could bring down an absolute shitstorm of outraged publicity on these creeps and end their careers.

Maybe. Or maybe the powerbrokers would turn the story against them, accusing Gertrude and Shirley of being a pair of mother-daughter vamps who used their sex appeal against a couple of hardworking guys with normal male urges. It didn't matter that Shirley was only twelve—the unspoken secret of her stardom was her attractiveness to older men (no exaggeration: the Vatican even sent a "morals envoy" to Los Angeles to make sure Shirley wasn't an undersized adult posing as a child). Gertrude wouldn't even have to stretch her imagination to guess how the Hollywood execs would push back if accused; all she had to do was walk into a theater and take a seat. "Recreational Sexual Abuse" and "Mouthy Dames Getting What They Deserve" were such common Hollywood plotlines at the time that audiences were actually surprised when the female lead *wasn't* jilted, jailed, humiliated, heartbroken, driven to suicide, or—best-case scenario—grudgingly accepted as butch enough to be one of the fellas.

"For the predators in these movies, consequences are almost always nonexistent. The men casually presume their right to the bodies of these young, beautiful women," as Dr. Marsha Gordon, the documentarian and professor of film studies at North Carolina State University who has made a specialty of pre-#MeToo cinema, has explained. "These repeated incidences of sexual exploitation appear to be commonplace, even expected. Female characters are rarely surprised when men grope or solicit them."

So Gertrude came up with a strategy to protect Shirley without having her driven out of Hollywood as a lying tramp: the two women would keep quiet, finish the film with MGM, and immediately return to the safety of Fox Studios. And it worked—until five years later, when Shirley was nearly raped by Louis B. Mayer's former son-in-law, studio head David O. Selznik. Selznik locked seventeen-year-old Shirley in his office and grabbed at her, pulling at her clothes until she managed to break free and bang on the door. Once again, Shirley remained silent. For nearly fifty years, she never spoke publicly about either assault. The studio execs knew a great deal when they saw one: they kept their lips sealed as well, trading any urge to boast for the freedom to assault again at will.

Say nothing, trust no one, stay out of sight—that's the free-pass playbook. But not for Gloria and Sergio.

When I first got on their trail, I assumed the only way they'd managed to avoid any legal jams for so long was by surrounding themselves in a fortress of silence and privacy. There was no way they could have groomed and abused dozens of young women right in the heart of Mexico's capital for more than a decade without *someone* noticing, not unless they were disciplined as monks and stealthy as ninjas. Instead, I arrived in Mexico City to discover they'd actually left behind enough of a public record to form a breadcrumb path into the woods and back to the witch's lair. A lot of it was embedded in the blather of entertainment news, in offhand remarks Gloria and Sergio and Mary Boquitas had made during TV appearances and in the midst of fan club newsletters and fluffy interviews. But if you read widely and closely enough, there it is: a timeline of contradictions and accidental revelations that tell a tale they'd meant to keep secret. It reminded me of that Julio Cortázar story, "Graffiti," about two young revolutionaries who communicate by scrawling secret little pictograms to each other in the tiny white spaces of spray-painted walls. If you knew where to look, the truth was right in front of you.

Nearly every lie that Gloria had told, for instance, was somewhere corrected in her wall of words by a fact she'd let slip. Like her birthday . . .

She was born Gloria de los Ángeles Treviño Ruiz in the northern Mexican border city of Monterrey on—

Well, that's where it gets fuzzy.

Gloria always says she was born on February 15, 1970. Even in her earliest media interviews, she was giving that date. But after she was arrested and her passport was seized, I discovered Gloria had actually begun shaving years off her age when she was still a teenager. It's kind of bewildering (what fourteen-year-old wants to pretend she's twelve?) until you realize something that Gloria must have figured out right away: in Mexico, singers are a dime a dozen, but child prodigies are entertainment gold.

So let's start her story again.

She was born Gloria de los Ángeles Treviño Ruiz in the northern Mexican border city of Monterrey on February 15, 1968. She was the first child—and the only daughter—of a young couple with big dreams and empty pockets. Manuel Treviño Cantú was an architectural student who'd fallen in love with Gloria Ruiz Arredondo, a seventeen-year-old aspiring ballerina. Manuel struggled to find design work by day while Gloria Ruiz was in the dance studio by night, but despite their hectic schedules they continued having children at a rapid rate. Soon, Gloria was joined by four younger brothers.

Manuel didn't have any parents or siblings to lend a hand with his growing family. He'd been orphaned as a young boy and raised by a variety of relatives who passed him along, from home to home, every few years. He had no tight bonds with any of them, so when money grew tight and things were looking desperate, Manuel and Gloria Ruiz were on their own. Gloria Ruiz's grandparents eventually agreed to help, but for only one of the children. So when Manuel and Gloria Ruiz set off to leave Monterrey in search of work, they took the four boys with them and left Gloria with her great-grandparents.

"It was fantastic!" Gloria would later recall. Being raised by two very elderly relatives, she discovered, had its benefits. "It was like living in Disneyland, because they let me do whatever I wanted!"

But privately, phone calls were being made and ultimatums issued. One morning, her great-grandmother said Gloria's father was coming by for a visit. When the car pulled up, Gloria panicked. Who was this man? Was he actually her father? It has been so long since she'd seen her parents, she couldn't tell for sure. And if it was just a visit, why were they loading so many suitcases in the trunk?

"It was horrible! I wanted to die!" she'd later say. "I felt like I was being kidnapped." She became hysterical, but her father got her into the car and began to drive. Instead of bringing her to join the family, however, he dropped her off at the home of an aunt and uncle who had raised him for a while as a boy. Poverty had forced Gloria into the same sad cycle of shifting homes that her father had endured as an orphan.

Gloria hated it there, and apparently her relatives weren't thrilled with the arrangement either. One night, she was awakened by a screaming argument in the kitchen. She couldn't make out the details, but sensed it was about her. Suddenly, her door flew open. A blonde woman swept into her room, gathered her belongings, and led her out the door. Gloria Ruiz had been summoned to reclaim her daughter.

Her parents were still penniless and jobless, so Gloria's mother began giving dance lessons. Gloria Ruiz turned out to be a delightful, encouraging teacher and her classes grew. Before long, she was earning enough to rent a little studio, which became her daughter's second home. When Gloria wasn't in classes herself, she kept herself busy by drawing quietly in a corner, scrawling out self-portraits, over and over, of little girls with wild hair and enormous round eyes.

But being the boss of her own studio and the family's only breadwinner didn't make Gloria Ruiz any more independent at home. Even though Manuel was usually unemployed, he still insisted that Gloria Ruiz be at the stove by 8 p.m. to cook his dinner. Gloria recalls walking home with her mother one night, the two of them feeling an increasing sense of dread as they realized they were going to be late, gradually increasing their pace until they were running. They arrived panting, hoping they'd made it on time.

They hadn't. Even though it was just a few minutes after the curfew, Manuel was furious. "If you like walking the streets so much, then stay there!" Gloria recalls her father shouting. He pulled Gloria inside and slammed the door shut in her mother's face, locking it. "And this was in the middle of December, when it was freezing outside." Gloria and one of her brothers snuck out a window and huddled with their mother in the cold, keeping her company until their angry father finally relented and let them in the house.

Gloria was ten when her mother decided she had to flee. Gloria Ruiz gathered up the children and escaped to her mother's house . . .

Only to be told to turn around and go back home. "'That's just one of the crosses that God has put in your path,'" Gloria would recall her grandmother saying. "My grandmother wouldn't give us a thing! Not a tortilla! Not a glass of water!" But Gloria Ruiz refused to return to Manuel. She found a tiny, unfurnished apartment and set out to make a life on her own. Gloria got used to doing her schoolwork by candlelight after the electricity was shut off, and to hiding in the bathroom with her mother and brothers when the landlord came knocking at the door demanding overdue rent.

Gloria Ruiz was only twenty-eight years old and still model-thin from her hours of daily dance instruction, and it wasn't long before other men were vying for her attention. "Well, my mother had to go in for a hernia operation, and I guess the surgeon who was treating her fell in love with her while she was on that table," Gloria would later say. Before the surgeon could propose, however, another doctor was also coming around. "He used to give me little gifts so I would help convince my mother to marry him." The surgeon won, however, and at age twelve, Gloria was delighted to hear they were leaving the dingy little apartment forever.

For the first time since she was a pregnant teenager, Gloria Ruiz could go to bed at night knowing there'd be food on the table for her children when she woke up and heat in the house. Finally, she could now focus her full attention on her ultimate goal:

Stardom.

But she had one more obstacle in her way:

Gloria.

6

CHISPITA JUNIOR

Her own time was over. Gloria Ruiz knew that.

But her daughter's was just beginning. If Gloria Ruiz couldn't get onstage, she'd settle for being a stage mom. They'd be the perfect team! Gloria Ruiz could use all of her audition experience and dance-world connections to get her daughter a crack at the spotlight . . .

Except that was the worst nightmare young Gloria could imagine.

Years of living out of a suitcase and sitting alone in a corner of her mother's dance studio had left Gloria timid and withdrawn, and her sudden access to a full refrigerator for the first time in her life allowed her once-frail figure to become plump. Years of bouncing around from school to school, plus her natural defense of drifting into daydreams, had left her a poor student with no idea how to catch up.

But one thing terrified Gloria more than going to school, and that was returning home. Gloria Ruiz graded her daughter even more severely than her teachers. If a test score was too low, Gloria got a beating. If she put on some weight, she was forced to wear a paper pig's tail pinned to her skirt. TV stars have to be able to read, Gloria Ruiz scolded her. They have to be thin and smart and beautiful! They can't flunk math and stuff their mouths with chocolate.

By age thirteen, Gloria was through. She was failing all eight of her classes and knew she was in for the whipping of a lifetime. She found a piece of rope and hid it behind the house. Before her mother got her report card, she'd decided, she would hang herself. Maybe her suicidal despair was adolescent self-pity, maybe it would pass before she looped that rope over a tree branch, but in the end, it didn't matter. Because suddenly one afternoon, a small miracle changed her life.

One of Gloria's older classmates felt sorry for the miserable new girl and took Gloria under her wing. She brought her home after school and gave Gloria a full makeover, schoolgirl-style. First, she unknotted the tight braid that had earned Gloria the nickname "Squaw Treviño" and brushed out her long, bouncy hair. She gave Gloria's eyes a smudge of liner and her lips a coat of gloss, then yanked up the button-down blouse tucked into her skirt and knotted it above her belly button.

Gloria looked in the mirror and fell in love.

Her "double life," as she called it, had begun. "I'd leave for school in the morning in my uniform, with my hair back in my nice schoolgirl's braid," she'd say. "But in the afternoon I'd put on some short-shorts or a miniskirt, shake my hair out, and put on makeup."

Immediately, the bullying stopped. "Every boy in the neighborhood was after me," Gloria would smirk. "But I didn't date any of them. I didn't like any of them enough to fall in love."

Intoxicated with new self-confidence, Gloria threw herself back into dance classes with a fire that impressed even Gloria Ruiz. Gloria began to slim down and speak up, developing her own version of the sass and street style she was learning from her older friends at school. As a mother, Gloria Ruiz may have felt a twinge of alarm at her tween daughter's sudden sex appeal . . . but as a budding talent manager, she was thrilled.

Gloria Ruiz began calculating next steps. Soon, she thought, Gloria might be ready to hit the show business circuit. Neither one of them realized it had already happened. Thanks to a bizarre coincidence, daughter Gloria's face was already famous.

At that moment, young women across Mexico were vying for the chance to become the next Chispita, the beloved telenovela orphan played by child actress Lucerito, later known as Lucero.

Chispita was so popular that when Lucerito launched her singing career at age fourteen, her TV fame made her an overnight pop sensation. Record sales skyrocketed, and her sold-out stage shows proved Lucerito had enough star power to carry an entire production on her own. Movie directors and record labels were fighting for the rights to her next project. It was time for Lucerito to leave the soaps and focus entirely on films and music—or at least, that was the path urged by her new manager: the twenty-eight-year-old hitmaker, Sergio Andrade.

While Lucerito weighed her options, Televisa held its breath. It's easy to make grownup characters in a series disappear; the writers just have to add a car accident to the plot, or a job transfer, and *poof*, they're gone. Yes, loyal viewers are shocked at first when a favorite actor leaves the show, but real life prepares us for that kind of change. We've all had to say goodbye to good friends, so we know how to get over it. But killing off a *child* character? That makes viewers go crazy. It's too harsh for audiences to absorb, too much like experiencing the death of a real child. Loyal viewers become so distressed, they often stop watching the show for good.

That's what Televisa was up against. If Lucerito left *Chispita*, *Chispita* was a goner. Unless . . .

Unless they could find another girl who looked just like her. Somewhere among the 20 million or so teenage girls in Mexico, there had to be at least one who looked enough like Lucerito to pull off the switcheroo. Swapping in a new Chispita was a gamble, of course, but what other choice did they have?

So in 1983, Televisa launched a nationwide Lucerito look-alike contest. They kept their true reason a secret. They never promised to put the winner on the show or even mentioned that Lucerito was thinking of leaving. But they did offer a very tasty first prize: a one-year scholarship to Televisa's talent training school, plus a full Chispita wardrobe up to—and including—a live dog exactly like the stunt pup on the show.

Gloria and her mother boarded a bus for the six-hundred-mile journey from Monterrey to Mexico City. When they stumbled off the bus and made their way to the studio, Gloria had to force her way through throngs of young fans who thought she actually was Lucerito. The resemblance was so uncanny that even Gloria's fellow look-alikes were amazed. Before the judging was even over, they began asking for her autograph, convinced that as soon as she won she'd be whisked away to stardom.

When the winner was announced, Gloria received good news and bad. "I really wanted the dog, and they never gave it to me," she griped. On the other hand, she did receive first prize and a one-year contract for training in the Televisa talent development lab.

Gloria Ruiz's lifelong dream was coming true, albeit backstage rather than center. Before she could really savor the moment and celebrate with her daughter, however, she had to go. Back home, she still had four young sons to raise and a dance studio to run. She gave Gloria a bus map of Mexico City and a fistful of pocket money, then left her alone and climbed on the bus for Monterrey.

Gloria—fourteen years old and now completely on her own—watched her mother's bus disappear down the road, then made her way back into one of the most dangerous cities in the world. The predators weren't just in the streets, though. They were also prowling the studios.

"Mexico is probably unlike any other country in the way it develops entertainers," says Sam Quinones, the author and cultural critic. "You don't freelance. You don't scrounge around like Madonna, hanging out at clubs and hoping for a record deal. The Televisa method for creating stars is to seclude young girls in singing and dancing schools, then have them emerge a few years later with a new name and appearance. That's the only way to make it."

Not surprisingly, these star schools are ripe for abuse by the men who run them. One of the few to break the code of silence and sound the alarm was Ga-Bí, the former singing star whose real name is Judith Enriqueta Chávez-Parks Flores. She was fifteen years old when she joined the cast of a Sunday variety show. On her first day of rehearsal, she was raped by a producer in his office while her mother, suspecting nothing, waited outside. When she emerged, Ga-Bí was too stunned and afraid to say anything. Her mother didn't find out until years later.

"That was my first experience as a show business professional," Ga-Bí would say. "Like thousands of other girls in Mexico, I kept my mouth shut, because that is what we were always taught to do. My first boss told me, *There are a thousand little Marias out there ready to take your place. If this life isn't for you, you're easy to replace.*"

7

THE MINI GIANT

Somehow, the teenage girl who arrived on a bus from nowhere survived on her own in Mexico City. In fact, she had a blast.

"It was marvelous!" Gloria would tell me years later, her eyes glowing at the memory. "It was a challenge, too, because every few months or so they gave you tests, and if you didn't pass, you were gone, but I loved it."

Gloria didn't know when she'd step in as the new Chispita, so she put in long days and extra hours on her star-school curriculum, determined to be a performance-ready singer and actor whenever she got the call. After months of prep, she was crushed when the network reversed course and killed the series instead. The potential blowback of swapping in a new actor, they decided, was too big a risk. If it failed, they'd all look ridiculous.

So instead of rocketing to stardom like Lucerito, Gloria ended up landing only walk-on roles in a few telenovelas. "I was scared, panicking," Gloria said. "I was sure they were going to send me back to Monterrey. I was wandering around, trying to figure out what to do, and I happened to run into Ricky Luis, a very good singer and a friend of mine from home."

"So," Ricky asked her, "what's next?"

"It looks like I'm going home," Gloria said.

Ricky had another thought. Sergio Andrade had just signed him to record his first album. While he was in the office doing the paperwork, he heard that Sergio was starting auditions for an all-girl pop band. Gloria didn't sing or play an instrument, but if she wanted to give it a try, Ricky would do his best to get her into the room with Sergio.

"Let's go, let's go!" Gloria erupted. "This has to be destiny!"

When they got to Sergio's studio, the waiting room was already full of young women. Ricky and Gloria squeezed into a corner and waited for Sergio to emerge from his office. Girls went in, girls came back out, but Sergio remained inside.

Hours passed. Several times, Gloria angled her way toward the office door between girls and tried to enter, but Sergio's assistant always asked her name, checked a list, and told her to sit back down. All the girls who'd been there when Gloria first arrived were gone, replaced by a fresh wave of recruits. Still no sign of Sergio.

At ten that night, Ricky got hungry and left. Gloria remained. Did Sergio have a bathroom in there? she wondered. A coffeemaker? A back door? How could he keep going so long without a break? And what on earth was he looking for, anyway? He only needed five girls. He'd interviewed *hundreds* already.

By midnight, the waiting room was nearly empty.

"Want to try tomorrow?" Sergio's assistant asked.

"Are you closing?"

"Not yet."

"Then I'll stay."

Finally, at two o'clock in the morning, Gloria was shown into Sergio's sanctum. Across the room was a piano, and behind it, an exhausted man with dark rings under his eyes and thick stubble darkening his face. He got up to greet her, and Gloria was surprised to see that the hit-making giant was no taller than she.

Sergio looked her over in return. "I know you," he said. "The little Lucerito twin. How's that working out?"

"Wonderful!" Gloria beamed, because if she'd learned one thing from Televisa's star school, it was to always be the brightest smile in the room, even when your back is screaming from twelve hours in a hard chair, and your stomach is rumbling from a full day without food, and your heart is broken because your show business dream is about to end with a bus ticket back to Monterrey.

"But I'm ready to try something new," she added. "Something outside of television."

"Huh," Sergio grunted. He took his seat behind the piano and led her through a few songs. *Not great, not bad*, he thought. *She's no songbird, but at least you can hear her.*

"What's next?" Gloria asked.

Sergio fought back a smile. Every other girl he'd seen for the past two days had ducked into the room bashfully, hopefully, or nervously, but this one was ablaze with energy and an almost reckless, nothing-to-lose attitude. Besides, she actually was a dead ringer for Lucerito. That couldn't hurt. He planned to launch *Boquitas Pintadas*—Little Lipsticked Mouths—in two months. He had to decide.

"I'm going to need a girl on keyboards," Sergio said.

"Perfect," Gloria said. She'd never touched a piano in her life.

"Do you play?"

Years later, when she was under police guard in a shabby Brazilian maternity ward, Gloria would look back on that moment as the greatest crossroad in her life. "There was no way that I was going to say, 'Um, Señor Andrade? Maybe?

Kind of?'" Gloria told me. "That's why those other girls didn't make it. They weren't sure. I was."

Gloria had a split second to come up with an answer for Sergio, something to set her apart from the hundreds of hopefuls who'd been filing in and out of that room for two days, but both her options were terrible. She could tell the truth and be dismissed right away. Or she could lie and be exposed as a fake as soon as this expert songwriter and pianist put her to the test. She was so tired it was hard to think, and she was all out of moves.

Except one.

"Show me," Gloria said, scooting in next to Sergio on the piano bench. "Show me what you want. I'll practice on my own, and I won't quit till you're happy."

"That," Sergio said, "is exactly what I like to hear."

8

LALO

"It's undeniable that Sergio Andrade is an outstanding musician and composer."

That's an astonishing statement, considering the source. I was in Mexico City, sitting across the desk from Patricia "Pati" Chapoy, a top TV Azteca executive and on-air personality. Locking down this interview was as crucial for me as getting into a jail cell with Gloria herself, because if Sergio Andrade has one arch-nemesis, it's this piercing-eyed woman who, at the moment, is giving me a carefully appraising once-over. Pati first met Sergio when he was barely out of his teens and has followed every twist of his career ever since. When Pati was a young music journalist, she was among the first to recognize Sergio's hitmaking potential. She'd later become the earliest—and for too long, *only*—voice to publicly sound the alarm that something wasn't right in the Sergio and Gloria world.

"*Mira*," she began before I'd even flipped open my notebook. She had an impressive executive's chair, the kind of hand-sewn ergonomic masterpiece that signals someone up top is glad to pay big bucks to keep her happy, but they might as well have given her a stool: Pati uses about three inches of the chair's real estate, perching upright and attentive on the extreme edge in the same posture I've seen Navy SEALs take when they're about to leap off a jump seat and out the hatch of a hovering helicopter.

"Look," Pati said. "There's no upside for me in any of this. There never has been. Many people have gotten along very well in this industry by following the philosophy that Sergio's business is Sergio's business. When I began asking questions, no one wanted to listen. When I persisted, I was told to keep quiet. When I *insisted*, I was attacked."

"So why have you spoken up?"

Her eyes flickered, a split-second tic that instantly disappeared but lingered between us. She was disappointed in me. *If you have to ask*, her eyes said, *you're no better than the rest of them.*

Back in the '70s, Pati was starting her TV career as a talent booker tasked with scouting up-and-coming performers and getting them on the air before anyone else. She heard about a young crooner who sounded interesting, an unknown from a rough port town who was singing some catchy original songs on the Mexico City piano lounge circuit. His talent was unmistakable, but his stage presence was, well . . . the kindest description Pati heard was "painful." He was short, and pudgy, and so shy that he'd stare down at the piano while singing, then jerk his head up at the end of the song in a frozen, terrified grin.

Pati wondered if this Sergio Andrade Sánchez was any relation to the hot TV sports commentator Eduardo "Lalo" Andrade Sánchez. The two shared the same family name, after all, and came from the same dead-end town. *That* might be a story, she mused: two nobodies from nowhere-ville, scrappy brothers trying to scratch their own way into show business. But the singer sounded like he'd be terrible on TV, so she never bothered to track him down.

Pati forgot about him until a few years later, when a blind teenager named Crystal finished her final song at a music festival in Puerto Rico and the audience erupted in a standing ovation. Pati was in the audience that night, and she fought her way backstage to find out where on earth this phenomenon had come from and see if she could book her.

"You'll have to speak to Maestro first," she was told.

"Maestro?" she asked.

"Maestro Andrade."

Oh, so it's Maestro now! Pati was intrigued. She began asking around, digging into his background. Was he just a hack riding the coattails of a talented young sensation, or did he actually bring some legitimate "Maestro" expertise to the table? Pati hung around the festival until someone pointed Sergio out to her and she managed to pull him aside to talk. She was now as curious about this mysterious musical mentor as she was about his blind young protégée. She sat down with Sergio, and never being one to waste words, she got right to it.

"So who are you?" she asked.

Sergio could answer that question in two words:

Not Lalo.

From the time he was a child, Sergio was defined by what he wasn't.

He wasn't strong and fast, like his brother Lalo. He wasn't lean and handsome and witty. He couldn't come through the door and shout, "THE HEART OF THE HOUSE IS HOME," or have his mother smother him with hugs even if he played a song on the piano that he'd written especially for her.

True, Sergio was good with words, but Lalo was much better, dramatic and witty and booming. Sergio was smart, but Lalo was clever. Lalo was a gifted athlete and natural team leader, while Sergio preferred to stay inside and read. By the time Lalo was in high school, he could already see himself as a future president of Mexico. His father agreed, so he uprooted the family and moved them all to the capital so Lalo could go to law school and still live under his thumb.

That's how the Andrade household operated: If you were the prince, the planet orbited around you. If you were his little brother, you kept quiet.

Their father was a short, stubby man and very sensitive about his height. So tall, handsome Lalo figured out early on that he could feed his father's ego by saying "I really take after you. Right, Papa? Eduardo one and Eduardo two!"

Papa's real mirror image was Sergio, and Sergio paid for it. His father's favorite punishment was to whip him with a belt, and then have Sergio get down on his knees, kiss his father's hand, and say "I love you, Papa." Sergio's mother doted on her boys, but she was still completely subservient to her husband. On Papa's orders, Doña Justina would punish Sergio by tying him to a table leg and beating him with a stick or electric cord.

Sergio escaped the abuse by winning acceptance at Mexico's National Conservatory of Music to study classical piano. He was desperate to keep living on his own and never sleep under his father's roof again, so while he was studying Vivaldi by day, he was also writing pop tunes by night. If it all worked out, Sergio hoped, his rock songs would support his classical training while the prestige of his classical training would help sell his rock songs.

By the time he turned twenty-three, both parts of the plan had clicked into place. Sergio placed third in the Yamaha

National Competition for pianists and he was hired that same year as a staff composer and arranger for RCA Victor Records. But before long, his side hustle began pushing aside his main gig. Sergio was surprised to discover that he enjoyed the challenge of working with crude tools—basic rock chords, barely trained singers, simple lyrics—to create soaring ballads that no one had ever heard before and then could never forget.

But the best part about being a pop music writer, he discovered, was the pop music singers. He was used to spending hours alone each day with his Steinway in an observatory practice room. Now, he could drop by RCA anytime he wanted and instantly be surrounded by professionally pretty women who couldn't wait to hear what *he*—not Lalo's little brother, but he, Sergio—had come up with.

Talent doesn't necessarily translate into self-confidence, though. Sergio was still awkward and self-conscious, and that is exactly what one singer in particular liked about him most. Ga-Bí had never recovered from the trauma of being sexually assaulted as a teenager when she first broke into show business. She wanted to keep her distance from entertainment hotshots, which of course was nearly impossible in a business with almost no women in positions of power.

And then this short, mumbling man appears one day while she's at CBS recording backup vocals on another singer's album. Instead of sizing her up with the same hungry gaze she was used to from all the other men in the business, this guy kept his face down and refused to meet her gaze. Ga-Bí asked around about the shy stranger and found out he'd just been hired away from RCA.

Ga-Bí was heading home later that evening when she heard a winsome little melody wafting through the open doorway of a rehearsal studio.

"*Encantadora*," she called out. "That's enchanting."

The stranger wheeled around with a look of such gratitude that it melted Ga-Bí's heart. "He wasn't considered an attractive man by other people in the studio, but I liked the way he looked," Ga-Bí would say. "He seemed extremely pleased, in fact surprised, when I told him I liked his smile."

Sergio and Ga-Bí began dating, and right from the start, Ga-Bí was charmed by the way Sergio let her take charge. Like his wardrobe. Sergio dressed exactly like a guy who didn't want to be noticed, all frumpy jackets and baggy pants, which Ga-Bí knew was going to dog him in the music business no matter how many ballads he penned.

"He liked it when I told him to wear such-and-such a shirt and necktie," Ga-Bí would recall. "And back then he used rather common colognes, like Old Spice or Brut, so I gave him a bottle of Aramis."

Sergio was so thrilled to be dating this beautiful, caring young woman that he took the big step and told his mother he was bringing someone special home to meet her. When they arrived, Sergio was delighted to find his mother had honored Ga-Bí by pulling out all the stops and preparing a beautifully elaborate lunch for her.

Except it wasn't.

"THE HEART OF THE HOUSE IS HOME," a voice shouted, as Lalo came banging through the door.

"From that moment on, Sergio and I ceased to exist for her," Ga-Bí recalls. Lalo was still in law school but was also becoming something of a sensation as a TV soccer commentator. In a country where every male is raised to believe they know more about the sport than anyone else, Lalo was beloved for his smart-alecky wit, remarkable statistical memory, and most of all, his natural joyfulness. Who doesn't love a guy who's having so much fun?

"This soccer is just the beginning," Sergio's mother raved while they were having lunch. "I knew from the time he was six years old that he was going to be something very, very special."

She fussed over him so much, Ga-Bí recalls, that even Lalo was embarrassed for his brother. "Mother, stop," he finally said. "Any more, and I'm leaving."

But Sergio had already gotten up, kissed his mother goodbye, and led Ga-Bí silently toward the door.

9

THE RUNAWAY

Ga-Bí did her best to keep it secret from Sergio, but she was none too pleased when her boyfriend suddenly became her boss.

CBS decided to let Ga-Bí try her luck at the International Music Festival in Puerto Rico. To prepare, she was assigned to work one-on-one with their new hire, that promising classical pianist. Everyone knew Sergio was her boyfriend, but that didn't disqualify him. The studio actually saw it as a plus. If you're going to be emotionally vulnerable and spend hours a day locked in a windowless soundproof room, they reasoned, who better to partner with than your lover?

Which makes perfect sense, of course, if you're the one in the power seat. If not, you might have very different feelings about seeing your career placed in the hands of a guy you only started dating a few weeks ago. And from what Ga-Bí could see, she already had good reason to worry: Sergio might be a musical genius, but showmanship? Not so much. Ga-Bí had seen him perform, and as much as she liked his songs, watching Sergio play them in public was unbearable. What did he know about wowing a major festival audience?

But Ga-Bí bit her lip. She and Sergio got to work, and for the first time in her career, she discovered how terrible she was. Not just as a performer—as a person. Sergio was constantly scolding her. She didn't project her voice. She didn't stand right. She didn't breathe right. She didn't even understand the lyrics he put in her hand. *And why*, he demanded, why was she so careless with the songs he'd given her as a gift from his own heart? Because she didn't love him, Sergio concluded. Or anyone. Ga-Bí must be cruel and selfish and incapable of love, because that's how she sounded when she sang: heartless and lazy and mean.

Ga-Bí was dizzy. She'd never heard anything like this before. All of her other producers praised her work ethic, complimenting her for staying late in studio and spending hours searching for the emotional center of even the sugariest of cotton-candy tunes. *They're lying*, Sergio sneered. They don't care if you make it to the top. To them, you're just another bimbo to flirt with and pat on the head. But not him. He cared. It hurt him to see her treated like a dumb pet. It hurt him even more that she didn't trust him.

Ga-Bí felt horrible. He was her boyfriend, and he seemed so wounded. He must want the best for her, right? She promised she'd do better, but no matter how hard she tried, Sergio's temper was unpredictable. She could never tell what would make him swing between playfulness and fury, so she learned to stay quiet, keep a wary eye on his moods, and wait for him to tell her what to do.

"It's very strange," Ga-Bí would say, looking back. "As a performer it's impossible to succeed without confidence, but mine was gone. I no longer had any confidence in myself. But I had complete confidence in Sergio. Whatever he said, I did."

Sergio broke Ga-Bí down and rebuilt her to his own specifications. At the festival, Ga-Bí wore the clothes Sergio selected, sang the song he'd chosen, and moved onstage precisely the way Sergio had dictated. And just as Sergio had predicted, it worked. Ga-Bí was awarded top female vocalist and Sergio was cited for best creative arrangement.

The following year, Ga-Bí released an album under Sergio's care that was well received. They returned to the same festival together and won again, an impressive repeat performance that convinced CBS that Ga-Bí's time had come. With Sergio guiding her, Ga-Bí was ready for the big time: a new album with top backing talent, a multinational tour, a big push into the U.S. market to make her a global name. But first, the studio urged her, take some time off. You earned it. Then let's get you and Sergio back in the studio.

Ga-Bí agreed. So she went on a trip—

And never returned.

For the past year, something had been gnawing at the back of her mind, something she couldn't quite put her finger on. Her star was rising like never before, so why was she so unhappy? Worse than unhappy: dirty. Dirty and dishonest, as if she were somehow cheating. None of it made any sense, so when she finally had a moment to breathe, she decided to get far away from her show business life for a while. A religious retreat in the mountains of North Carolina seemed perfect.

And it was there, while sitting in quiet meditation, that it all snapped into focus. Ga-Bí had been taught since her Catholic girlhood that she was made in God's image, which meant she should love and respect herself as much as she loved and respected God. But during her time with Sergio, she discovered she was actually lazy and selfish and stupid, and the only way to wash away her sins was to obey the commandments of the Almighty.

Not God. Sergio. He'd become the ultimate authority in

her life about everything from the thoughts in her head to the food on her plate.

Ga-Bí was furious and disgusted. Not with Sergio. With herself. After she was raped on her first day in television, she swore to herself that she would never, ever make herself that vulnerable again. But bit by bit, the man she loved and admired had taken advantage of her trust and turned her back into the same scared, compliant girl she'd been before.

Ga-Bí needed more time to think, so she extended her time in North Carolina a little longer while she worked on a strategy to protect herself in the future. Then, something happened: the old Ga-Bí showed up. For the first time in nearly two years, her constant anxiety faded and her playfulness and confidence began to return. A question she didn't want to answer started teasing at the corner of her mind, until she finally couldn't put it off any longer and confronted it head-on:

Is it worth it?

If she went back to Sergio, he'd make her famous. She had no doubt about it. He'd already proven he was a master of "the game," as Ga-Bí called it, and to play along, all she had to do was follow his orders. She'd never have to make another decision. She could just leave everything in Sergio's hands as he turned her into the kind of woman he wanted.

There was only one hitch: the old Ga-Bí would have to go.

Today, Ga-Bí is still in North Carolina. She became so attached to the place that opened her eyes, it became her home. She soon met and married a kind, caring army officer from nearby Fort Bragg, and decided to take the one skill she wanted to retain from show business—cosmetology—and make it her new career.

Looking back, Ga-Bí shudders to think how close she

came to never escaping. She was fortunate, she realized, because she was first. With her, Sergio was still learning the rules of "the game," still getting a feel for the extent of his power and the limits of what he could get away with.

The next girls wouldn't be so lucky.

10

CRYSTAL

When Ga-Bí dropped out of sight in 1981, Sergio learned an important lesson. With twenty-year-olds, you never know when they'll snap to and suddenly begin thinking for themselves. He never made that mistake again.

Sergio soon discovered another upside to Ga-Bí's sudden departure. Thanks to Ga-Bí's transformation from a forgotten child actor into a two-time festival champion, Sergio was earning a low-key reputation among show business insiders as a musical fix-it man. Sergio now had the credentials, and the free time, to work with more accomplished performers who needed help reaching the top ranks. And Raúl Velasco, the starmaking host of the massively popular variety show *Siempre en Domingo*, had exactly the singer in mind.

Crystal's real name is Gaudelia Díaz. She and her younger brother were both born blind to poor day laborers in Acapulco. At age five, she was sent to a special school for the visually impaired in Mexico City. She'd barely been there a month when the school's theater company needed to fill a child's role for a musical. Even though she'd never acted before or sung in public, five-year-old Crystal instantly and eagerly volunteered.

Forget about stage fright. Crystal had such a blast in her first musical that as soon as the curtain dropped, she began preparing for the next. By age seven, she was comfortable on piano. By nine, she'd added guitar and mandolin and advanced voice. So one day, when a movie casting director called the school's theater director in search of a young actress, he had the perfect candidate.

Crystal was chosen to co-star in *¿De Que Color Es el Viento?* (What Color Is the Wind?), a movie about two blind children from different social classes who bond through their disability. The charming young newcomer was a big hit, but when the producers began making arrangements for a sequel, Crystal's father put his foot down.

"He was afraid the movie industry would lead me down the wrong path, and he insisted I go back to my studies." Crystal was the first in her family to have a chance to break out of poverty, and her parents were convinced the path to a better future was education, not entertainment. Grudgingly, Crystal obeyed. She became a superb student-athlete, earning top grades while showing exceptional talent in skating, track, and gymnastics. But she'd never given up the show business bug, and when she was sixteen, her parents finally relented and allowed her to enter Valores Juveniles, Mexico's national TV youth talent search.

As soon as she got onstage and began to sing, Raúl Velasco could tell she had star potential. She had such a gorgeous, confident voice and natural charisma that he couldn't believe she had zero professional training and had only been in front of the camera once, as an eight-year-old. Remarkable! Still, to go any further she'd need a full performance makeover. Don Raúl put in a call to Sergio Andrade.

When Crystal was told to report to Sergio's studio, she was disappointed. "I really wanted Chucho Guerrero as my musical director," she recalls. "Chucho had the name at that time and Sergio wasn't well known." Oddly, one thing reassured her: when she arrived for their first meeting, he sounded seriously pissed. From all the way down the hall, she could hear him shouting through the door of a rehearsal room.

"He was extremely demanding," says Crystal. "He would always be in the studio, working long hours with much older musicians. He would really yell at them, but they listened and respected him because he knew what he was doing."

Sergio had a harsh tongue but a flawless eye. After his first few sessions with Crystal, he pronounced her ready for her big stage debut. He wanted her to enter the International Music Festival, the same showcase where Ga-Bí had made her name, but they'd only have a tight window to prepare. The first task was coming up with a song, and Sergio delivered.

"When he sang 'Suavemente' to me, I liked it a lot," Crystal says, "It's such a beautiful song, and Sergio had written it so it ended with my name, Crystal."

Crystal readied herself to try it, but Sergio stopped her. You're not a singer, he instructed. You're a musical instrument to be tuned and plucked exactly as I wish. Every note, every nuance that comes out of your mouth better sound exactly the way I tell you. "In Mexico, your musical director tells you how you have to sing, even a big star like Luis Miguel," explains Crystal. "He told me exactly how I should sing his songs, and they turned out beautifully."

Crystal's version of "Suavemente" made her an overnight sensation. It brought down the house at the International Music Festival and soon shot to #1 on the Latin charts. It became an even bigger hit when Herb Alpert famously recorded it in the U.S. By the time they returned from the festival, Sergio had a new nickname: "Mr. Midas."

Secretly, he also had a new girlfriend.

"I admired him so much, I fell in love," Crystal would say. Crystal was eager to let her parents know that their teenage daughter now had someone looking out for her: her twenty-eight-year-old boyfriend. But Sergio said no, absolutely not. "He told me to be discreet because it wasn't good for my career to let anybody know. He said we'd sell more records if people thought I was single."

Crystal was heartsick but kept her mouth shut. "Like the old saying goes," she'd shrug. "Worship God, but obey your lover."

Sleeping with Crystal in private didn't change his treatment of her in public. If anything, his temper got worse. "He'd yell at me in front of everyone, in front of my mother even, and no one ever said anything. So I got to think it was normal."

Her real punishments, however, were always behind closed doors. "If I disagreed with him, if I dared to criticize him," Crystal would explain, "he had different ways to discipline me. It depended on his mood. When he wasn't that angry, he'd leave me at a park bench. Other times he'd lock me in the car for hours and tell me not to move." Sergio had quickly figured out that for a blind teenager in the chaos of Mexico City, a car was an extraordinarily effective disciplinary device. Used properly, it was simple, terrifying, and left no marks. "It was a Mustang he had, with automatic windows, so I couldn't open them to get more air."

Whenever Sergio wasn't imprisoning Crystal in a bedroom or abandoning her in a park, he'd lean close to her ear and threaten even worse. While Crystal was rehearsing for the Yamaha International Song Contest in Tokyo, Sergio was furious when Crystal's sleepiness from jet lag affected her sharpness on the piano. He slapped the keyboard cover down on her fingers, which only made her more nervous. If she made one more mistake, Sergio hissed, he'd break her arm so she couldn't go onstage and humiliate them both.

Trembling, Crystal played the tune perfectly.

Back home, meanwhile, a surprise awaited Sergio. The tween TV sensation Lucerito—"Mexico's Sweetheart"—was ready to make her musical debut. Because of Sergio's success with Ga-Bí and Crystal, her parents wanted him to mastermind her first album. Right from the start, though, something was strange about Sergio's method of working with the thirteen-year-old girl.

"He would lock himself with her in the studio and stay there for hours. Nobody said anything," Crystal would recall. "I never talked to anyone about what was going on in there, but everyone thought it was very peculiar."

Finally, Crystal's suspicions boiled over. She confronted Sergio one morning in his office. "I may be blind but I'm not stupid," Crystal stormed. "You're screwing Lucerito."

Sergio gazed back, his eyes black and emotionless.

"How do you know?" he asked.

"You spend hours alone with her every day in the rehearsal room, with the door locked and—"

"No," Sergio interrupted. "How do you know you're not stupid?"

Sergio was so cold and menacing, so quiet and direct, it took Crystal's breath away. What was wrong with her, he asked, that would allow her to ask something so stupid, so juvenile and cruel? He spoke almost as if to himself, genuinely perplexed that he'd never realized until that moment that Crystal was so foolish and malicious.

Crystal opened her mouth to reply, but Sergio cut her off. Who ever said you're smart? Where did you get that idea? You're pretty and you can sing. So can a bird. That doesn't make the bird smart. You know the difference between you and a parakeet? The only difference?

You, Crystal said meekly.

Me what?

You're the only difference between me and a parakeet, Crystal replied.

Do you need me to prove that again?

No, Sergio.

Maybe I should take you for a drive.

No. Please no.

It's all in your mind, Sergio said. And we need to help you with that, so you don't keep saying things that you don't understand. Yes?

Yes.

Good, Sergio concluded. Get in the car.

11

FRAGILE DOLLS OF OBLIVION

Lucerito's debut took off like a rocket.

For a bubblegum effort aimed squarely at middle-schoolers, *Te Prometo* sold so briskly that within months it was already a gold record. Sergio had written every song and made sure he was quadruple-credited as "Composer, Arranger, Producer, and Musical Director." Just for the sake of salesmanship, any other manager would have pretended that Lucerito had written her own songs straight from her heart, but Sergio's ego wouldn't allow it. Lucerito's only job, he made clear, was to do, say, and sing exactly what he told her to do, say, and sing.

Sergio kept her working. In less than a year, Lucerito was out with her follow-up, another smash album called *At Such a Young Age* (*Con Tan Pocos Años*). Lucerito's young fans loved it, but sales took a hit after parents raised a ruckus about the title, a creepily sexual choice for an album by a fourteen-year-old who still looked eleven. Sergio tried to explain, but his ego took control of his tongue and made things worse. Much, much worse.

"I see nine of the songs are yours, but one is by Lucerito herself," a TV reporter asked during a studio interview. "Have you been helping her develop as a songwriter?"

"Actually," Sergio said, "I wrote that song as well."

"With Lucerito, you mean."

"No," Sergio insisted. "Just me. Me alone."

"Oh." The reporter paused, as anyone would when a pop star's manager suddenly blurts out on live TV that he and "Mexico's sweetheart" have defrauded the public.

Sergio forged on. "You see, some gossips were spreading rumors that I wrote that song about Lucerito because I'm in love with her." To put the matter to rest, he decided to say Lucerito came up with the song on her own. There! Problem solved.

"Well, that's . . . that's . . ." The reporter stammered, dumbstruck, his mind short-circuited by that unexpected jolt. *What the HELL is Sergio talking about?* No one had been spreading any rumors about a thirty-year-old manager romancing his ninth-grade client until the thirty-year-old manager suddenly brought it up himself. But from that moment on, rumors went wild. Despite the firestorm he'd triggered with that first self-inflicted fiasco, Sergio sat for more live interviews in an attempt to put out the flames. Every denial that came out of his mouth, however, only stirred up suspicions. Any adult who has to deny sleeping with a minor, the thinking went, has probably done *something* sleazy to put themselves in the hot seat.

The only lucky break for Sergio was tacit support from Lucerito's family, who maintained a dignified silence despite feverish attempts to get them to speak. That gave Sergio a little breathing room to come up with a new public-relations plan to salvage his career and hopefully keep law enforcement out of the picture. He quit making any public statements, and instead launched an entirely different three-part strategy:

PART 1: OPERATION CRYSTAL

Sergio reversed his ban on PDA and allowed Crystal—who was now eighteen-going-on-nineteen—to reveal their relationship to the world. He couldn't be up to anything fishy with Lucerito if his girlfriend was right next to him in the studio every day—right? Sergio deployed Crystal with the kind of power move only he could pull off: he quickly wrote two new hit songs for her, which landed Crystal back in the Top 10.

PART 2: BE EVERYWHERE, ALWAYS

To suggest he was too busy, too public, and too respected to have any underage skeletons in his closet, Sergio threw himself into a manic array of new projects. He launched the young rock guitarist Ricky Luis; the progressive performers Hernán Visseti and Ciclón; and a new act called Grupo Okidoki formed by the grown kids of a nostalgic favorite, Humberto Urban. Astonishingly, Sergio wrote nearly all the songs for these new clients. Instead of freezing under pressure, his stamina and creativity were off the charts. Rock critics who, weeks earlier, were obsessing over his morals were

> now rhapsodizing over his talent. As if that wasn't enough of a flex, Sergio even recorded an album of his own, accompanying himself on piano and mastering all the tapes alone.

But the true whirl of his magician's cape was:

PART 3: THE BOQUITAS PINTADAS

> Sergio came up with the name, of course, and it's exactly what you'd expect of him: obscure, ickily sexual, and kind of brilliant. Sergio plucked it from the lyrics of an old Argentinian foxtrot, "Rubias de New York," which describes four irresistible young women.

"Mary, Peggy, Betty, Julie, blondes from New York," the song goes. "I don't know how to live without them." The *rubias* are "fragile dolls of oblivion and pleasure" with "blossoming lips":

> Deliciosas criaturas perfumadas
> *Delicious scented creatures*
> Quiero el beso de sus boquitas pintadas
> *I want the kiss from their painted mouths*

Sergio had named the group before there even was one. Which made sense, because the Boquitas were only intended to have one real star: Sergio himself.

The Boquitas were actually more of a boast than a band. This new group, besides distracting everyone from Lucerito, would also scratch an itch that had been nagging at Sergio's ego: the one thing that had always been missing from Mr. Midas's résumé was a surprise. The performers who came to him already had a good amount of training under their belts. Even the young ones—Ga-Bí, Lucerito, Crystal—were either TV veterans or song contest favorites by the time they arrived in his hands. The question would always linger over how much credit Sergio really deserved for their musical success.

But not this time. Sergio's plan was to pluck five young women from obscurity and puppet-master them into a supergroup. The Boquitas (whoever they turned out to be) were always intended to showcase *his* talents, not theirs. He would put five girls on instruments of his choosing, then teach them how to perform his songs. The more raw the Boquitas, the greater Sergio's triumph when they eventually soared.

And as soon as attention shifted to the Boquitas, Sergio would be safe to turn his own attention back to Lucerito. Because in a studio full of teenage girls, he figured, who'd make a fuss over just one?

Sergio was right. About his studio, at least.

The moment he began casting Boquitas, his studio turned into an all-night clubhouse full of chattering, giggling, hopeful young women. Sergio spent so much time auditioning, some nights he didn't even make it home. His solution? If he couldn't make it to his house because of the girls, he'd just move the girls to his home.

Sergio had all the furniture removed from the first two floors of his house, leaving nothing except a couple of hard benches along the walls like church pews. His new publicity director, the former rock journalist Rubén Aviña, was assigned an office in a small back bedroom that was furnished with a sofa, but no table, chair, or desk. He ended up sitting on the floor to type.

"Sergio and I weren't living together then, and he was using his house as his studio," Crystal would recall. "Every day it seemed like there were more girls there. Everywhere you went in that house, more girls came out. I didn't want to ask, because he wouldn't like it and I might get punished, but I had to wonder—are all these girls really musicians?"

Crystal's younger brother had the same question. Now that Crystal's relationship was out in the open, Sergio felt more comfortable having her brother, who was also blind, accompany her to the studio. "Sergio was very fond of him, and the two would joke around together," Crystal would say. "That's when you would really see Sergio's tender side." Sergio called her brother *El Ciego*—the blind guy—and whenever Crystal came through the door, Sergio would call out, "*Ay ya*, where's my blind buddy?"

El Ciego didn't know much about his sister's situation with Sergio, but even he could tell there was something strange about all the teenybopper bustle throughout Sergio's home. Whispered conversations filtered through the doors, and the bathrooms were always thick with the scents of perfume and fruity lip gloss.

"These girls smell like trouble," he warned Sergio. "Something bad is going to happen if you have all these young girls running around."

"Indeed, they smell like trouble," Sergio smirked. "But they also smell like strawberries."

12

THE 5TH BOQUITA

Rubén Aviña was right in the center of this bizarre tween carousel, watching it whirl around him as he wondered: Does Sergio really know what he's doing? Do *I*?

Today, as he tells me the story in the midst of his tidy, book-filled office, it's a coin toss whether he was the perfect choice for Sergio's public-relations representative or the absolute worst. Everything about him seems genuine and believable, from that focused-but-friendly gaze in his warm eyes to the quietly confident moustache we associate with brainy good guys like Gabriel García Márquez, Kurt Vonnegut, and Magnum P.I. I can sense he's a bright, good-natured person who wants to see the best in everyone—but that doesn't mean he doesn't see.

"I loved working for Sergio," he tells me. "At first." The studio was nuts, but in a fun way. Singers and musicians and eager newcomers were constantly barreling in and out the door, and the only thing more unpredictable than who would pop in next was which Sergio would show up each morning. Would it be Merry Songwriter, with a fresh new tune burbling from his lips? Or Show Biz Savant, eyes ablaze with his latest vision for a TV spectacular? Scowling Genius was also a regular, fuming and muttering darkly to himself, replaced hours later by Kindly Collaborator, the astral opposite twin who'd drape a friendly arm across Rubén's shoulder as he suggested tweaks to a press release in progress. But there was one Sergio that Rubén did his best to avoid, and that Sergio was too unpleasant to soften with a nickname. Much of the time, Sergio was so mission-focused on training his performers that he seemed robotic. But every once in a while, Rubén would catch a glimpse of Sergio's eyes playing across the girls' bodies with a stare so hungry and gleeful, it was sickening.

Rubén really liked his job and hated the thought of quitting, but he had to set limits. I absolutely will not lie for Sergio, he decided. And if I see him touch or hurt anyone, I'm going to the police. Those two lines in the sand were easy to draw. But things got a lot trickier when it came to the 5th Boquita. *Does anyone else see this?* Rubén wondered. *Or is it just me?*

Crystal's mother spotted it right away. She took one look at Sergio's new group and her jaw dropped.

Crystal, she hissed in her daughter's ear. *This girl looks just like Lucerito. They could be twins!*

Crystal and her mother had stopped by Sergio's house because he'd sent word that henceforth Crystal would need a personal assistant and he, of course, had selected one. When they arrived to meet this mystery stranger who would, under Sergio's orders, have full run of Crystal's home and be at her side 24/7, they ran smack into the newly selected Boquitas Pintadas, there to start their first rehearsal.

Crystal's mom instantly recognized two of the Boquitas. She always kept a sharp eye out for her daughter's competition, so she knew that Pilar Ramírez had appeared on the kids' show *Chiquilladas* and that Claudia Rosas had been drummer for the short-lived bubblegum band Las Vicuñitas. The remaining Boquitas she'd never seen before. One was Mónica Rodríguez, a teenager from Sergio's hometown of Coatzacoalcos. The other was a tall, fiery-eyed fifteen-year-old named María Raquenel Portillo.

But it was the 5th Boquita who riveted her attention. Of all the girls on earth that Sergio could have selected, he had somehow found the mirror image of the tween he'd just sworn wasn't his secret girlfriend.

So reckless, Crystal's mother thought. *So stupidly risky.*

"You want to have sex with these girls, Sergio," she said.

"Of course not," Sergio protested. "This is a professional studio."

Crystal's mom wasn't some desperate stage mom. She was a hardworking day laborer who'd lifted two blind children out of poverty, and she hadn't done it by letting herself get pushed around.

"I know you, Sergio," she insisted. "And I know what's going on."

Crystal managed to shush her mother and get her out the door. Neither one of them was fooled, though. Whoever this new girl was—this Gloria Treviño—they had a gut feeling she wasn't there for her voice. Crystal's mother wasn't going to make a scene at that moment and embarrass her daughter, but she wasn't going away either. She'd be back the next day, and the next, and keep coming up with excuses to drop in unannounced until she got to the bottom of whatever Sergio was up to.

But if you want to catch Sergio off-guard, you only get one chance. From then on, the Boquitas were nowhere to be seen. Whenever Crystal's mother came through the door, all she found was a quiet waiting room full of hungry hopefuls. The five Boquitas were phantoms.

"I knew they were around there somewhere, taking music lessons and learning their instruments," Rubén would recall. "But I never saw them. They were closed off in a studio with a piano. That's where they would spend the entire day, never even leaving to have lunch as far as I could tell. They were five little ghosts, those Boquitas Pintadas."

One afternoon, there came a knock on Rubén's door. He opened it and found a pretty, wild-haired young woman with freckles across her nose and a portable synthesizer hanging around her neck.

"Do you mind if I practice here?" she asked Rubén. "There's no place else for me to go."

Sure, Rubén said. He took his seat back on the floor and continued tapping out his press releases while Gloria de los Angeles Treviño Ruiz took a seat on the sofa and began searching out chords on her keyboard. Before long, she flopped back on the sofa and began leafing through a magazine.

"Better watch out I don't tell Sergio how you rehearse," Rubén chided.

The girl laughed, and the two began talking. "It's really tough," Gloria confided. "We get here at seven in the morning, and don't take a break until four in the afternoon." Then it was back in the room for the second session which lasted "until death," as she put it. "Sometimes we don't get out of here till four in the morning. Then I'll get two hours of sleep and be dreaming of piano keys the whole time! Usually, I don't even have time to eat. I'm always going around starving."

From that afternoon on, Gloria would use Rubén's officc as her regular hideaway. Rubén got the feeling Gloria was more interested in talk than privacy because, within moments of arriving, she'd launch into some story about her topsy-turvy childhood. It was kind of strange, he thought, how often Gloria's tales ended in some bitter disappointment, as if joy was always the setup for a tragic punch line.

Gloria would light up, for instance, as she talked about a treasured little dog she'd named Reina (Queen) . . . but then told how Reina was killed by a car. She adored living with her great-grandparents . . . but she was shifted to the home of a despised aunt . . . then reunited with her parents! . . . who later divorced . . .

Being a Boquita was just another example. Gloria was elated when Sergio picked her, but now that she was part of the group . . . wow. The road to pop stardom was a lot rougher than she thought. Rubén always assumed Sergio was putting together a Menudo-style girl group, five pretty faces whose musical talent was a fourth-place priority behind sex appeal, dance moves, and hairstyles.

But apparently Mr. Midas meant business.

"We had to learn not just to play, but to dominate our instruments," Gloria would recall. "Our music instruction was very thorough. He drilled us on musical history, theory, notation, harmony, and composition. Sergio demanded nothing less than perfection."

But why? Rubén was perplexed. He'd been around scores of pop performers in his time, and they basically came in two flavors: Artists and Acts.

Artists are true musicians who become performers. *Acts* are performers who imitate artists. (The apotheosis of all Acts was reached with Milli Vanilli, two singers who didn't even bother to sing.)

Turning an Artist into an Act is way easier than turning an Act into an Artist. In fact, off the top of his head Rubén couldn't even think of an Act that had gone Artist. If an Act you are born, as an Act you shall remain. So if Sergio wanted real musicians, why didn't he simply hire them in the first place?

Rubén wondered about this every time he passed the rehearsal room on his way home at night and heard the Boquitas still in there, plunking along as Sergio roared orders at them. If teenybopper beauty was the key to their success, who cared whether they were actually strumming their own guitars? No one ever expected Ricky Martin to let rip with a guitar solo, yet Menudo sold millions of records. Sergio, he felt, was making the girls miserable for nothing.

Only later did the light bulb flash and he realized what Sergio was up to: Amateurishness wasn't the Boquitas' problem. It was the *point*.

The Boquitas Pintadas would be proof of Sergio's brilliance. If he could pluck five girls off the street and transform them from raw talents into a bona fide band, what *couldn't* he do? No other musical director would even attempt a transformation like that.

Birthing the Boquitas would be a brutally painful process, however. And like all births, only for the women.

Crystal was no longer allowed to just drop by Sergio's house. Because he was so busy with Boquitas boot camp, Sergio explained, plus his ongoing projects with Lucerito and the rest of his performers, he wanted Crystal to schedule her time with him through the personal assistant that he insisted she hire: Nora Miranda.

So everywhere Crystal went, Nora was by her side. Sergio was so pleased with Nora's chaperoning that after a few months, he assigned her to start tending to the Boquitas Pintadas as well. Anytime she wasn't with Crystal, he wanted her keeping an eye on the rest of the girls in the studio.

"Nora was our world," Crystal would say. "Anything we needed, Nora was there to provide it."

Crystal had no idea where Sergio found Nora or why, exactly, he suddenly felt that it was no longer suitable for Crystal to rely on her mother, who had come down from their home in northern Mexico to live with Crystal and do the exact same job that Nora had now taken over. But Crystal followed Sergio's orders without question. Even her mother, who usually had no problem standing up to Sergio, backed down this time after he hit a sensitive nerve: maybe, he suggested, a working-class woman from the backcountry wasn't sophisticated enough to represent a star like Crystal in show business settings.

Nora was pleasant enough company and fine with normal, day-to-day tasks, but to be honest, she wasn't exactly qualified for the job. Crystal was surprised to discover that Nora had never worked in the music industry. Or with the blind. Or even as a personal assistant. As far as Crystal could tell, she had no special skills that would make her leap from a pool of other applicants as the one and only person Sergio could trust with the happiness and safety of a top client who also happened to be his girlfriend.

So what made Nora so special in Sergio's eyes?

Sergio Jr.

Nora's secret spilled out late one night after Crystal had a show in Tijuana. Instead of traveling all the way back to Mexico City, Crystal decided they'd stop over at her parents' house. After Crystal had gone to bed, Nora began talking with Crystal's mom at the kitchen table.

Sergio, Nora said, has a lot of hurt from his childhood. That's why it's so hard for him to express love. Or relate to his son.

His . . . *what*? Crystal's mother was stunned. Sergio has a child?

Our little boy, Nora said.

She'd given birth to Sergio Gustavo when they were dating eight years earlier, shortly before Sergio met Ga-Bí. Sergio was very clear: he told Nora she could have the baby or not, it was up to her, but she shouldn't count on him for anything. He was focused totally and only on music. She named the boy after him, hoping he'd soften, but—

"It didn't matter," Nora said. "Sergio has never seen him."

The next morning, Crystal woke up to the news that her personal assistant had once been impregnated and abandoned by the manager who was now her thirty-year-old boyfriend. For a nineteen-year-old, that was a lot to absorb before breakfast.

No te preocupes, Crystal's mom reassured her. Don't worry. We'll find you a new manager. I'll get your things from Sergio's house myself. You never have to see that man again.

Mamá, with respect, Crystal said. No.

Sergio loves me, she argued. If he neglected to mention that the woman he'd hired as her constant companion had also been his girlfriend and was raising their secret love child, well . . . who was she to say that was wrong? Sergio is brilliant. He does things for reasons we don't always understand.

Crystal's mother was aghast. I can't stand by while you do something this foolish, she said.

Crystal steeled her nerve. You don't have to, she replied. I'm legal age now. I own my own home. And . . . She paused, suddenly realizing she had another major decision to make. And I have Nora, she concluded. If Sergio thinks she's right for me, she's right for me.

Distraught but true to her word, Crystal's mother left Crystal on her own with Nora. After she'd gone, Crystal wondered why Nora had ever shared that secret about Sergio with her mother in the first place. She never asked Nora about it, but it nagged at her mind for weeks.

And then suddenly, it all became clear.

I was right, Crystal realized. Sergio really must be a genius, because who else would ever come up with such an ingenious scheme? Who else would recruit his still-obsessed ex-girlfriend as the one person he could trust to not only keep tabs on Crystal for him, but also to drive out her mother, spy on the Boquitas, and—

Cover up the fact that Sergio had secretly married his fifteen-year-old bass player.

13

MARY BOQUITAS

María Raquenel Portillo was perfect.

Not because of her looks, although her raven curls and piercing dark eyes made her a striking beauty.

Not because of her voice, despite her natural contralto that let her glide from sweet highs to growling lows.

And not even because of her age, which, at fifteen, put her smack in the sweet spot between all of the thirteen- to seventeen-year-olds who seemed to constantly fill Sergio's home studio most days.

No, what made María perfect was something else. She had the one invisible quality that Sergio was learning to prize above all else:

Silence.

María could keep a secret. She never breathed a word about her relationship with Sergio. Not to her friends, not to her fellow Boquitas, not to Nora. How she managed to bottle it up for so long is hard to imagine. It must have been excruciating for Maria to spend all day in a small rehearsal room with four teenage girls and never once let slip that the man they all idolized was now *her husband*.

But María kept her mouth shut and eyes down whenever Sergio was in the room, avoiding even the slightest affectionate glance that could expose their romance. Those were Sergio's instructions. She was his special one, he told her, and all special things had to be kept private. Not because they were hiding anything. "For artistic purposes," he said—apparently the same artistic purposes that silenced Crystal after he began sleeping with her when she was seventeen.

If anyone found out about them, Sergio told María, it could tear the Boquitas apart before they even got started and stain her reputation as a performer. And as for breaking the news to Crystal . . . well, they had to be merciful, right? Crystal was young and blind and depended so much on Sergio. As soon as he made sure Crystal would be okay on her own, Sergio promised, he'd let everyone know how much he loved María.

María obeyed with fanatical devotion. That left just one loose end for Sergio to handle.

Going public with Crystal had bought him some peace, but that would blow up in his face if anyone suspected it had been a smokescreen. All it would take was a whiff of rumor about him and one of the teen Boquitas and all the Lucerito stuff would come roaring back to bite him. Sergio couldn't risk having the family of another young singer asking questions that could catch the ear of the media.

So Sergio made a bold move. Instead of waiting for any gossip to reach María's parents, he brought it right to their door. He came over one evening and asked to marry their daughter. Not only did he receive their "blessing and best wishes," as he'd later say, but something even better: their promise to keep quiet. Anything that rocked the Boquitas' boat right now, he warned, would sink María's shot at stardom.

A few days later, Sergio and María slipped away to marry in a courtroom ceremony. Then it was right back to work.

The newly wed María entered the rehearsal room as she always did, trying her best to hide any clue that she was now a married woman. She wasn't wearing his ring or carrying his last name, but Sergio did come up with a secret symbol to show she belonged to him. From that day on, she was Mary Boquitas.

Rubén Aviña, Sergio's new publicist, was impressed. Judging from what he could hear through the door of the tiny studio, Sergio's experiment was working. Rubén's rock critic's ear told him the Boquitas were nearly stage-ready. He had no idea how they'd handle an audience, but in the safety of their tiny studio, they were getting more polished and powerful by the day.

"Should I set a little something up?" Rubén asked one evening after the Boquitas had finished another marathon rehearsal. The next step for any new group, of course, was to book some club gigs so they could work out the kinks in front of the fewest eyes and figure out their performance chemistry.

"Don't call any clubs," Sergio replied. "Call Raúl."

"Raúl . . . ?" Rubén was mystified. "You mean Raúl *Velasco*?"

"Exactly."

"Really? Why?"

Sergio pointed toward his 16-channel Soundcraft mixer and reel-to-reel tape recorders. "You think we've just been practicing? I've got a full album ready to launch."

"But—"

"Call Raúl," Sergio insisted.

Sergio was proposing a massive, do-or-die gamble. He was so eager to flex his talents that instead of soft launching the Boquitas in front of friends and family, he wanted to throw them to the wolves. To the wolf, more precisely: Raúl Velasco, host of the most popular show in Mexico, *Siempre en Domingo*.

Before there were influencers, there was Raúl. For decades,

he'd been an entertainment icon with a track record for sniffing out newcomers who'd go on to become stars. Sergio had seen it for himself with Crystal and Lucerito. Getting on Raúl Velasco's show could make your album a hit. Getting him in your corner could make you unstoppable.

Despite Rubén's misgivings, he set up a meeting for Sergio at Televisa's studios. "I have a new girl group, Don Raúl, and you're really going to like them," Sergio said, as he slotted a demo video into the machine and hit play. Don Raúl watched the first few minutes, then looked at Sergio like he was out of his mind.

"They look like tiny prostitutes, man!" he snorted. "That's what you're selling with this group." Raúl Velasco prized his reputation for spotting edgy new acts, but Sergio had gone way too far. Sexy was fine. But he drew the line at prosti-tots.

"They're going to be big," Sergio insisted.

"You want them on my family show? On Sunday night? A group called 'Sexy Little Lipstick Mouths'? No way. It's never going to happen."

Sergio had too much respect for Don Raúl to argue. Instead, he went behind his back. Within days, Don Raúl received a terse message from Televisa's top management.

Schedule Sergio's girls. Now.

If Televisa wanted any of Sergio's singers, they'd have to take all of them. Mr. Midas wasn't playing around.

The only thing Sergio couldn't do was join the Boquitas onstage. With their TV debut approaching fast, the Boquitas needed to rally around a floor general. Typically that's the lead singer's job, but privately, the youngest and last-picked of the Boquitas decided to fill those shoes herself.

Gloria still had the emotional scars from being on the bottom of the Mean Girls totem pole, and she wasn't going to let it happen to her again. She'd seen how it worked at school, the way one or two girls took charge and everyone else fell into step with their fashion, hair styles, and slang, so she began putting the same tactics to work herself. To rise to the top and become queen bee of the Boquitas, Gloria began tearing them down behind their backs.

"Pilar and Mónica are a pair of hardcore weirdos," she'd whisper to Rubén Aviña and anyone who'd listen. Pilar was gay, Gloria explained, while Mónica was a religious freak with an eating disorder. Mónica was always bingeing on pastries and yammering about "some kind of cult or other." Gloria was pretty sure the two of them had converted each other to their individual tastes. "Mónica made Pilar renounce the Virgin Mary," Gloria gossiped. "And in return Mónica gave herself over to Pilar's"—Gloria searched for a euphemism—"preferences."

And oh my God! What was up with María—sorry, *Mary*. She was so shy and silent, keeping her eyes glued to the floor whenever Sergio was talking to them. How on earth was she going to sing like that with a TV camera in her face? She was going to freeze and make them all look stupid, Gloria was sure of it.

If Gloria was right, then the Boquitas really were jelling into a rock band. At least in one sense: after just a few short months they were thick in the kind of backstabbing and intrigue that most groups take years to develop. Already, they had a guitarist sleeping with the pianist; a bass player sleeping with the manager; a manager cheating on his celebrity girlfriend; a national TV host calling them whores; and a girl who'd barely made the cut gleefully dishing dirt on them all.

And then in an instant, all that vanished. On the night of their *Siempre en Domingo* appearance, the Boquitas Pintadas took the stage and showed the world what Mr. Midas was all about.

Pilar and Mary Boquitas stepped to the mic together and, side by side, tore into "All's Fair in Love" ("En el Amor Todo Se Vale"), one of Sergio's new songs. Somehow, he'd created an irresistible head-bobber that was also an anthem to emotional abuse. The three backup Boquitas crooned along as Pilar and Mary described a girl who gleefully tormented her boyfriend, singing lines like:

Yes, I lied and treated you like dirt the other day,
Just to see if you'd beg me to stop

The Boquitas were rocking, and their songs were pretty catchy if you didn't listen too closely to the low-key diabolical lyrics. Also, Sergio must have taken Don Raúl's prosti-tots comments to heart, too: rather than going for sex appeal, he dressed the Boquitas in trendy '80s mall fashion, with lots of distressed denim, neckerchiefs, and baggy animal print blouses.

Watching from the wings, Raúl Velasco had to admit he might have overreacted. He actually seemed to be enjoying the show—until Pilar and Mary stepped back, and Gloria took the mic for "Caveman Love" ("Amor Cavernicolo"), about a young woman who's so submissive to her brutish boyfriend that she's ready to clobber strangers on demand. "Who do you want me to smack?" Gloria sang. "Don't bother hiding your club, there's no need to bother."

Don Raúl's jaw dropped. Was this baby-faced teen crooning about rough sex and grooming? Don't bother hiding your "*club*"?

Gloria had actually written "Caveman Love" herself, as well as another song, "Nightfall" ("Se Hace Noche"), about a girl who slips away from her family to spend the night with her lover. The only thing more surprising about the raunchiness of teenage Gloria's songs was the fact that Sergio even considered them for the album. For the first time, he released his iron control and granted not one but two songs to some kid who'd quite literally wandered in off the street. Crystal and Lucerito never got that kind of treatment, even if it was in Sergio's best interest to share the credit a little.

But Gloria was different. Maybe Sergio had found a young woman who actually thought the way he did.

Crystal and her mother tuned in to *Siempre en Domingo* and listened in silence as the Boquitas performed. Don Raúl's prosti-tots comment had found its way to Crystal, of course, as well as to her brother, her mother—everybody. In a pre-social-media era, nothing traveled faster than hot gossip, and Don Raúl was a master at sparking the flames. His tongue was vicious, and all the more dangerous because he often turned out to be right.

Now, the voices inside Crystal's head urging her to leave Sergio were right in front of her face. Even one of her backup singers begged her to please, please stop kidding herself and get out.

It's not that simple, Crystal told her. She was penniless, and all of her amps and touring equipment were locked up in Sergio's house.

"Sergio handled the money, and never gave me any," she said.

"This is crazy!" the singer replied. "How can the No. 1 selling artist be broke?" I'll take care of this, she assured Crystal.

The singer recruited her friend Juan Gabriel, a street-tough musician who'd fought his way up from nothing. "Don't worry, Crystalisima," Juan Gabriel told her. "I'll get you back together."

He and his boys would get her equipment back from Sergio so she could perform again, and in the meantime, he'd float her as much money as she needed. "Five or six thousand dollars isn't much today, but in 1984, it was a lot for him to offer," Crystal says. Then, he added one last gesture to boost her spirits: he invited Crystal to be his guest of honor at his televised concert.

Show the world you're smiling and unbroken, Juan Gabriel urged her. He was right. The cameras kept swinging back again and again to celebrity singer Crystal at the foot of the stage, beaming with joy in a circle of Juan Gabriel's best friends.

At dawn the next morning, Crystal's phone rang.

"My office," Sergio snarled. He hung up.

Crystal went. She felt around for a chair.

"Stand," Sergio ordered. He launched into an interrogation. How do you know this man? Have you slept with him? Kissed him? Those men who came for your equipment, how about them? His questioning went on so long, Crystal grew woozy and nauseous.

"Sergio, I'm going to be sick," she said.

"Then get out."

"Enough!" Crystal's brother said after she got home, weeping.

He had Juan Gabriel come over, and together the two of them talked to Crystal for hours, reminding her over and over how successful she was, how valuable she was to them, how much friends and family and fans adored her. She was addicted to a dangerous relationship, and they were going to stand by her until the spell broke and the old Crystal returned and began to think for herself again.

"My brother stayed with me the whole time," Crystal would say. "He would not leave my side for days, until I came to my senses. I wasn't even aware that other people cared for me. I only had eyes for Sergio."

But no more. Sergio tried to bully her to come back by

threatening to withdraw her from that year's International Music Festival, but Crystal didn't buckle. He then upped the pressure: if she didn't return to him, he would take "Better Times," the song they'd written together about a blind person hoping for a brighter future, and give it to Yuri, a young blonde beauty hungry for a hit. True to Sergio's threat, his coaching and Crystal's song gave Yuri her first big success.

Crystal shrugged it off. She began booking events and went back on the road. She felt a new power stirring inside, a playfulness she hadn't experienced for years, and it rekindled her childhood love of running. She got so fast that before long, she qualified to represent Mexico at the Paralympic Games in three different events.

Weeks passed without a word from Sergio, then months. Crystal breathed a sigh of relief. Just like Ga-Bí, she'd finally broken free. Sergio was out of her life forever.

Until late one night in the summer of 1986, when she was awakened by a frantic pounding on her front door. A voice she hadn't heard in three months and hoped she'd never hear again was calling her name.

"Crystal, please. Please! You have to let me in," Sergio implored.

"No," Crystal said from the other side of the door. "Absolutely no."

"They're coming for me," Sergio pleaded. "If you don't let me in, they're going to kill me."

14

BLIND DEVOTION

"*They*?" Crystal asked. "Who's *they*? What are you talking about?"

She could hear Sergio panting raspily a few inches from her ear, as if he'd collapsed against the door in exhaustion.

"Sergio, who?" Crystal repeated.

Nothing. And then, faint as a whisper:

"Please."

Crystal's hand wavered near the lock, uncertain . . .

She clicked it open. Sergio staggered inside, limp with fear and soaked in sweat. He hugged her, draping himself over her in a long, damp embrace of relief. His clothes felt torn to her touch and badly rumpled, as if he'd been roughed up, and his face felt swollen against her cheek.

Finally, he sighed and said, "I need to lie down." Without another word, he walked down the hall to Crystal's room. She could hear him undressing, dropping his clothes on the floor, then the bedsprings creaking as he pulled back the sheets and slipped inside.

"Come," he called. "I need you with me tonight."

Crystal turned around, felt her way down the hall to her

guest room, and locked the door behind her. She didn't know what Sergio was up to, but she wasn't climbing into bed with him to find out.

When she woke up the next morning, the news was everywhere.

"Credible sources are reporting that Mr. Midas, the music impresario Sergio Andrade, has been accused of seducing, mistreating, and exploiting young girls in his care." The scoop had been broken by *TVyNovelas*, Mexico's most popular and influential entertainment weekly, but within hours, every radio and news channel in the country was broadcasting it as well. "One well-known singer who'd enjoyed considerable success with Andrade suddenly terminated all contact with him," the story continued, "and her family is said to be irate and exploring all options."

Nobody had to guess the name of the "well-known singer." And Sergio had already discovered what kind of "options" the family of Mexico's tween sweetheart would explore if they ever got their hands on him again.

Of course, that was just one side of the story. Before printing their scoop, *TVyNovelas* had given Sergio an opportunity to reply. This was his chance to let loose with a fire-breathing rebuttal and deny all the rumors, threatening anyone who dared spread such malicious gossip about a good and innocent man.

Instead, Sergio offered this:

"There has been a wave of commentary about me unlike anything I'd ever have imagined. They've called me everything from exploiter to child abuser," Sergio said. "I think that these things will eventually collapse from their own weight. If I really am that way, time will tell. If not, likewise."

If I really am that way???

Time will tell???

What the hell was that? Crystal, listening to the news on the radio, couldn't believe what she was hearing. As soon as Sergio emerged from her bedroom that morning, she pounced.

"Are you sleeping with Lucerito?" she demanded.

He released another of his long, soulful sighs, then launched into an impassioned tale about his painful childhood and reverence for music and the Christ-like journey of the true artist who must suffer so others can soar, going on and on until Crystal had to remind herself what she'd asked in the first place. Somewhere in Sergio's aria of an answer to her simple yes-or-no question, Crystal was pretty sure she heard a "No"—and if not in his actual words then certainly in his voice. This, Crystal decided, was the sound of a bewildered man in genuine pain.

"So what happened?" she asked.

"Well, you know what kind of imagination I have . . ." he began.

According to Sergio, he was having one of his usual phone chats with Lucerito, nothing special, just about new songs and tour dates and their plans for her future, and *maaayyybe* at some point he said something like "Hey, what if we went on tour and never came back? What if we took off and traveled the world together?" It was just chitchat between friends! Like, where-would-you-go-if-you-could-go-anywhere kind of stuff.

But apparently Lucerito's sixteen-year-old brother overheard enough of the conversation to be alarmed. He bolted straight to their mother, and that's when all hell broke loose. Lucero León confronted her daughter, and Lucerito's explanation that no, no, Sergio was only talking about traveling the world together when she was older didn't put out any fires.

Lucero León was both a Mexican mother and a show business professional, so she knew this was a two-phone-call situation. First to her lawyer, to make sure every last cent that Sergio owed them was paid. And then to her brother, to make sure Sergio got a little payback of his own.

Sergio was either tipped off or extraordinarily lucky because by the time Lucerito's uncle barged into the studio, Sergio was gone. As Lucerito's uncle searched the office, he was transfixed by the piles of books on Sergio's desk. Nearly all were about hypnosis and child psychology. "What the hell kind of a musician needs to be playing around with little kids' brains?" he wondered.

Despite his narrow escape from family justice, Sergio figured it would all blow over if he lay low for a day or two. But when he got word that a *TVyNovelas* reporter was looking for him, he reversed course. He decided to return the call and deal with the problem head-on. He was sure he could put out the fire with a few well-chosen words, and who was better at choosing words than him, the master songwriter? A little understatement and chagrin and he'd be out of the woods.

Lucerito's family didn't see it that way. They must have gotten an advance copy of the magazine, Sergio told Crystal, because as he was walking to his hotel late that night, three guys suddenly appeared from the dark and began pummeling him. "Time will tell? You're damn right, *cabrón*," one of them said. "And when it does, we'll be back."

Sergio managed to break free and flee into the hotel, but he knew he'd need a better place to hide. That's when it hit him. Everyone found out months ago that Crystal was through with him, so her house was the last place anyone would expect to find him. He only needed a day or two underground, he assured her, to give him time to walk back his stupid magazine comments and prove his innocence once and for all. Otherwise, he was dead.

Crystal felt a tug at her heart. "I believe you," she said.

She wasn't completely wrong. Looking back later, Crystal is confident that Sergio was genuinely terrified for his life. "It's one of the few things he ever told me that I think was really true," Crystal says.

But the longer Sergio hid out in her house, the more she heard about him and young women. The reason no one ever heard from Ga-Bí anymore, it was said, was because she'd fled the country to break free of his mind control. And that brother-sister pop group he managed that suddenly vanished? The sister reportedly got pregnant by an older man she refused to name. Who else could it be? The entertainment press barely had to add any dots to that story for readers to connect them.

The Lucerito family, however, was a stone fortress. They surrounded her in a protective huddle, no one breathing another word in public about Sergio. For him, that was even more terrifying. The silence was only broken much later by Lucerito herself, who offered this thinly veiled remark: "An evil person can even make fools out of grownups because he hits them with a wall of words about everything they're going to study, learn, accomplish. Thanks to my mamá, who is very sharp about this stuff and can't be fooled, I wasn't involved in any garbage and awfulness."

A few people came to Sergio's defense but only made matters worse. Yuri, the rising star who'd gotten lucky when Sergio gave her one of Crystal's songs, claimed she'd never had a problem with him. "No one ever abused me because my mom carried a gun, and that's why they called her '*Mamá Gallo*'

[Mother Hen]," Yuri said, seemingly deaf to her implication that when working with Sergio it helped to pack heat.

Gloria Trevi's assessment was just as accidentally awful. "Women with artistic aspirations or just out for money would throw themselves at him, trying to achieve with their bodies what they couldn't with their talent," she said. "They all wanted to trap the youngest and most famous producer of the eighties, the boy genius, the starmaker. Women of all ages and status and professions were pursuing him."

But Sergio, she stressed, was a man of restraint. "He didn't sleep with all of them."

And yes, while there was a, um . . . situation . . . with a singer who was on the young side, Sergio only had the most honorable of intentions. "They loved each other, and had a true, romantic, consensual relationship," Gloria said. The real villain, in her opinion, was the mouthy mother who butted in and got everyone riled up. Because in the process of taking down Sergio, that certain angry mom torpedoed Gloria as well.

"She went to Televisa and demanded that Sergio be blacklisted," Gloria claimed. "No one at Televisa was even allowed to take his phone calls anymore. Which meant if Sergio was your manager, you were blacklisted, too."

Sergio's artists began scrambling to terminate their contracts and sign with new managers. Within days of the *TVyNovelas* article, Mr. Midas's client roster was empty. Even the Boquitas Pintadas, whose single "I Can't Forget Him" ("No Puedo Olvidarlo") was steadily climbing the Most Requested charts, had to face their new, bizarre reality. With their manager on the run and no chance of going back on TV, their short ride was over.

The Boquitas were through.

For nearly a year, Sergio remained invisible.

Mexican media were clamoring for paparazzi photos or news tidbits it could share of the fugitive music mogul, but Sergio had pulled off a truly remarkable vanishing act. Only one person had any clue what he was up to, and she desperately wished she didn't. Horrible as Sergio was as a boyfriend, as an ex he was even worse. He'd conditioned Crystal to believe torture, cheating, and psychological abuse were part of a relationship, but she didn't know they'd continue after the relationship was over.

"We were not lovers, but he mistreated me as though we were," she would say. "There were nights we had sex. Sometimes he came into my room, or I was watching TV and he'd start," she'd recall. "The second night it happened, I realized he was demeaning me, but in my strange way of thinking back then, I thought, 'He's here, I've agreed to that, so I might as well accept it all.'"

During the day, Sergio would scan the street for suspicious-looking lurkers and menacing cars, then slip outside when he felt the coast was clear. Crystal knew better than to ask where he was going, but something about his excitement left little doubt what he was up to. "At least he wasn't bringing his girls into my house and trying to make me accept it," she'd say. "At least he didn't humiliate me that way."

But one thing finally pushed her over the edge. A gossip columnist had sniffed out a rumor that Sergio was actually married, and before Crystal could even process the news, a marriage certificate had been unearthed: the man who'd gone into hiding because of his dubious connection to one teen singer was secretly married to another one: fifteen-year-old María Raquenel Portillo, aka Mary Boquitas.

"When I heard about this María Raquenel," Crystal would say, "I'd had it with him. She was barely fifteen. I said, No, thanks."

If he didn't get out of her house at once, she demanded, she'd expose his whereabouts to the world. Sergio shrugged and began packing. He didn't mind leaving because by then, the heat on him was letting up. Word had reached him that the furious family of the "well-known singer" was starting to quiet down. Someone had explained that carrying out a public vendetta against Sergio wasn't going to help their daughter's reputation, and since nothing had actually happened, why not let it go and get her back on TV? The someone who'd done the explaining was believed to be none other than the "Heart of the Home" himself: Sergio's silver-tongued big brother, Lalo.

During the years when Sergio was blowing up as a musical mastermind, Lalo was enjoying his own meteoric rise. He'd put himself through law school as a TV soccer announcer, and his on-air popularity was so great that after graduation, Televisa had kept him as in-house legal counsel. But Lalo soon outgrew even that promotion—not to mention his nickname—and began positioning himself for a career in politics. With his twinkling charm and ferocious intelligence, Eduardo Andrade Sánchez quickly became a power player, with the accent on "power"—the kind of guy who could reach for his phone and unload a world of regret on anyone who messed with his little brother.

Sergio had always hated living in Lalo's shadow, but now there was finally some upside. With his big brother's muscle at his back, Sergio felt it was safe to come out of the shadows and start rebuilding his career. And the timing couldn't have been better. Because by 1988, Gloria really needed his help.

15

PIG-EYE TACOS

"Well, *mija*, your adventure is over," Gloria's mother told her when the Boquitas broke up in 1986. "It's time to come home."

Gloria was now further from the top than when she'd started. At least when she arrived in Mexico City two years before, she'd been a promising young Lucerito look-alike with Televisa's powerhouse backing. Now, she was just another cute girl from the provinces who'd tried, and failed, to captivate the country with nothing more than a pretty face and giggly natural charm.

Gloria hadn't even been the most remarkable performer in a rather unremarkable group. On most of the Boquitas' songs, Gloria's voice was barely noticeable, a faint adolescent echo chiming in on the chorus. No one was hungrier than Gloria's mother to see her make it big, but as a former dancer, Gloria Ruiz also knew just what kind of danger an ambitious teenager could be lured into while grasping desperately at the fringes of Mexican show business without the support of Televisa's star school or Sergio Andrade's hit factory.

"No," Gloria told her mother. "I want another chance."

"Don't you understand?" her mother said. "You already had two. Twice as many as I got. It's over."

Did Gloria really believe her mother had enjoyed spending all those years teaching pirouettes to factory workers' kids for a few pesos a night? She'd taken her best shot, and when she couldn't become a famous dancer, she set out to become the next best thing: a wealthy wife. It had taken a little while, but she finally found her rich doctor. Now it was Gloria's turn to start her Plan B—and quick, before her teenage beauty began to fade and, God forbid, she followed in her mother's footsteps and found herself penniless and pregnant.

"No," Gloria repeated. "I'm still young. I can do it."

"Well, not with my money. You're on your own."

For the past two years, Gloria Ruiz had been covering Gloria's living expenses. The Televisa scholarship barely provided enough for housing, and after that ended, Gloria had no income at all. During the Boquitas Pintadas' months of training, Sergio hadn't given them a dime, and their album hadn't sold enough to earn royalties. Without her mother's allowance, Gloria was broke.

"I had just turned seventeen when they threw me out of my boardinghouse because I couldn't pay the monthly bill," Gloria would recall. "I went to another one, and when they threw me out of there, I moved to another. I was looking everywhere for a job as a housemaid, or waitress, anything." All the cute outfits she'd gotten during her time at Televisa, she sold to secondhand shops. "I had to scrub out my bra and panties at night, so I'd have something clean to wear in the morning," she said. "I was a true vagrant."

At her most desperate, Gloria began begging on the street. She discovered that if she went early in the morning to Polanco, the ritzy neighborhood full of art galleries and luxury hotels, she could sweet-talk spare change out of elderly rich women who always said she reminded them of their granddaughters. She avoided men, however, and got off the streets before dark to avoid being mistaken for a prostitute. Before heading back to whatever boardinghouse she'd landed in, she stopped by taco stands that were closing for the day to see if she could get stale tortillas and throwaways for free.

"During my hungry years, I ate tacos stuffed with pig eyes, or the tongue or the throat," she would later tell *Más* magazine. "My God, I was so famished they tasted delicious!"

But thanks to Sergio, she still had one card to play. During Boquitas rehearsals, Sergio would halt everything at 10 a.m. each day and turn on the television. A dynamic new dance exercise had been created for at-home moms, and Sergio insisted that the girls never miss a workout: Jane Fonda and her aerobics craze had crossed the Rio Grande. Sergio liked the upbeat pace of aerobics but more specifically, the fashion choices that came with it. He had a feeling those blazing neon tights, sheer bodysuits, and gymnastic routines were going to cross over into music. He wanted his Boquitas to be ready.

So whenever Gloria wasn't pleading with old ladies for pity pesos, she was walking around Mexico City looking for work at aerobics studios. After a few weeks, she finally got an offer: as a janitor. The former Televisa star-in-training began scrubbing toilets and wiping down mirrors, but it wasn't long until she talked her way into subbing in as a last-minute replacement for an absent teacher. This was her one chance to make a big impression, so she came out firing. Gloria bounced around the room, screaming encouragement and kicking for the ceiling. The studio owner was pleased enough to offer another class right away. "Same energy," he added. Gloria grit her teeth and hid the fact that she'd already left it all on the floor.

"Sometimes he'd have me in there twelve hours a day," Gloria would recall. It was brutally exhausting, but at least instead of mopping floors and scrounging for coins, she was now getting paid to practice dance moves and perform for an audience.

She was also writing furiously in her notebooks, making use of the breaks between aerobics sessions to jot down song ideas she'd come up with during class. She'd been writing verses since she was five years old and had learned to read and arrange music during her year with the Boquitas. Her tough new life, meanwhile, was giving her plenty of hard-knocks and girl-alone material to draw on for lyrics.

When she'd written nearly thirty new songs, Gloria felt she was ready. She began cold-calling record producers but couldn't get past their receptionists. She even left a few Hail Mary messages for *Siempre en Domingo*'s Raúl Velasco, but that got her nowhere. If anyone even remembered her name, they knew her as Miss Second Fiddle: the low-rent Lucerito, the backup Boquita. If she could only get through the door, she'd show them that kid was gone. She couldn't afford to have her hair cut, so she let it go long and loose. She couldn't buy clothes, so she refashioned the ones she had, feeling liberated by the trash-chic style of Madonna and Cyndi Lauper to experiment with clashing colors and artfully torn skirts.

"I was no longer a little girl with little girl dreams," she'd say. "I was now a woman who'd paid her dues, and Sergio always said that was the key to success: talent and hunger."

Maybe it was time to track him down.

16

DIABOLICAL LAMBS

Early one evening in 1988, Sergio Andrade slipped headphones over his ears and settled in behind the mic for his regular daily show, *My Personal Collection*, at radio station XEW.

He'd stage-managed a clever return to show business. Not by jumping into the same high-profile, Mr. Midas starmaker role as before, but by easing his way back as an on-air personality. There, in the seclusion of his soundproof booth, he could show off his musical chops with little risk of contact with young singers or angry parents. Plus, every time he eased the needle onto a record, he reminded the music industry that as the man who chose what songs got on the air, Sergio was still a force to be reckoned with.

That evening, as usual, he'd paused the music so he could go off on one of his mini-lectures about vocal styles, or classical composition, or whatever else was on his mind, when suddenly he was interrupted by a loud banging on the door. A wild-haired girl was knocking with one hand and waving happily through the window of the sound booth with the other. Sergio froze for a beat, wondering who the hell she was and what she wanted, until slowly, he recognized the ecstatic grin and playful eyes.

Well, well—the scrappy kid from Monterrey was still in town.

Gloria, he could see at a glance, had changed a lot over the past year. Physically, she'd matured from a freckled schoolgirl into a busty, athletic young woman. And just from the way she'd connived her way past XEW's front desk and was now insisting he open the soundproof door, she was clearly no longer the obedient tween who'd waited quietly on a bench outside his office all day.

Sergio put on a record and let Gloria into the booth. Almost immediately, she opened her backpack and pulled out a battered binder with drawings scrawled all over the cover, kids-style sketches of round-eyed girls and soaring birds and rainbows. She wasn't there to catch up.

"Could you look at my songs?" she asked. "Maybe during a break I can sing some for you?"

Sergio pointed toward the binder. "Everything in there is songs?"

"Yes. I've been really—"

Sergio cut her off. "Give it to me. I'll choose."

Gloria handed it over. Sergio flipped through, skimming past the first few teen-self-pity songs with barely a glance, until a title with a glint of darkness caught his eye:

"What Am I Doing Here?" ("¿Qué Hago Aqui?")

Sergio read the lyrics, then started over and considered each line again. It was deftly phrased and nicely rhymed, but something more: it was a song that Sergio never could have written himself. For all his skill, Sergio had a secret weak spot. He could write about what young women did and said, but he had no idea what they *felt*. When it came to adolescent emotions, the best he could do was bundle old clichés into fresh melodies and hope nobody noticed.

But Gloria's words? This was a voice Sergio could never fake. "What am I doing here?" Gloria wrote. "In this home where I can't stop crying, where my parents can't stop fighting, where they talk by shouting?"

Sergio stopped reading for a sec, cued up another record for his listeners, and then dug back into the binder. He stopped when a snippet of "What Will I Do Without Him?" ("¿Que Voy Hacer Sin Él?") leaped out at him: "I know very well he'll forget about me, but I don't know, I don't know, what I'll do without him."

That's the most danceable sad song I've ever heard, Sergio thought. He checked his watch. Okay, he told Gloria. Wait outside till I'm finished. Then let's find a piano.

"The instant Gloria sang those songs for me," Sergio would later say, "I knew if I could make her record, she'd be a sensation."

That's his version. Here's hers: "Sergio told me, 'These are very good, but you have to understand, the music business is in crisis right now. The record companies aren't spending, and if they did, it wouldn't be for another woman.'" The Latin market was way overstocked with female vocalists, he explained, but for Gloria that meant a real silver-lining opportunity:

> Too Many Singers + Not Enough Material = Lots of $$ for an Unknown Teen with a Full Notebook

"Let's sell some of these to a more experienced singer," Sergio suggested, "and use the proceeds as development money."

That way, they could spend time training Gloria as a solo performer and rent a studio without getting a record label involved. They'd have a much better chance of landing a production deal if they showed up with a polished performer and a recording in hand, Sergio told her. Plus, they'd retain more control of the product.

"I'll do whatever I have to," Gloria said. "Except selling my songs."

Okay, Sergio said. I've got another idea.

The coast was clear, Sergio figured, for him to come out in the open and pick up where he'd left off. He secured a converted house that would become one of the most notorious addresses in the country:

108 Adolfo Prieto Street

"Sergio Andrade opened an art school where he offered classes in singing, dancing, acting, music, and aerobics," Gloria would say. "It turned into an academy with a tremendous number of students."

Sergio's new compound had performance spaces on the first floor, an office and bedroom upstairs, and a yard out back. Finding staff was easy: besides Gloria, he also had Mary Boquitas, whom he'd continued seeing on the sly while hiding out in Crystal's house.

"He had me doing a little of everything," Gloria says, "even handing out badminton birdies and teaching aerobics." Whenever Sergio barked "*¡Vamonos!*" Gloria would drop whatever she was up to, even if she was in the midst of leading an exercise class, and grab anything she guessed Sergio might need—briefcase, sunglasses, daily calendar—because she didn't dare bother him to ask where they were going.

"One always spoke to Sergio with extreme courtesy," Gloria

would say. "Sergio drew the line and demanded respect. Our relationship was boss and subordinate."

Even Mary Boquitas had to address her husband not as Sergio, but as Señor. "At work, Sergio treated Mary just like everyone else," Gloria says. Actually, worse. Normal employees are paid. Mary and Gloria got nothing. Sergio said that because he was just getting back into the business after his long "sabbatical," he needed all his money to keep the school afloat. Instead of paying Gloria and Mary, he told them to give up their boardinghouse rooms and sleep in his basement. They agreed.

Down in their underground bunkhouse, Gloria and her onetime bandmate and frenemy became best friends. Mary began pouring out her heart about her marriage to Sergio, which had evolved from secret liaison into bewildering head game. Sergio rarely allowed Mary to spend the night in his bedroom and often mentioned he was thinking of divorce. Sometimes, he even mused out loud about his sexual attraction to some new teenagers who'd turned up at his studio. But at the same time, Sergio was also domineering and bitterly possessive, yelling at Mary in jealous rages until she dissolved into tears.

Gloria, as usual, was quick to defend Sergio with her topsy-turvy logic: so many eager women had given Sergio so much easy sex that he could no longer trust anyone. "His experiences had brought him to the conclusion that, if not all, then at least ninety percent of women were unfaithful piranhas," Gloria explained.

"And," she concluded, "I believe he was afraid that his partner would do with another man what these women had done with him." In Sergio's eyes, women are naturally predatory and treacherous and deserve what they get. And because Sergio was a genius, it had to be true.

Mary, nevertheless, was still desperate to rekindle their romance, and spent hours at night asking Gloria's advice. Those conversations made Gloria increasingly uncomfortable—because she'd begun sleeping with Sergio herself.

"When did it start?" she'd reflect. "I don't know. At first, our relationship had always been strictly work-related and a little stormy. I was a rebel by nature and impulsive; he was methodical and demanding. That's why all during the Boquitas Pintadas period, I was often at the end of my rope with him. What kept me there was my desire to become an artist, to triumph, to become famous. I know I irritated him, but he put up with it because he could see the artist in me. We mutually tolerated each other."

Even though she was juggling endless responsibilities at Sergio's school, he still expected her to carve out long hours to work on her music. As a Boquita, Gloria had mostly lingered in the background. Her only chance to make it as a solo artist, Sergio told her, was to come out roaring, commanding the stage with full diva power and blowing her audience back in their seats. Otherwise, she'd be gone in a week. "You have to make that guy in the back row want to kill for you," Sergio insisted. "Every pair of eyes has to think you're looking right at them."

The more Sergio tore apart her singing, the more infatuated Gloria became. "He wasn't the best-looking guy in the world," Gloria would say, "but he was a leader—a boss—and that is very attractive to women. He was famous and wealthy, a musician and a poet. And not to mention, an excellent lover."

Gloria knew how dangerous it was for Sergio to be around so many young women—except she was concerned about the risk to *him*. "There didn't seem to be any cure for Sergio," she'd shrug. "He was intelligent, sensitive, talented, hardworking, didn't smoke, wasn't obsessed with sports, but he had one weakness—women." It was all those diabolical lambs, in other words, who kept leading the poor wolf astray. "One woman can be a man's curse," Gloria would say, quoting a saying Sergio had taught her. "Many, his destruction."

Sergio didn't hide what he was up to from Mary and Gloria; he gloated about it. "There were a lot of stories he told me, a lot that he held back, and a lot that I discovered without wanting to, either because people told me or they happened right before my eyes," Gloria would say. "So I had to get my thoughts and feelings toward Sergio in order and figure out my future."

By now, she had spent nearly a year as Sergio's live-in assistant and second-string girlfriend. She'd just turned twenty, and hadn't performed since she was seventeen. Was she going to be his servant in the basement forever? As obedient as she was, a part of her mind still wondered if all of this was leading anywhere—all the hunger pangs and exhaustion and verbal abuse, plus the humiliation from sneaking off for sex with her best friend's husband. Did Sergio take her seriously, or was she just another piranha to him, Number Whatever of the dozens of girls in the studio hoping for his attention?

She told Sergio she was thinking of going away for a while to sort out her life. He countered with an offer. He'd record her album right away—if she could get her parents to pay for it. Not that he didn't have full faith in her talent, Sergio assured her. It was only because his star school was still finding its footing and he couldn't spare the cash.

"I really don't think my father likes me singing," Gloria replied. "And my mother and I aren't talking to each other."

"What's this?" Sergio asked. "Since when?"

"Since I wouldn't go home after the Boquitas ended."

Sergio knew Gloria's mother. She'd visited Sergio's studio often during the Boquitas Pintadas days, and unlike Crystal's mom, Gloria Ruiz had no problem with all the young women vying for Sergio's eye. To her, that was the sign of a true star-maker. Sergio remembered a flamboyant, aggressively blonde ex-dancer who thrilled at the chance for fame by association.

"I'll sort this out," Sergio said. "Let's go to Monterrey."

17

ALINE AT THIRTEEN

"You came at just the right time!" Gloria's mother gushed.

Gloria had planned out a whole pitch, complete with tears, pleas, and props. During the drive up from Mexico City, she'd rehearsed in her mind how she'd get down on her knees and beg for one last chance, promising to come home this time if she failed as a singer. She'd even brought a microphone from Sergio's school as a visual.

She never got the chance. Gloria Ruiz was overjoyed to find Mr. Midas at her front door, and within minutes, they were sipping coffee in the living room while Sergio described his plan for making Gloria a star. Her songs are guaranteed hits, Sergio raved, and her stage presence is ready to go. "Her moment is *now*!" Sergio paused. "If only I had the financing."

Gloria Ruiz's eyes lit up. She stumbled over herself in her haste to mention the inheritance she'd just received. It wasn't very big, but it was all hers, separate from Gloria's stepfather, so she was free to spend it any way she pleased.

Instantly, Sergio was all business. "You start packing," he told Gloria's mom. "You start rehearsing," he told Gloria. "I'll start making calls."

The next day, the three of them—Sergio, Gloria, and her over-the-moon mother—were on a flight to L.A., heading for Milagros Sound Studio.

Gloria Ruiz stared at her daughter in amazement.

As soon as Gloria stepped into the recording booth and slipped on her headphones, she lit up. Anything Sergio suggested, Gloria not only obeyed but outdid, shaking her body and growling her vocals as if her mouth was about to foam and her eyes roll back in her head. What ever happened to the shy Squaw Treviño who'd been bullied in school and overshadowed by four boisterous boys at home? How did she turn into . . . this? This magnetic spotlight grabber who sang with a voice that could drown out a bar fight?

"Well, Mom, I owe it all to you," Gloria could have explained. "A girl really learns to go for it when she's begging on the streets and stealing her best friend's middle-aged husband."

Any self-consciousness Gloria had, or discomfort with eyes on her body, had disappeared after spending twelve hours a day talking strangers out of their money on the streets of Mexico City. During those years on her own, the cute-as-Chispita look-alike named Gloria Treviño had hardened into "Gloria Trevi," a street punk who made "rock" seem as much a description of her heart as of her music.

Sergio rented the studio by night when it was cheaper. By day, Gloria and her mom searched Salvation Army thrift shops for Gloria's new wardrobe. Gloria Ruiz was no help at all, constantly plucking gowns and cocktail dresses from the racks, until Sergio explained that they wanted Gloria to look like the prettiest woman who's ever lived under a bridge.

Thick-soled boots; ripped stockings; crop tops in colors that can be seen from space. Gloria's old life on the streets would become her new look onstage.

Gloria's panhandling experience also made her Sergio's top recruiter. Once, during a trip to Pachuca with Gloria and Mary Boquitas to attend a performing arts convention, Sergio suddenly veered toward a fruit stand.

"We were walking past some street vendors when he pointed to a girl who was selling fruit with her mother," Mary Boquitas would later say. "She was very young and pretty. Long black hair, really adorable, with a lovely smile. Sergio told us to chat up the girl and become friendly with her, while he conversed with the mother. That's when we first met Sonia Ríos."

Mary and Gloria tried to convince Sonia to leave the stall for a while to join them at the convention, but she shyly insisted she had to stay and help her mother. Eventually, they gave up and said goodbye—but not for long. "We kept leaving the convention and going back to that fruit stall," Mary says. "Finally, after various visits, the great maestro said the words that many parents are dying to hear."

"Your daughter is very intelligent," Sergio told Sonia's mother. "She has tremendous potential, but she will never have the opportunities here that she could encounter in Mexico City. I am willing," Sergio continued grandly, "to accept her as a student in my academy." Sonia's mother was stunned but uncertain. Sergio gestured toward Gloria and Mary. "You have nothing to fear. She can live with them like a little sister. They'll take very good care of her."

"That same afternoon, with the blessing of her mother, she got into the car with us," Mary says. "To be honest, I really didn't think she'd stay for very long. I never dreamed that

Sergio would make her a permanent part of our strange little world."

About the same time, a single mother back in Mexico City had just landed a promotions job at XEW, the same radio station where Sergio had his evening program. Her name was Jossie Hernández, and she had a thirteen-year-old daughter, Aline. After Jossie started at the station, Aline became a regular visitor, dropping by after school to see her mom and listen to just-released albums.

One afternoon, Jossie called Aline at home because a rumor was spreading that teen heartthrob Pablito Ruiz was stopping by the station later that day. If Aline wanted to see him, she should come right away. Aline hurried over with two of her friends, and they joined the group of fans who'd already clustered outside the station. While they waited, a sleek white sedan slowly approached and parked directly across the street.

Was that him? For a long time, nothing happened. Then the back door of the car opened and a young woman stepped out. She walked toward them, smiling, and made her way directly toward Aline. As Aline tells the story, the young woman laid a hand on her arm and said, "You know what? I've been watching you from my car and . . . Well, I have a school and I go around looking for girls to launch as models."

Aline stared back, dumbstruck. "Don't you want to be a model?" the woman asked. "Or an actress, or a singer?"

Aline couldn't believe what she was hearing. Was she really being plucked off the street by a talent scout who wanted to groom her for stardom? Did that kind of thing really happen?

"Well, yes, sure," Aline stammered. "I mean, I can't believe it, but yes, I've always wanted to be a performer. The truth is,

I've been writing songs since I was a kid, and I love to sing, and dance—"

"Great," the woman interrupted. "What's your name?"

"Aline."

"How old are you?"

Aline paused a beat, tempted to lie, but opted for the truth. "I'm thirteen."

"Perfect!" the woman exclaimed.

Aline was happily surprised. She was certain that her height had fooled the woman into thinking she was older and that she would reject her as soon as she learned how young Aline really was. Instead, the woman seemed delighted. She scrawled down Aline's phone number and promised to call. If Aline's mother had any concerns, the young woman promised, she'd come over and speak with her personally.

"Okay," Aline agreed. "And what's your name?"

"Gloria," the woman answered. "Gloria Treviño."

Aline was so breathless when she saw Jossie, her mother assumed she must have gotten an autograph from Pablito Ruiz after all. Aline burbled out the news that she'd been picked from dozens and dozens of girls to attend a special model/actress/singer school with Gloria Treviño—

"Who?" Jossie asked. "Who's Gloria Treviño?"

Something fishy was going on. Jossie didn't know who this woman was, and it brought to mind something else that had been nagging at her. She'd only been at the radio station a few months, but that was long enough to know that Argentinian pop stars didn't just pop in on short notice—and if they did, XEW would be sure to keep it quiet to avoid a mob out front. Jossie couldn't recall who shared the tip, but she distinctly remembers being told it was okay to let Aline and her friends know.

That was Red Flag #1 and Red Flag #2—and #3 was that weird white car. Aline said it looked like the woman was sitting inside watching them, as if the car wasn't just parked there for convenience but deliberately positioned as an observation point. If this Treviño really was a talent scout, how did she know a crowd of girls would be in front of the station at exactly that time? And what was she looking for, anyway? How could she tell from all the way across the street that thirteen-year-old Aline chatting with her friends was The One?

"I don't want you to have anything to do with her," Jossie told Aline. "What if she kidnaps you? If she calls, you give me the phone."

But Aline never heard from the woman, and after a week had passed, she came around to her mother's belief that she'd either fallen for a hoax or escaped an abduction. That was until early one evening when there was a knock on the door. Jossie opened it to find a beaming young woman who introduced herself as Gloria Treviño. Jossie brought her into the living room and grilled her about what was going on. Gloria said she worked for a talent school run by "the maestro, señor Sergio Andrade." That caught Jossie's attention. She'd never met Sergio in person, but she knew the kind of awe he inspired at the radio station.

Jossie was so impressed, in fact, that she missed Red Flag #4. It was waving right there in front of her, but she was so dazzled by her daughter's one degree of separation from a famous hitmaker that she didn't stop to consider which was more likely. Either—

> (1) It was just a coincidence that the only time Jossie had ever been encouraged to have her daughter drop by the station was the same day and hour that Sergio's assistant happened to be outside—

Or,

> (2) Sergio had seen Aline around the station, found out her mother's name, then concocted a fake celebrity appearance rumor as bait and dispatched his minion to lie in wait.

But Jossie was so dazzled by Sergio's fame that she no longer suspected a thing. She agreed to allow Aline to go for an audition the next morning at 11 a.m. When Jossie and Aline arrived at 108 Adolfo Prieto Street, a very different Gloria opened the door. All her smiles and warmth from the day before were gone, replaced by a somewhat stern formality. Jossie couldn't shake the feeling that it had something to do with her, because Gloria spoke directly to Aline, not to her.

"Mr. Sergio Andrade," she said, "is waiting for you in his office."

Jossie and Aline headed for the stairs, but Gloria stopped them. "You'll have to wait down here," she told Jossie. "Aline might get nervous with you there."

No, Aline protested, she'd actually be more comfortable with her mother in the room. Gloria was firm: Aline had to audition alone.

Jossie shrugged and took a seat in the lobby. Aline, carrying her little overnight bag, followed Gloria upstairs. Aline hadn't known what to pack for the audition because she wasn't sure what she was auditioning for. Model, actress, singer? So she'd stuffed a bag with the kinds of things the kids wore in the movie *A Chorus Line*: a leotard, some sneakers, a pair of tights.

Gloria led her into a rehearsal studio. Aline looked around, expecting to meet the kind of maestro she'd seen in movies:

elegant, cultured, maybe a little aloof. Instead, she found a guy who looked like a trash collector. He was short, chubby, and stubble-faced, wearing shabby clothes and giving off, Aline would say, "a really strange, anxious vibe."

Sergio began by asking her age, and why she wanted to become an artist. Aline stammered out an answer, but Sergio gave no reply. Instead, he directed her to improvise a scene. "Just make up something, whatever comes to mind, and act it out," he said. Aline was bewildered, but an old-timey movie Indian like Tonto came to mind so she did her best impression, hoping at least to amuse Sergio a little.

Gloria and Sergio watched her, stone-faced.

Next, Sergio asked her to sing. Aline had prepared a song just in case, so this time she was ready. She closed her eyes and barreled into an a cappella version of a hit by Bibi Gaytán, doing her best to imitate the Timbiriche frontwoman's hair-flinging, body-writhing showmanship. Once again, Gloria's and Sergio's faces were blank. Neither said a word. Aline wasn't sure what to do next.

"Umm, I also dance?" she offered.

Sergio nodded. Aline handed Gloria a tape she'd made, hoping raw energy could make up for whatever was lacking in her singing and acting. But before the first song even ended, Sergio gestured to Gloria to turn it off. Gloria led Aline to a side room and closed the door.

"Aline, you know what?" Gloria said. "For this part of the audition, you're going to take off your clothes."

Aline was speechless.

"We have to see which parts of your body are going to need special exercise and attention," Gloria went on. "It's very normal."

Aline was petrified. No one ever got naked in *A Chorus Line*.

"Don't be afraid," Gloria urged. "The only ones who will see you are me and Sergio. And if you want, I'll leave the room."

"No!" Aline said. "He's the one I'm worried about."

"Sergio is a professional maestro," Gloria responded. "For him, this is very typical, very normal."

Aline felt tears welling up. "I can't do this."

Gloria sighed. "All right. Just go out in your bra and panties. Pretend you're in a bathing suit."

That didn't help. Aline had only recently begun wearing bras and hadn't put one on that day. Could she wear her leotard? Gloria huffed again, exasperated, and left the room. Aline slipped on the leotard and wrapped herself in a towel. When she returned to the studio, Sergio told her to drop the towel. She let it fall. Sergio had her turn sideways, then three-quarters, and walk across the room.

"Okay," he said. "Get dressed."

The audition was over. Aline, crushed and humiliated, picked up her towel and returned to the side room to change. She was still fumbling into her clothes when Gloria burst in.

"Sergio really likes you!" Gloria told her. "You've got it!"

"Really?" Aline was shocked. After botching her improv, leaving them cold with her performing, and refusing to strip naked, what had she done to impress them? The entire morning seemed to be one disaster after another, but Sergio, miraculously, was offering her a scholarship anyway.

"But there's one thing," Gloria continued. "Don't tell your mother everything about the audition. You can tell her you sang, and danced, and did that thing about the Indian, but don't tell her I wanted you to take your clothes off. See, for artists that's the most normal thing in the world, but for people in the outside world, especially parents, they just don't understand."

Aline didn't want to risk that, did she? "Your mother might not let you come to classes," Gloria explained, "and you'll miss out on the opportunity of a lifetime. Sergio sees something very special in you."

Aline was overwhelmed by a surge of affection. Minutes earlier, she'd been cringing and trapped, intimidated by Gloria and afraid to disappoint her. Now, suddenly, Gloria was no longer her torturer. She was her savior.

"Gloria seemed the most beautiful person I had ever seen," Aline would recall. "I saw her as a true friend."

18

BATTLE FOR THE MIND

By the time I got wind of Aline's story and arranged to meet her and Jossie, I'd already been investigating the allegations around Sergio and Gloria for nearly a year. The more I discovered about their creation of the clan, the more I kept sticking on one word: *How?*

For the most part, I grasped the way Sergio's system worked. He used Gloria and Mary Boquitas as bait for new recruits. He promised to make them famous, then bamboozled their parents with official-sounding blather about scholarships and rigorous training at his "star school." In the audition room, he'd deploy Gloria's street-smart powers of persuasion to convince the girls to swallow their terror and strip naked in front of a middle-aged stranger.

All that I understood—in theory. But in actual living conditions, I couldn't get my mind around the final and most crucial part of the process. Once the shock of the ordeal wore off and the girls returned to the safety of their homes, how did Sergio know they wouldn't turn him in? Or at least unburden themselves to *someone*—an older sister, a best friend, a trusted aunt? How did he gain so much command of their will in so little time?

Predators don't pick their targets at random, so a key part of the equation had to be his choice of victims. By now, Sergio had experimented with enough girls—and badly miscalculated with one in particular—to be able to spot his prey with an expert's instinct. Sergio was hunting for a special combination of factors, none of them unusual on their own and most invisible to anyone who hadn't learned to think like him. To see through his eyes, you had to get into his head—and that's not a comfortable place to be. I'd been there for twelve months by this point, and in one way it was paying off: when I first met Aline, I spotted Sergio's pattern immediately.

What bonded Aline and Gloria most was a number.

Both were slender brunettes raised by tough, single mothers who yearned for stardom, and both began performing shortly after losing their fathers. Gloria threw herself into dance lessons and a full makeover not long after her parents' divorce, while Aline became fixated on pop stars after her father's sudden death when she was six.

But crucially, both entered show business at age thirteen, that perilous year when girls are shifting between safety and sexuality and their egos are eggshell thin. It's precisely because that year is so volatile that director Catherine Hardwicke chose to focus on it in her film *Thirteen*. To ensure she was representing it accurately, she made the unusual step of writing the script with thirteen-year-old Nikki Reed, who'd dropped out of school and left home at thirteen because she was enduring the same turmoil that Hardwicke wanted to depict.

"You used to have fun running around in overalls and pigtails, and suddenly you go to school and boys are making fun of you if you're not a hottie, or don't have a good ass or whatever," Hardwicke would explain. "And so *bing*!—the light bulb goes off that if you're a girl, you suddenly gotta change things. And it's confusing. So she started getting really angry with her mom, really angry at her dad, angry at her brother, hating everybody, hating herself, and became kind of obsessed with living up to the beauty thing."

And if there is one person on earth who can make things worse, adds Nikki Reed, it's your mother. Ironically, the tighter you two are, the more that relationship is in jeopardy. "You can be so close to your mother, you have to break away," Nikki would say. "You can't stand to be in the same room."

That's why Erik Erikson, the famed developmental psychologist, believed it was precisely at that point, right when a young woman is transitioning from child to teenager, that she's most at risk for manipulation. And why? Because she's torn between her identity and her "role": between how she sees herself, in other words, and how she wants to be seen.

Erikson believed "Identity vs. Role Confusion" is the danger zone when judgment is poor and insecurity is high, when a maturing body and new attention from the opposite sex can leave a thirteen-year-old wondering who she's supposed to be. Which maybe wouldn't be so bad, except for this: if you don't know who you're supposed to be, you're easy prey for someone willing to tell you. Erikson can get a little wordy on this point, because it's a big one: "In their search for a new sense of continuity and sameness, adolescents have to re-fight many of the battles of earlier years," he explains. "Even though to do so, they must artificially appoint perfectly well-meaning people to play the roles of adversaries, and install lasting idols and ideals as guardians of a final identity."

In other words: being thirteen is a crazy time, because your drive to be Not a Kid makes your parents seem like villains.

And that kind of battle leaves the door wide open for true villains, who ooze in and give you the "respect" and "understanding" you're not finding at home.

Sergio didn't need a PhD to figure all that out for himself.

Maybe he had a copy of Erik Erikson's *Childhood and Society* on his desk with all those other child psych books that Lucerito's uncle found, but it's just as likely he discovered it from personal trial and error. Working his way backward, two years at a time, he went from

- Ga-Bí (19),
- to Crystal (17),
- to Mary Boquitas (15),

—until he finally homed in on the exact age when a young woman was less likely to resist, more likely to blame herself, and culturally wired to keep secrets from her parents.

That's exactly what Aline's own mother had done. Jossie was only twelve when she fell for Heriberto Hernández, a twenty-two-year-old electric company lineman. Jossie's parents refused to let them date, so Jossie became adept at slipping out of the house and seeing Heriberto on the sly. For six years, she hid this romance from her parents, even after secretly marrying Heriberto at age eighteen. Right after the courthouse ceremony, Jossie returned home as if nothing had happened. Heriberto and Jossie finally came clean when she was nineteen, and less than a year later, Aline was born.

Shortly after Aline's sixth birthday, Heriberto was killed in a horrific car crash just a few blocks from their house. Aline was not only grief-stricken but terrified: her mother kept keening that her husband's death was foretold by "evil omens" and caused by "dark forces." Heriberto died because she had lied, she told Aline. They were being punished for all the years of heartache she'd caused her parents. Aline would never get over the feeling that a watchful presence was out there, ready to settle the score for bad behavior.

But Jossie couldn't afford to mourn for long. She was now a thirty-year-old widow with two young girls to support and not much education and no job skills. She did have a sharp mind and radiant charm, and that was enough to talk her way into a job she'd seen advertised for a promotions aide at XEW. Coincidentally, she showed up at the radio station to launch her second act just after Sergio Andrade arrived to begin his.

Aline, meanwhile, was developing a new life of her own. For months, she had nightmares about her father's death and woke up screaming. Nothing helped . . . until Michael Jackson released *Thriller*. Aline loved the album and taped a poster of the singer on the ceiling above her bed. She began sleeping with a light on so that whenever her eyes popped open in terror, she'd be comforted by Michael Jackson's smile. Music became such a healing force for Aline that she began writing songs of her own and lip-syncing to the radio.

That wasn't good enough for Jossie. When she saw this change in Aline, she got behind it 100 percent. It wasn't enough that Aline was now inviting friends over to dance in the living room after school. No, Jossie wanted them on *Siempre en Domingo*. With zero experience of her own, she began coaching Aline and her cousin as a duo. By the time Aline was eleven, Jossie was hauling her to talent contests, designing and sewing her stage costumes, and even hiring a professional musician to help polish Aline's songs.

Nothing worked. Aline and Jossie always came home disappointed, never managing to attract the attention of anyone who could give Aline a start in show business. "After all my dreams, reality seemed very ugly," Aline would say. "Being a performer seemed almost impossible, something very distant and impossible to reach."

Until that day a white sedan pulled up and a young woman with a blinding smile stepped out.

"So you promise not to say anything?" Gloria asked as Aline was drying her eyes and stuffing her leotard back into her overnight bag.

"I promise," Aline said.

Just that quickly, Aline switched her loyalty from her mother, whom she considered her best friend, to Gloria, this stranger who'd just left her in tears. Such a whiplash change in trust is utterly unsurprising for Catherine Hardwicke, who focused on precisely that kind of bewilderingly fast transfer of affection in her movie *Thirteen*.

"One dynamic she really seems to understand is the intensity of girls' friendships during this time," one film reviewer pointed out. "Finding a new best friend is almost like falling in love, the feeling is so intoxicating and all-consuming." But supercharging that dynamic was an element that has been CIA-proven to work on anyone, regardless of age or gender: psychological abuse.

"One of the more horrible consequences," notes psychiatrist Dr. William Sargant, is the flood of affection that victims often feel toward the captors who torment them. Sargant worked with prisoners of war, consulted for the British spy agency MI5, and compiled his decades of research in the landmark study *Battle for the Mind: A Physiology of Conversion and Brainwashing*. But the biggest surprise for Sargant was discovering that two of the most powerful weapons in the brainwasher's arsenal are a pair of simple, everyday sensations that most of us feel all the time: shame and guilt.

Take Christianity. When Dr. Sargant delved into techniques used by master interrogators and Communist regime "re-educators," he kept getting a sense of déjà vu. It finally clicked: a lot of what he was seeing was similar to his own experience growing up in the Methodist Church. The best way to convert someone isn't by telling them what's so great about your religion; it's by pointing out what's so bad about their character. Everyone has some secret anxiety that they're not smart, or kind, or brave enough. Hit this hot button of insecurity, and you can escalate that self-doubt until the person you're trying to convert no longer trusts their own judgment on anything.

Anyone who comes from a religious background, Dr. Sargant realized, is conditioned from childhood to respond to this tactic. You're told there is an all-powerful master out there who knows your heart better than you do and will judge your behavior and punish your misdeeds. Christians are taught they're bad from birth, born with original sin and prone to plenty more, since nearly every natural desire is against church rules. But there's hope! Your wickedness will be forgiven . . . as long as you seek forgiveness by doing whatever you're told by the same ministers who planted that seed of shame in the first place.

Aline's entire audition was perfectly designed to make her feel inadequate and alone. Her mother was forced to wait downstairs. Gloria's sunny charm was switched off and replaced by a stony glare. Sergio was expressionless and nearly mute, offering no hint of personal connection. When Aline was asked to strip, Gloria cranked up Aline's anxiety even further by offering to step out of the room, planting the suggestion that Aline would be left totally alone with Sergio. Even though Gloria was making her miserable, Aline was still desperate for her company. "The need for companionship," Denise Winn points out in *The Manipulated Mind*, "doesn't vanish when the guard or interrogator is the only one in the room." Quite the opposite: as stress increases, companionship is needed even more to serve as an emotional buttress. The tormentor becomes, as Winn puts it, "a substitute friend."

And when Aline was feeling crushed and rejected, that's exactly who came through the door. Aline believed she had failed the audition but before she could slink out in shame, Gloria suddenly reappeared in a burst of loving friendship. That substitute alliance was soon put to the test, though. On the drive home with her mother, Aline felt a ball of dread in her stomach. She'd learned the hard way that when people lie, loved ones die. Could she really risk deceiving her mother and not mentioning the nude-modeling request? She thought about it and made up her mind.

"I decided to keep the whole thing a secret," Aline would say. "A secret between me, Sergio, and Gloria."

It was a choice all three of them would bitterly regret.

19

THE BASEMENT GIRLS

The following Tuesday, Jossie picked Aline up after school and dropped her off at 108 Adolfo Prieto for her first sessions at the studio. Aline would have classes two afternoons a week, alternating between voice, acting, and "physical expression." When she arrived, Aline found the place filled with young girls, all between the ages of thirteen and eighteen. Gloria, a twenty-one-year-old pretending to be nineteen, was the oldest.

Aline immediately felt out of place, because so many of the girls were wearing clothes identical to Gloria's, all of them in rumpled skirts and worn-out T-shirts. By her second week, Aline realized these outfits weren't just similar: they were literally identical. Some of the girls would stay late for "extended training," and sleep over in a bunkhouse down in the studio's basement. When they dressed for school in the morning, they'd swap clothes with each other so it looked like they were coming from home, plucking whatever else they needed from a communal closet of Gloria's and Maria Boquitas's hand-me-downs.

"That must be part of the artistic life," Aline figured.

The hostility, however, was harder to understand. Aline had

classes with four other girls and even though they were all more or less her age, they wouldn't speak to her. Mary, who'd been friendly enough on the day of her audition, was now giving Aline the cold shoulder.

With Gloria's suddenly manic schedule demanding most of Sergio's attention, he couldn't manage both the studio and his love life on his own anymore. He needed a gatekeeper, someone who could watch over the girls and keep outsiders at bay, just like when he'd hired his ex-girlfriend and the mother of his baby, Nora Miranda, to keep an eye on Crystal's business and make sure she stayed out of his. But Nora had a weak spot: she'd gotten too close to Crystal's mom and revealed the secret about Sergio's son.

This time, Sergio found a better lieutenant.

Mary Boquitas had proven under fire that unless Sergio gave her permission to open them, her lips were sealed. Even back when Lucerito rumors were flying and the press was voracious for tidbits about Sergio, Mary never told anyone that she'd become his teen bride. She didn't even breathe a word about it to Gloria until Sergio told her first. Even if it meant lying to her best friend, Mary would follow Sergio's orders.

"This is the way Sergio likes it," Gloria told Aline, by way of explaining Mary's iciness. "We should all be paying attention to the maestro, not the other students."

Gloria seemed exempt from that code of silence. Between classes, Aline and Gloria would meet to chat. It seemed like Gloria wanted to know everything about her, peppering Aline with questions about her family, her school, her daydreams. In return, Aline brought Gloria candy and bags of potato chips from her school's vending machine. Gloria devoured the snacks so ravenously that some days Aline didn't eat her lunch at school and brought it to Gloria instead. Gloria was so grateful for the sandwiches and fruit that Aline, timidly, asked if she wasn't getting enough to eat at home?

"Of course," Gloria assured her. She was living with an elderly aunt on the outskirts of town, she claimed, and sometimes got home too late to cook. But something seemed fishy. Gloria was always ravenous, exhausted, unkempt, and *there*. She was in the studio whenever Aline arrived and still there when she left. Aline never saw her leave.

"Artists." Aline shrugged.

That's all Gloria would ever say about her personal life. Otherwise, whenever they weren't discussing Aline, she was talking about Sergio: his genius, his poetry, his bruised, sensitive soul. Wasn't he amazing, Gloria gushed, so smart, *lo máximo*?

Wellll . . . to be honest, Aline thought he was an asshole. *He's so rude*, she thought. *So ugly and brutish.* Sergio was constantly raging and shouting, berating the instructors and belittling the students until one or more girls were in tears, if not the entire class. Aline kept that to herself. To Gloria, she ventured: "You work so hard. I don't know why he's so mean to you."

No, no, Gloria insisted. Sergio had a tender soul hidden beneath a bruise of suffering. Once Aline saw his true nature, she'd realize that Sergio was a wonderful man. His temper, Gloria said, was really pain; Gloria said that Sergio had been badly hurt by the women he'd loved. Gloria also knew a secret that would change Aline's mind, she said: Sergio was taking such a special interest that he was considering giving Aline personal lessons.

"Do you know what kind of honor that would be?" Gloria asked. "He doesn't mentor just anyone. If he picks you, that means he's ready to make you his next star. Just like he's doing with me."

"With you?" Aline asked, incredulous. "You're a singer?"

That was the first she'd heard that Gloria was a performer. The way Gloria acted around Sergio, so servile and attentive, always answering "Yes, sir," and "As you wish, sir!" Aline naturally assumed she was staff, not talent.

But by that summer of 1989, Sergio had already landed a multi-record deal for Gloria with BMG. The record company was so excited about Sergio's rough cut of *¿Qué Hago Aqui?* that it was rushing the album into production and planned to release it that coming fall. Even while Gloria was running around as Sergio's gofer, she was also rehearsing for an upcoming TV appearance and a concert tour that would begin when her album launched.

To answer Aline's question, Gloria slipped a tape of "Dr. Psiquiatra" into a Walkman and plopped the headphones over Aline's ears. Wow! The song was fantastic! Aline couldn't believe that a woman who could sing like that, and was about to have a solo album released by a major label, would still take the time to pal around with an awkward tween like her every afternoon.

"And you could be next!" Gloria said. "That's why I've got to tell you, you're getting your career off to a bad start."

"Bad?" Aline asked, suddenly fearful. "What am I doing wrong?"

"You really mucked things up when you wouldn't undress at the audition," Gloria said. "Very unprofessional."

Gloria kept explaining nudity was no big deal in show business. It was all part of performing, just another tool for letting the manager understand what he was working with. What was the big deal? Hadn't Aline ever seen a naked woman before? She hadn't? Well, in show business, people undress around each other all the time. Sergio was the best because he never overlooked anything—he had to know absolutely everything about Aline, so he could bring out her strengths and hide any flaws.

Finally, Aline said, "Okay."

"Great," Gloria said. "We can make up for your audition right now. Get undressed, and I'll go get Sergio."

Aline slowly began taking off her clothes, dreading the moment the door would reopen. What was Sergio going to make her do? How long was this going to last? It was already 7:30 at night—what if her mother arrived just then to pick her up? She stepped out of her clothes and waited, holding a towel in front of herself.

Sergio and Gloria arrived within minutes. Sergio looked her up and down, studying her with the same impassive gaze he'd had during the audition. Drop the towel, he ordered. Aline let it fall to the floor. Turn around, he commanded. Show me your profile. Walk across the room. Aline obeyed. Whenever she glanced up, Sergio was stone-faced, staring intently. Get dressed, he finally said. Then he left the room without another word.

Aline hurriedly dressed, finishing just moments before her mother pulled up in the car. Aline slid into the passenger seat.

"How were your classes today?" Jossie asked.

"Okay," Aline replied quietly. "Normal."

Aline dreaded returning to the studio the next day. She was flushed with embarrassment and didn't know how she'd look Sergio in the eyes, or even Gloria. But Gloria welcomed her with a beaming smile and even Sergio greeted her from across the room with a jaunty wave. That evening, Aline was getting ready to leave when Gloria said Sergio wanted to see her. Aline was rigid with nervousness as she entered his office, but Sergio had her sit down and put her at ease by asking about her tastes in music. He seemed friendly and interested, and

Aline began to relax. More than relax: she felt the same glow of affection that came over her with Gloria at the end of her horrific audition.

Maybe when someone sees you naked, the two of you develop a little bond of complicity, Aline thought.

Sergio asked Aline about her songwriting, as if they were two colleagues talking shop, and told her about some of his own compositions. Aline was shocked to discover how many of the hits she'd loved for years had actually been written by Sergio. Aline knew he was successful and influential, but only then did it dawn on her that Sergio was the true power behind the stars she'd grown up envying.

Sergio seemed to see Aline differently as well. Nearly every afternoon, he found a moment to pull her aside and chat. You're helping him, Gloria told Aline one day while they were sharing Aline's lunch. Dropping her voice to a whisper, Gloria said that Sergio's heart had once been badly broken, and he'd never gotten over it. It had happened nearly ten years ago, Gloria told her, when Sergio had fallen in love with a very young singer.

"You must remind him of her," Gloria said. "She was the same age as you."

Gloria went on to tell a story that sounded remarkably similar to the Lucerito rumors. Sergio and the girl managed to keep their romance a secret, Gloria said, until her brother eavesdropped on a call and blew everything up. The parents' fury was bad enough, but what really broke Sergio's heart was the girl's reaction. Sergio expected the girl to declare her love for Sergio, but according to Gloria, she denied her feelings and blamed it all on him. Since then, Gloria lamented, Sergio would never risk giving his heart to another woman.

I should know, Gloria confessed. I was in love with Sergio myself.

Aline couldn't believe it. *Really?!* This gorgeous, sunny, magnetic teenager was in love with this chubby, angry old man?

Oh yes, Gloria assured her. And how about Aline—was she getting a crush on Sergio, too? Aline studied Gloria's face to see if she was kidding. Sergio was thirty-three and Aline was thirteen. She'd never had a boyfriend; the closest she'd come to any kind of intimacy was kissing the Michael Jackson poster in her bedroom.

But for the next few days, Aline kept pondering Gloria's crazy idea that maybe Sergio had a thing for her. She would never do anything about it, of course, but Aline couldn't help wondering what it would be like to be the girlfriend of the great Sergio Andrade, to be onstage singing songs he'd written especially for her.

Not many days later, Sergio summoned Aline to his office. He had her sit next to him at the piano. He'd just written a new song, he told her, and would like her feedback. He closed his eyes and sang in Spanish,

I'm so afraid of losing you,
Before I've even won you.
I'm afraid you won't approve,
so I never make the first move.
And so we remain this distance apart—
Because I can't conquer the fear that fills my heart

"I had goosebumps," Aline would later say. Flustered and tongue-tied, she sat there mutely. Was it really about her? She struggled for something to say, any compliment she could give without sounding like an idiot if Sergio had actually written the song about someone else, or no one at all.

"It's so, um, beautiful," she finally stammered. "I'd love to sing it for my vocal arts exam, if that's okay."

Sergio's face turned to granite. "No," he said, turning away from her. "My creations aren't thrown around like that."

Aline was mortified. She apologized, over and over, to Sergio's back as he stared down at the piano. Aline left the studio and searched for Gloria to find out what to do. "I feel horrible," Aline said.

"If you're upset with yourself, you must have feelings for him," Gloria counseled. "Go talk to him. He's *lo máximo*, the best."

Aline went back upstairs. She found Sergio in his office. He nodded, baleful and silent, when she asked to come in. He remained seated behind his desk while Aline stood in front of him like a misbehaving student and stammered out her apology. "Things are happening to me that I've never experienced before," she said. "This all probably sounds silly to you, but—"

"Who's confusing you this way?" Sergio asked.

"You."

For a long time, Sergio was silent. Finally, he looked up at her and said, "Are you sure you know what you're saying?"

"I think I do," Aline replied, even though she'd lost track of what they were talking about.

"Think about it," he warned her. "I'm a man who has suffered, and I don't want you toying with me."

Aline's mind was swimming. Sergio jerked to his feet and strode to the piano. He slid onto the bench and, once again, began crooning the song he'd played earlier for Aline. He looked Aline right in the eyes when he reached the last line—"Because I can't conquer the fear that fills my heart"—and then got up, walked over to the thirteen-year-old girl, and kissed her.

Aline, stunned, remained frozen. It was her first kiss.

Abruptly, Sergio broke away and went to the door.

"Mary!" he shouted. Mary Boquitas appeared almost instantly. "Take the car and drive Aline home," he ordered.

"My mother will be coming later," Aline said.

"Call and tell her you have a ride," he said. "That's all for today."

Aline stumbled out of his office and followed Mary downstairs, thoroughly confused about what was going on. Only later, as she and Mary rode wordlessly through the streets of Mexico City, did it dawn on Aline that Sergio wanted her to think before facing her mother.

"Do you love me?" Sergio asked Aline a few days later.

"I do, Sergio," she replied. He'd begun asking so often that she now just answered automatically.

"Show me," Sergio commanded.

"Show you . . . ?"

"I'm going to leave the room," Sergio said. "When I come back, I'll know you love me if you're sitting naked at the piano. If you're not willing to show me your body, you're not ready to open your heart."

With that, he left the room.

Aline prayed he was joking. She stared at the door, hoping that any second Sergio would pop his head back into the room with a big prankster's grin. But as the minutes ticked by, Aline began to fret. Disobeying Sergio would certainly trigger one of his tantrums about why he, El Maestro, was to be obeyed without question. But what if she actually stripped and one of the other girls burst in? Or Gloria? Or her mother!

Sergio re-entered the room moments later. He found Aline sitting on the piano bench, naked and blushing furiously. Sergio locked the door. He slid onto the bench beside her and began to caress her. Aline "was like a statue," she would later say, frozen with fear and embarrassment. She remained shocked and rigid as Sergio lifted her and laid her down on the piano bench. It was all part of a test, he told her, a test of her truth and devotion. When Sergio penetrated her, Aline says, she burst into tears.

Sex, Aline soon discovered, wouldn't be her only test.

Sergio began ranking Aline's behavior, hour by hour, as an indicator of her "mindfulness and sincerity." How she was dressed, the look on her face when she greeted Sergio, her demeanor around the other girls—all of these and many others were indicators of her "inner heart," as Sergio put it. Aline found the tests bewildering. She wore very little makeup and put it on the same way all the time, but Sergio would some days scold her for looking like a tramp, and others for not making an effort to look attractive for him.

One afternoon, Sergio informed Aline that she'd acquired far too many demerits. Aline dropped to her knees to beg his pardon, exactly as Sergio had taught her. Sergio shook his head and began slipping off his belt. He'd once told her that the day would come when she'd deserve a beating, but Aline had never believed he'd actually whip her. Now, seeing his belt come off, Aline was terrified.

"No, Sergio, please," she implored. "Please don't!" He grabbed her by the shoulders, turned her around, and began flogging her. The more Aline begged him to stop, the harder he whipped her, until she bit her lip until he finished.

That night when she got home, Aline had such painful welts on her bottom she couldn't sit. She went right to her room, complaining of a headache. Her mother was becoming a little concerned about how quiet and withdrawn Aline had become since starting her after-school program, but she put it down to normal adolescent mopiness. After all, Aline was just thirteen.

Once the shock of the beating wore off, Aline began to think that Sergio might have been right. He'd said it was for her own good, that she needed discipline and punishment if she was going to mature and learn. She shouldn't feel bad about it, Sergio assured her; he treated Gloria and Mary the same way. If he didn't care about her, he said, he wouldn't bother.

That part made sense, Aline thought: it's exactly what her father would have told her. But the part about group sex—that was a little tougher to grasp.

It was Gloria who first brought it up. Aline was at home one Saturday afternoon when Gloria dropped by. She would do that on occasion, pop around to check in on Aline and chat with her mother, always unannounced and at random times. Aline and Jossie were flattered by the visits, especially since they knew Gloria was furiously busy at the time preparing for her album debut, but in the back of her mind, Aline couldn't shake the feeling that Sergio was behind it all, dispatching Gloria as a spy to make sure Aline wasn't seeing any boys and her mother wasn't getting curious about what was going on at the studio.

It was during one of those impromptu visits, while Gloria and Aline were lounging in Aline's room, that Gloria began talking about how wonderful it was to be Sergio's girlfriend. Aline nodded in agreement—until she realized that Gloria wasn't talking about her. She was talking about herself. Yes, Gloria said, she was romantically involved with Sergio as well. What, hadn't Aline known?

Aline was stunned. The next day, she asked Sergio if it was true. Instead of answering, he called in Gloria and Mary. They arrived quickly and stood on either side of him behind the desk, as if they already knew why they'd been summoned.

"If you truly love me, and you want to remain with me,"

Sergio told Aline, "then you have to accept me with them. Because Gloria and Mary arrived before you, and they're very important to me. You choose."

That, as Aline would later recall, was the moment that so many things that confused her suddenly made sense. So that's why all those girls slept over, and shared each other's clothes, and eyed her so competitively from the moment she'd first come through the door.

Aline looked from Sergio to Gloria. That had to be why Gloria always seemed to be at the studio, day and night, wearing rumpled, passed-around clothes. She didn't live with some aunt on the outskirts of town, Aline suspected. Gloria and Mary were living right here in the studio, along with who knew how many other girls, so they'd always be at Sergio's command.

Sergio waited for Aline to answer, Gloria and Mary flanking his chair like a pair of loyal soldiers, and Aline suddenly wondered what that felt like, to be bonded so tightly to Sergio that he could rely on you to carry out his every wish and make him happy without the need for constant beatings and, in return, receive the guidance of his genius.

"Tell her everything I've done for you," Sergio said, as if reading Aline's thoughts.

"You've fed us," Mary said. "And you taught us so much."

"But you never gave us anything for our birthdays, like you did for Aline," Gloria added. She sounded wounded.

"You even wrote a song for her," Mary said, her voice now as forlorn as Gloria's. They both began crying, mumbling through their tears about how lucky Aline was. Aline began weeping as well, not for herself but for Gloria and Mary. "They seemed so lonely," Aline would later recall. "So unprotected and desperate for affection."

Somehow, the thirteen-year-old who'd been coerced into

sex on a piano bench by a middle-aged man and his two accomplices now felt like everything had changed, and instead of being a victim, she somehow had the power to help all these broken hearts. And so, weeping with sympathy for Mary and Gloria, she agreed to stay a little longer and try to make this strange relationship work.

"That's good, very good," Sergio reassured her. "Because when Gloria's album comes out, everything is going to change. And when that happens, she's going to need you."

20

THE TIGER

"Throw that skinny bitch offstage!"

Before Gloria was halfway through her first song, every drunk in the bar was howling for her to SHUT UP AND GET OUT! She could barely hear herself over the shouting but the louder she sang, the more the crowd screamed. Some hecklers got the bright idea of raiding the bar for ammunition, so from out of the darkness Gloria found herself being pelted by lemon and orange slices from the drink stations, followed by the drinks themselves. She ducked the hurtling glasses, wondering when Sergio would come to her rescue.

But Sergio was leaning on a wall in the wings, arms folded across his chest, taking in the show as if everything was going exactly to plan.

Which it was. Pretty much.

"There is no school for this kind of training," Sergio had told Gloria. "Not for the kind of star I want you to be. You're not out there to entertain. You're out to start a revolution."

A few days earlier, Sergio had called an all-hands meeting in the studio. He had news and marching orders. The news: BMG set a launch date for Gloria's album, so it was really happening. And soon. The marching orders: As of that moment all of them, from singers to secretaries, were full-time record promoters. Sergio wanted them to hit the streets and find places for Gloria to sing—bars, weddings, strip clubs, quinceañeras, he didn't care, as long as they gave her a mic and put her onstage. Once a gig was booked, they had to badger every friend, neighbor, and stranger to come fill the seats.

Because here's the dirty truth, Sergio told Gloria: people are always more interested in the artist than the art. It didn't matter how pretty her songs were. To get anyone to pay attention, she had to be more than a singer; she had to be a sensation. She had to be so shocking and sexy and scary that people would be clamoring to find out what she'd do next. And the best way to learn that skill, Sergio figured, was by facing an audience who didn't want to be one.

That's why, on this night, the aspiring diva was taking live fire in a rock bar from a gang of rowdies. She racked her brain for a tune that might quiet them down, some familiar old favorite that would get them singing along, but all she had memorized was her meager Boquitas repertoire and new songs from the still-unreleased album.

"Okay, okay," Gloria said. "Do you want me to leave?"

"YESSSSS!" the crowd shouted.

"Well . . . GO FUCK YOUR MOTHERS!"

Gloria scooped up fistfuls of the soggy napkins and lemon rinds they'd hurled and flung them back. She grabbed a can of soda and doused everyone she could reach. In the stunned silence that followed, Gloria turned to the little backup band that Sergio had hired for the night. "Play 'Dr. Psiquiatra,'" she ordered.

Since they hated her anyway, she might as well sing whatever she wanted. And what she wanted was a song she had to beg Sergio to include on the album. Not that he didn't like it.

But he had serious doubts that a goth tale about a teenage girl being abused by a middle-aged doctor would go over big with the middle-aged men who ran the music industry.

Doctor Psiquiatra, Gloria bellowed.

> *Don't keep staring at my legs.*
> *NO, NO, NO, I'M NOT—*
> (beat, beat, beat)
> *CRAZY!*

Gloria figured the drunks must still be regrouping after her outburst because for the first time, she got to the end of a song without being drowned out by boos. But she wasn't going to push her luck, so after the last note, she bounded offstage while the crowd was mustering a counterattack. Behind her, she could hear the roars building.

The bar owner stomped over. Gloria braced herself and hoped Sergio wouldn't be too furious because she'd stunk up the place and cursed everyone out.

"You were fantastic!" the owner gushed. "Rough start, but you really won them over." The bedlam behind her, Gloria realized, was the rowdy house bellowing for an encore.

Word began to spread about this wild woman with her ripped stockings and tousled hair, coming onstage looking like she'd just been in a street fight and was ready to start another one if the audience didn't shut up and pay attention.

Gloria was the anti-Boquita, which is exactly what Sergio wanted. Sergio did not repeat mistakes (professionally, at least), and he'd learned a bitter lesson by heeding the Don Raúl Velascos of the world. He'd packaged the Boquitas as sweethearts and serious musicians and they never caught fire. This time, Sergio was gambling that Gloria's rawness would come across as something new: a street-tough kid who could really sing.

For months she kept up a grueling pace, road-tripping so hard that she often slept only four hours a night between shows, but it was paying off. Gloria was drawing bigger crowds, and thanks to Sergio's radio connections, some of her songs were already getting airtime. Before her album was even released, "Dr. Psiquiatra" hit No. 5 nationwide.

That's when the call came in. Raúl Velasco was ready to put aside past grievances and invite Gloria to make her TV debut as a solo artist on *Siempre en Domingo*. The don was no fan of Sergio. But Gloria was getting too big to ignore.

"I couldn't believe it!" Aline would say. "My fairy godmother, my friend, my sister was going to appear on *Siempre en Domingo*! Who knew how many millions of people in Europe and all of Latin America were going to see her!"

And Aline was right there with her. On the night of Gloria's appearance, Aline accompanied her to Televisa's studio and helped her get dressed and warm up. Aline and Sergio then waited with Gloria in the wings during the countdown for a performance that could make her Latin music's Next Big Thing—or doom her as a Never-Was.

"Stay calm," Sergio whispered. "Relax. Breathe."

Gloria relaxed. She breathed.

And then she came out screaming. "I felt like I was exploding," she'd say. "I jumped, I dropped and rolled around, I tore my stockings so my panties were showing."

Even Aline was astonished, wondering for a few moments whether Gloria really was in the midst of a hysterical episode after weeks of pressure and exhaustion. Gloria was gyrating around so wildly, the spotlight couldn't stay with her. Several times she leapt completely out of camera range. Up in the booth, urgent orders were sent to camera operators to keep their lenses as tight as possible on Gloria's face and avoid showing her from the waist down as she writhed on the floor.

"Are you crazy?" Raúl Velasco asked after Gloria finished her first song. "Crazy for real?" He waited a few moments before leaning his mic toward her to answer, slowing things down in an attempt to regain control of his own show.

Gloria panted, catching her breath. Softly, she replied, "No, I'm not crazy. Just desperate."

"Desperate?" Don Raúl asked. "Desperate for what?"

"Desperate to be happy. To sing. To . . . to . . . grab your glasses!" Gloria snatched them from his face, leaving the elderly icon blushing and blinking on live TV. The production crew was aghast. As Don Raúl staggered around, squinting and humiliated, two producers rushed over and ushered Gloria offstage.

"Most singers get to do two, three songs," Gloria would grumble. "I couldn't even hear what they were telling me, the applause was so loud. I just knew they wanted me to go. Right away! So I left."

Showing your panties is one thing. Blinding the host is another. But ruining the Tiger's dinner—that's what did it for Gloria.

The Tiger was Emilio Azcárraga Milmo, Televisa's owner and "the Rupert Murdoch of Mexico," nicknamed for his white-streaked hair and ferocious temper. As the head of Mexico's only TV network, the Tiger reigned as one of the most powerful people in Mexico, a TV tyrant who could sway elections and mint new stars . . . or end careers before they started.

That Sunday, the Tiger had been hosting a dinner party. Among the guests was Cardinal Ernesto Corripio y Ahumada, the seventy-two-year-old archbishop of Mexico City. Ordinarily, the Tiger would never turn the TV on while entertaining, but *Siempre en Domingo* was his pride and joy, a show he had personally shaped by handpicking Raúl Velasco as host. It was also the first Mexican-generated TV show to challenge the dominance of American and Spanish imports, and as such Azcárraga saw it as a model of what Mexican programming should be. He rarely missed it.

So as the Tiger and his dinner guests watched that night, Gloria Trevi was busy making a statement of her own. The archbishop, needless to say, was appalled. "He said it looked like Televisa was showcasing a street whore," Gloria was later told.

The next day, Sergio got word from Televisa: Gloria was banned.

Not just from one show: all of them. Mexico's only television network was blacklisting Gloria. *And don't try crying to Lalo this time*, Sergio was warned. This death sentence wasn't up for appeal. It had thundered down directly from the Tiger himself.

Sergio wasn't happy about the ban. He was thrilled.

He quickly reactivated his publicist from the Boquitas Pintadas days, Rubén Aviña, and had him spread the story about this rebellious new sensation—this Mexican Madonna—who was so out of control, she'd nearly given the archbishop a coronary right in the Tiger's living room. Radio and print news ate it up. Within days, Gloria was on front pages across the country.

"Everyone thought that without television I'd be nothing, but my songs were selling like hotcakes," Gloria said. "This was coming from my heart, and people were reacting to my heart, so I couldn't just change."

Overnight, she became a phenomenon. "Dr. Psiquiatra" shot to #1 on the charts, and remained there for a staggering three months until it was bumped down a notch when her "What Will I Do Without Him?" ("¿Qué Voy a Hacer sin Él?") surged to the top. A few weeks later, another Gloria tune—"The Last Kiss" ("El Último Beso")—rose to #1. Suddenly, this unknown teenager who'd only performed once on TV had a Beatles-like hold on the top three spots on the Mexican hit parade.

All kinds of journalists—not just music but news, culture, and even religion reporters—began flocking to Gloria's shows. Plenty of singers become famous, but not many become infamous. The more Televisa kept her out of the public eye, the more her legend grew, and Gloria knew exactly how to feed it, with a natural feel for hitting the sweet spot between outrageous and obnoxious. For a girl who'd never finished high school and had spent the past few years in near-isolation under Sergio's watchful eye, Gloria had an astounding talent for wrapping even the most experienced and respected reporters around her finger. For that, she relied on her true superpower:

Gloria is a terrific liar.

That's not an opinion; that's scientific fact. When it comes to baffling with bullshit, Gloria has a gift. One of her early masterpieces was crafted right after her first album came out when a reporter for the *Los Angeles Times* interviewed Gloria about the inspiration for "Dr. Psiquiatra."

As a young woman in the music industry, the reporter asked, have you run into that kind of abuse yourself?

Gloria looked perplexed. What do you mean?

Ummm . . . The reporter was perplexed as well. What seemed like a straightforward question about very straightforward lyrics had somehow run into a brick wall. The reporter tried again. Was the song based on your own experience?

Oh yes, Gloria agreed. She then went on to spin a ridiculous story that wouldn't have fooled most ten-year-olds, but as delivered by Gloria was convincing enough to make its way into the paper.

"The album's first hit, 'Dr. Psiquiatra,' was inspired by one of her final acts before leaving Monterrey: the spontaneous liberation of lab animals slated for dissection in her ninth-grade biology class," the *Los Angeles Times* reported. Gloria claimed she'd raced around the classroom, freeing the creatures and shooing them out of the school. When threatened with expulsion by the principal, the tween freedom fighter stood her ground. "You're teaching sadism to children," Gloria claims she said. "Why don't you make a how-to video instead?"

Red flags are flying all over this story, the most obvious being—

> 1. The song obviously has nothing to do with animal rights or biology class, and everything to do with lascivious men preying on young women.

And,

> 2. The frogs and fetal pigs provided for school dissection are already dead, of course. Unless the class was about reanimating zombie pets, these cadavers couldn't leap from their trays if they wanted to.

But that's why Gloria is such a fabulous fabulist. Imagine being interviewed by one of the most influential newspapers in North America for an article that could help skyrocket your career and, at that moment, deciding to look into the reporter's eyes and try to get away with an utterly preposterous, *easily fact-checkable* lie. For very good reasons, Gloria wanted to avoid any questions about sexual misbehavior between young women and Older Men in Charge, and her success at slipping out of that corner demonstrates why, when it comes to fooling people, she's in a very special category.

Because we all fib a little. But it's another level altogether to make up crazy stuff that can convince even professional skeptics like an *L.A. Times* reporter. Lying like that requires a certain number of rare qualities—eighteen, to be precise. They were compiled by Aldert Vrij, the Dutch psychologist known as "Dr. Deception," who spent decades doing a deep dive into the behavior of the world's best bullshit artists. Over and over, he found the same traits.

Like—

- **Beauty.** Really good liars are really good-looking. Dr. Deception discovered that pretty people are judged as more believable than the rest of us, a phenomenon that suddenly explains TV weather forecasters and presidential "spokespretties."
- **Expressiveness.** Our lives are dictated by snap judgments. We like to think of ourselves as calm and careful judges of character, but the truth is, we form our opinions within minutes of meeting someone. Consequently, you're more likely to make a lasting first impression as trustworthy if you're warm, extroverted, and entertaining.
- **Decoding.** Con artists have an instinct for reading faces and picking up on signs of disbelief, which triggers the next two traits:
- **Verbal confidence.** Like improv actors, liars trust their gut. They don't stammer around saying *um* and *ah* and *like* and other filler words. Instead, they come out confidently with whatever phrase

comes to mind, and they find a way to make it work because they are . . .

- **Fearlessly foolish.** Dr. Deception was surprised to discover that because of the way we're hard-wired, skilled liars often have better luck getting away with a ridiculous, over-the-top tale rather than something more realistic. Our brains were formed in a time before language, back when survival depended on using our body language and facial cues to communicate do-or-die stuff, like *Bears live in that cave!* or *Sounds crazy but rub those sticks together and fire comes out.* You had to convey those messages exactly right, even without words to rely on, or else you'd pay a social penalty that's way more severe than our modern little wrist-slap of getting canceled. If you were wrong back in the Stone Age about crying—or not crying—wolf, you could be driven out of the tribe at best, torn to shreds at worst.

It's kind of odd, but all these evolutionary influences have turned us into creatures who are nervous about lying yet fond of liars:

1. We've got a built-in deterrent for lying because it makes us physically uncomfortable, causing our stomachs to cramp, our foreheads to sweat, our chests to get tight; and,
2. We've also got a built-in affection for entertainers because our ancestors relied for survival on people who could deliver Big Important Warnings in vivid, dramatic fashion.

> The more riveting you were, the more likely you'd be liked and believed.

For honest people, that's exactly how it should work. But for liars, that friendship bond is a loophole to exploit. Even though a nagging voice deep inside may be whispering "Hoax!," the pleasure centers of your brain are lighting up and urging you to keep listening. That's the whole reason stand-up comedy even exists. We know that Chris Rock and Amy Schumer are juicing their stories or flat-out making them up, but the tools they employ—rich detail, emotional commitment, and surprising plot twists—capture not only our attention, but our hearts. We like a bold storyteller for the same reason we like dogs; because for two million years, they kept us out of trouble. Today, a really good liar can exploit that factory pre-set in our brains specifically because a story is too good to be true.

But here's the catch. As simple as these tools sound, they're a lot easier to list than to learn. If you're not born a liar, you're probably a bad one. And Gloria was a superstar.

"She was so spontaneous, both onstage and in person," says Humberto Leal Valenzuela, the news director for Juárez's RadioNet, who was often assigned to cover her. He was there for her first concert in Juárez and was as shocked as anyone when she flew into a rage soon after walking onstage because someone in the front row was making noise. She charged into the wings, returned with a can of soda, and dumped it on his head, then flounced offstage in a furious diva huff—

Before running back a moment later, laughing. *Gotcha!*

As her victim sat there, stunned, Gloria pulled her blouse off and used it to mop his face, then left it with him as a souvenir as she jumped back onstage to perform in only her bra and skirt.

"We've baptized a new believer!" she shouted.

The crowd roared and surged to their feet. "Five minutes into the show," Humberto Leal Valenzuela marveled, "and already she had a standing ovation."

Gloria stopped by Humberto's office the next afternoon for a sit-down interview, as became her habit for the next few years whenever she was in Juárez. Humberto genuinely liked Gloria and grew to regard her as a real friend—or at least she always treated him as one.

"She would come into my office, throw her feet up on my desk, and just start talking about anything that crossed her mind," Humberto would recall. "You have to understand how incredibly unusual that was for a young entertainer. First, to be so relaxed with someone who is going to review your work and could hurt your career. And secondly, she would talk about things other singers would never mention. It was never about hairstyles or any of that silly nonsense. She dove right into politics, drugs, abortion—whatever was the hot topic of the moment."

But instead of the usual trendy tripe that Humberto had heard many times from self-impressed celebrities, Gloria told a story of living on the streets and spoke from her own first-hand experience when it came to social issues. "Her positions were pretty well thought out, so much that I couldn't tell how serious she was about her political ambitions," Humberto says. "She wasn't talking yet about being the first female president of Mexico. That would come later. Back then, she just wanted to be the first pop singer elected as mayor of Monterrey."

Something was weird, though. The one question Gloria refused to answer was the one everyone cared about most:

Did she have a boyfriend?

It was a mystery. Mexico's most popular sex symbol didn't seem to be having any herself. In public, she was always flanked by Sergio and Mary Boquitas. Otherwise, she never turned up in photos—or even gossip—with anyone who could plausibly be a romantic partner. Whenever Humberto or any other journalist asked, Gloria would deflect with a joke, a wink, or a scowl.

"I'm an artist," she'd say. "Not a boy toy."

Her silence when it came to love was absolutely unshakable. Even later, when she released a 260-page memoir with plenty of details about everything she did, ate, saw, and thought during her "hungry years" as a starving artist on the streets of Mexico City, Gloria devoted exactly one sentence—twenty-one words, .025% of the entire book—to any affairs of the heart. "At 18," she writes, "I broke up with my boyfriend because he wanted to get married and I wanted to be an artist."

Really? What's his name, where did they meet, how long were they together? Gloria doesn't give a clue. This nameless, faceless boyfriend exits the conversation almost before he enters—

As if he never existed at all.

21

THE WHIPPING BOYS

Late one night in June 1989, while everyone in the house was asleep, Sergio Andrade awoke to the sound of someone weeping and stumbling outside his bedroom. He opened the door to find Gloria. Her face was streaked with tears and drool ran from her mouth.

"Idiot!" Sergio shouted. He shook her by the shoulders. Gloria was limp in his hands, moaning and muttering.

"Stupid! Stupid girl!" Sergio yelled. He slapped her across the face, hard, then backhanded her viciously across the other cheek. He continued slapping her, again and again, as Gloria's head flopped from side to side.

From downstairs in the basement, Mary Boquitas heard the commotion and came running. She arrived to find Sergio punching Gloria in the stomach, and when that only caused her to gasp and gag but not vomit, he rammed his fingers into her mouth until she choked.

"How could you do this?" he bellowed.

Together, Mary and Sergio held Gloria up and worked their fingers into her throat until she began retching up the pills she'd swallowed. Mary threw Gloria's arm over her shoulders and walked her around the room to keep her conscious. Sergio trailed behind, still raging, so furious that he suddenly grabbed Gloria by the hair and spun her around, smacking her so hard in the face that she and Mary Boquitas nearly fell to the floor.

"Answer me, stupid," Sergio said. "How could you do this to me?"

Gloria murmured something, barely moving her lips. Sergio slapped her again. "Wake up! Speak up!"

"You don't care," Gloria muttered.

"Idiot," Sergio snarled. "What do you know?"

"You only care about her," Gloria said.

She pointed to the door of Sergio's bedroom, where thirteen-year-old Aline Hernández watched in silence.

At the time, Gloria was in the midst of a media tsunami. The homeless street girl was now the most imitated fashion icon in Mexico, and offers were flooding in from promoters across Latin America and Europe. Everyone was dying to book the outlaw singer who was so dangerous, her own country wouldn't put her on TV.

By the end of its first week on sale, *¿Qué Hago Aqui?* was No. 1 on the charts, and concert promoters throughout the country were calling Sergio every day, promising to fill any venue he wanted, for as many shows as he wanted, on any night they could get the new Mexican sensation. Two million copies of the album would be sold, and wherever she performed, Gloria was selling out the house.

Faced with such staggering public acclaim, the Tiger finally surrendered. Gloria could return to television, he told Sergio, but only if she behaved like all the other female singers. That meant a tasteful dress, neatly styled hair, and a "professional demeanor." No torn nylons. No peek-a-boo panties. And for heaven's sake, no manhandling the host.

Sergio had Televisa wrapped around his finger, and he knew it. "No promises," he replied.

The Tiger bristled . . . then relented.

Big mistake.

Gloria made her triumphant return to Televisa's airwaves on a talk show hosted by Verónica Castro, one of Mexico's most revered actresses. Gloria was wearing a short skirt and a crop top, and her hair was a magnificent mess. Grande dame Veronica was offended, but she bit her tongue and icily led Gloria through a series of sugar-cookie questions. Finally, she couldn't hold back.

"Don't people mistake you for a prostitute?" Verónica Castro asked.

"I have no problem with prostitutes," Gloria shot back. "Unless they have a problem with me."

That should have given Verónica a whiff of danger, but she pressed on. "Well, I believe they should be taken off the streets."

"At least they sell their bodies to get food for their families," Gloria retorted. "Not to get their own talk shows."

Verónica Castro gasped. A grinning Gloria shot her fist in the air. "*VIVA LA PROSTITUCIÓN!*" she shouted.

Gloria's adoring army of "Trevitas" was ecstatic about her return to television, however short-lived it might be. These mini-Glorias were springing up all over, starting with the students at Sergio's star academy who were thrilled to see their gym equipment checkout girl taking the country by storm. If they needed any other proof that Mr. Midas was a legitimate starmaker, Gloria was it.

Elsewhere, schoolgirls and nightclub partiers alike were

adopting Gloria's trademark torn tights, clunky boots, and flouncy thrift-store skirts and packing her concerts in bigger and bigger auditoriums. Word had spread that Gloria live wasn't a show; it was a near-religious experience.

The lights would drop, the auditorium would go black, and from the darkness a drumbeat would echo.

Bar-a-bat-a-batta-ba!

Guitars picked up the rhythm as the voices of three backup singers—Aline, Mary, and Sarai, one of the new girls—leaned into their mikes and chanted, "G! . . . L! . . . O! . . . R!—"

Then a spotlight would blaze center stage as Gloria, a frenzied blur of angry hair and ruined clothes, would suddenly appear, screeching, "*GLOOOOORRRRRIIIAAAAA!*" She'd drop to her knees, fighting the air and tearing at her own clothes, again screaming:

"*GLOOOOORRRRRIIIAAAAA!*"

That was usually the calmest moment of the night. Gloria's shows would start around nine and go until one, two in the morning, whenever she and the crowd had roared themselves into exhaustion. As soon as she'd rasped out her last encore of the night, Gloria would collapse in the arms of her roadies. "Because of the way I sang, danced, and ran around, I'd finish the show soaked in sweat and soda," Gloria would say. "Security crews would rush me off in their arms, with barely any clothes on, since my skirts, shirts, and nylons were torn apart, victims of my desperation and tantrums."

She'd be hustled right out the arena's back door, not even stopping to change clothes, hoping to outrun fans swarming every car in sight, stopping traffic in search of their idol. Sometimes, police would have to slip Gloria into an ambulance and sneak her out under cover of sirens and flashing lights.

During these early shows, Gloria developed an odd signature move. She'd pull a man out of the audience and lead him onstage. As he stood there, thrilled and a bit confused, Gloria would rub against him, easing him out of his shirt . . . sliding the belt out of his pants . . . working her hands around his waist, stroking and caressing, singing and staring him straight in the eyes as, a little at a time, she pushed his pants down his legs until they were around his ankles.

But it didn't stop there. Gloria would wrap the man's belt around her fist and begin whipping her trapped victim as he struggled to escape. If he bent over to pull up his pants, she'd lash his bottom. If he tried to hobble offstage, Gloria would follow, shrieking maniacally and slashing away with the belt. But suddenly, she'd stop. She'd drop the belt and wrap her victim in an apologetic hug, embracing him warmly . . . then intimately . . . then hungrily, pushing him backward until, with his ankles still entwined in his pants, he had no choice except to follow her lead and lower himself to the floor. Gloria would climb onto his lap and keep pushing until he was flat on his back, holding him down by the shoulders as she writhed against him, thrusting her hips.

"I love to see men in the role of women," Gloria would say. "I love to see the look on their faces when I put them to the floor. They suddenly experience what a woman has to deal with all the time and get this panicked expression on their face of '*No, no, no!*'"

Oddly, Gloria had no trouble finding fresh victims even after this routine was no longer a surprise. "I think guys like feeling what it's like when roles are reversed," she'd say. "Now it's the man who's on the bottom. And me, a woman, is stripping off his clothes. A woman seducing and trapping them. The next time they're with a girl, I bet they'll be a lot sweeter because now they know how it feels."

"Really?" one reporter pushed back. Did Gloria seriously believe that publicly humiliating men would make them go home and act more kindly toward their girlfriends? Gloria fixed her interviewer with a devilish grin. "I do it because I like it. And it amuses me. And it gives the girls an eyeful of skin for a change."

But lost in all her sass was the real question that everyone kept missing. Not "*Why?*" but "*Where?*" Where did this torture fantasy come from? The shaming, the belt lashing, the stripping and domination of a defenseless person—no one seemed to wonder how a teenager seemed so familiar with sexualized abuse. To Gloria's shrieking fans, this was all about girl power and feminist fearlessness. They had no idea that the hidden world of 108 Adolfo Prieto Street was playing out before their eyes.

Only three people knew that Mexico's biggest pop star still lived in her manager's cellar.

On nights when Aline told her mother she was "having a sleepover with Gloria and the girls," Gloria had to watch as Aline accompanied Sergio upstairs to the master bedroom while Gloria turned and descended to the basement. When Aline had to hurry home, Gloria would be summoned to Sergio's bed as his second choice. Gloria couldn't even escape having her nose rubbed in Sergio's new relationship in the recording booth, because whenever she was working on a new song, Sergio insisted that Aline be at her side singing backup.

Concert trips were even worse, Aline would say. "After each show, we'd get back to the hotel long after midnight and inevitably, Sergio would want to make love to me even though I couldn't stand it. It hurt me, a lot. And if that wasn't bad enough, sometimes it would occur to him to have Gloria join us."

Gloria would never defy Sergio, but that didn't mean she

was completely docile. Behind Sergio's back, Gloria reverted to her old Boquitas behavior of savaging the people she publicly pretended to love. "Aline acts all awkward and innocent," she whispered to Mary and the other girls in the studio. "But she's actually a sneaky slut." Gloria spread a rumor that Aline liked to watch porn with her guy friends and first had sex with a stranger on a kitchen counter in the middle of a party. And then one day, Gloria emerged from the basement with a sly new song she'd written for the second album. Without naming anyone, she said it was about a girl who'd slept with nearly a dozen guys but told each that he was her first. She already had the perfect title, too: "The Most Virgin of Virgins" ("Virgen de las Virgenes").

But beneath her scorn, Gloria was suffering. When she looked in the mirror, her own appearance repulsed her. She must be "deformed," she would later recall feeling, because "no man has ever loved me." She sank into a depression, fixated on "the treachery of my few friends, the disaster I'd made of a love life, the horrible feeling that I don't matter to anybody."

One night, she got out of her basement bed and went upstairs. She rummaged through the bathroom cabinets, gathering all the pills she could find—sedatives and sleeping pills and pain medication—and dumped them into a pile on a coffee table.

"There had to be about seventy," she guessed. She began choking them down, gagging but forcing herself to swallow, until she blacked out.

"Stupid! Stupid!" she heard someone screaming as she came to.

Sergio was forcing her to drink milk. "Why is he doing this?" she wondered dimly. "He knows I detest milk."

Exactly. Gloria gulped down a few swallows and retched them back up. Sergio kept drowning Gloria in milk, then he hauled her to her feet and walked her in circles around the living room. Over his shoulder, he ordered Mary to get a bucket and mop up the vomit. He barked at Aline to stop gawking and go back to bed. As soon as Mary finished cleaning the floor, Sergio turned Gloria over to her and returned to his room. Instead of taking Gloria to the hospital, he left her in the care of one teenager as he got back into bed with another.

That night was an awakening for Gloria. As she'd later tell the story, she realized this was all her fault. Sergio had asked her to show real love and selflessness, and she'd failed. But never again. She vowed that from that moment on, she'd be a better person. She'd be more like Mary.

"Forgive me, Sergio," she prayed. "Forgive me."

22

ALINE, SOLO

Sergio kept Gloria's collapse a secret by making her vanish.

Before anyone found out about her suicide attempt, Sergio stunned Gloria's fans by announcing he was canceling the rest of her tour. Gloria needed absolute privacy and concentration to work on her second album, he said. Therefore, until further notice, there would be no more shows, no more interviews, no more appearances of any kind.

And with that, in August of 1990, Gloria and her girl gang disappeared.

The house on Adolfo Prieto was suddenly vacant. Sergio left word that the studio would be closed and all classes terminated until he returned. However, to a few carefully selected students he delivered a very different message: if they were willing to travel with Sergio and Gloria to an undisclosed location in Los Angeles, they could join her as backup singers on the new project. But if Sergio got any inkling that they'd told anyone about the trip, he'd shut it down immediately and send everyone home.

Sergio knew that Aline's mother would require special handling, so he told Aline he'd talk to her himself. A few weeks earlier, Jossie had left her job at the radio station to launch her own ceramics business. Sergio had immediately offered to help out by volunteering his own private chauffeur to drive Aline home after rehearsals so Jossie wouldn't have to spend her evenings stuck in traffic. Now, he was phoning with another offer: since he was hiring a studio for Gloria's album, he'd like to record some tracks for Aline as well.

"She's nearly ready for her own solo project," Sergio told Jossie. But for Aline to travel with them, Sergio would need not only her passport but also a notarized affidavit granting him legal guardianship of a minor. Jossie paused, wondering why Mexico's top starmaker was personally booking flights for one of the backup singers, not to mention interrupting his work with Latin America's hottest new sensation so he could produce, arrange, and record an album for a fourteen-year-old who'd never played an instrument, written a song, or done anything more than shake a tambourine between two other girls.

"Mary and Gloria will watch out for her," Sergio promised.

"Okay," Jossie finally agreed.

But another mother wasn't buying it. For some time, Emma de Becerra had been increasingly uncomfortable with the stories she'd wrung out of her twin teen daughters, Ivette and Ivonne, about the goings-on in the studio. They told her the other girls were "a little strange." Several of them seemed to live in the basement, while Gloria and Mary acted like Sergio's servants, never making a move "unless Sergio first gave them permission." Whenever Emma came by to pick up the girls, she'd always find Gloria or Mary at the door with some excuse about why she shouldn't come inside. So when the girls came home one afternoon and said they had been invited to L.A. but needed Emma to sign over legal guardianship to Sergio, Emma refused. Within an hour, she got a call from Sergio. He was furious.

"You're going to second-guess me?" he shouted. "You think you know what's best? Sign it or I'm done with them." Emma was so stunned, she didn't even reply. She hung up on Sergio and told her daughters they were never, ever returning to Sergio's star school.

When they arrived in Los Angeles, Aline discovered that instead of putting a road manager in charge of the trip, Sergio insisted on handling everything himself. He personally checked the girls into a Best Western hotel and doled out their room assignments. In the lobby, he handed each pair of girls a key and sent them off, leaving Aline for last.

"You'll be staying with me," he told her. He coached her on exactly what to tell her mother and stepfather. "Don't let them know the name or phone number of the hotel," Aline says Sergio told her. "Tell them I need you to concentrate on your album, and you can't be getting calls at all hours." Aline made the call according to instructions. Luckily, she says, her stepfather answered and bought the story.

In the studio that night, Aline says, Sergio was a different man. He clapped headphones over his ears, and for the next eight hours he was unapproachable. He was completely absorbed in the music, never cracking a joke or even a smile, snapping at anyone who broke his concentration. Still, even though Sergio demanded uninterrupted focus, he also insisted that Aline and Mary and Sonia Ríos, the teenager they'd recruited from the fruit stall in Pachuca, remain with him. That's one reason he liked working from midnight till dawn: not only was the studio cheaper, but there were fewer people around to get curious about the young girls surrounding him. Even when Gloria was recording solo tracks and there was nothing for the other girls to do, Sergio insisted that they all remain. "We were dying," Aline says. "Those hours seemed endless."

No one else ever entered the studio. Most producers enlisted a rotating cast of friends and fellow musicians to collaborate and offer feedback, but Sergio worked completely alone. No pals, colleagues, or grown-ups of any kind. Aline thought he was the most solitary person she'd ever known. Over the past year, she had only ever seen him with teenage girls.

During work hours, Sergio's stamina was amazing. Sergio would stay at the mixing board till dawn, Aline says, then head back to the hotel and start making business calls to Mexico and New York, where the workday had already begun. After only a few days at Sergio's pace, Aline was woozy with fatigue. She wasn't allowed to sleep until Sergio was ready to go to bed, and even then, he'd only get a few hours of rest. Aline became so sleep-addled that once, in the middle of the night, she accidentally violated one of Sergio's strictest orders:

She answered the phone.

"Aline?" said the voice on the other end of the line.

"Mamá?" Aline replied, startled. How on earth had her mother found out where she was?

It was no thanks to Sergio. Jossie had repeatedly asked Sergio for contact information before Aline left, but Sergio claimed they were still ironing out details for the hotel and recording studio and he'd call as soon as they were locked in. When Jossie later heard that Aline had left a message with her stepfather about not being allowed to share the name of the hotel or even a phone number because "the artists couldn't be disturbed," Jossie felt a surge of panic.

For a while, she'd had a growing sense of uneasiness, largely because of Gloria. Why was Sergio paying so much attention to her daughter, even if he truly believed Aline had star potential, when he was already managing the biggest blockbuster talent in the country? And the more famous Gloria became, the more Jossie's suspicions grew. Something wasn't right, and when Jossie discovered that she'd been manipulated into signing over legal guardianship to a man who was now concealing her daughter's whereabouts, she knew she'd made a terrible mistake.

Jossie tried calling the Adolfo Prieto Street studio, but no one answered. She began dialing hotels across Los Angeles, but none had a Trevi or an Andrade registered. Suddenly, Jossie remembered a conversation she'd once had with Aline about the studio where Sergio had recorded Gloria's first album. The name was unforgettable: "Milagro Sound." The sound of a miracle.

Jossie called a cousin in L.A., who managed to track down a number for Milagro. By that time, it was three in the morning in California and nearing daybreak in Mexico City, but Jossie called the studio anyway. She had just missed Sergio, someone at the studio told her; he must have gone back to the hotel. "By chance do you know which one?" Jossie asked. They did—and Sergio's room and phone number. Jossie punched in the numbers, ready to blister Sergio for making her worry—but when she heard Aline's sleepy voice answering the phone in Sergio's room, she went cold.

"What are you doing there?" Jossie asked. "Isn't that Sergio's room?"

Aline stammered a denial. No, no, she said; the hotel must have connected her to the wrong room. Aline sounded confused and panicked. "Okay," Jossie said. "I understand." She said goodbye, hung up the phone, and taxied straight to the airport. By that afternoon she was in Los Angeles, heading toward the Best Western hotel.

23

BRANDY

Aline was strolling back from lunch with Gloria and Sonia Ríos and the rest of the girls when suddenly she froze in panic. Pacing back and forth outside their L.A. hotel, smoking angrily, was her mother.

Sergio was trailing behind the girls, far enough back for Gloria to hiss him a warning. By the time Jossie spotted him, Sergio was ready. He rushed toward her, all smiles and delighted eyes, and began smothering her with a barrage of happy talk as if running into her on a sidewalk in Los Angeles was the luckiest of coincidences. He never asked how she'd found them or why she was there. Instead, he prattled on about how great Gloria's new album was sounding and how much progress Aline was making. She was showing so much star potential, in fact, that as soon as Sergio finished with Gloria, he wanted to roll tape on her right away.

But! Regrettably, he'd have to explain all that later, Sergio said, checking his watch. He was already late for an important meeting. A manager's life, he shrugged. Always another fire to put out. First thing tomorrow they'd talk more, okay? And with that, Sergio turned and hurried off.

Jossie watched him go, not buying it. He didn't even give me a chance to complain, she thought to herself.

Jossie wheeled on her daughter. Aline swore that she'd been sharing a room with Gloria and Mary. Gloria nodded along in agreement. Jossie still wasn't convinced, but she'd calmed enough to hear Sergio out. She checked into the hotel and told Aline to gather her bags. Aline would stay with her until Jossie had a chance to sort things out with Sergio. If she wasn't completely convinced that Aline was safe, Jossie was bringing her home.

Early the next morning, Jossie knocked on Sergio's door. No one answered. She tried Gloria's room. Oh, Gloria told her, Sergio's gone. He was called back to Mexico on urgent business and wouldn't be back for a few days. Jossie was stunned, then furious. Okay, she told Gloria. I've had enough. I'm taking Aline home with me today.

"But, señora, that's impossible," Gloria replied. "Sergio has Aline's passport." Sergio always held all the girls' papers, Gloria explained. Since he hadn't returned Aline's, he must have accidentally taken it with him. Aline would have to stay until he got back.

"I'm not leaving without my daughter," Jossie insisted.

Gloria merely shrugged. "As you wish, señora."

For the next three days, Gloria and the other girls were polite but aloof, treating Jossie like a neurotic old woman who had to be tolerated while they went about the professional, no-nonsense business of recording an album with a respected producer. Aline, on the other hand, was in a rage, accusing Jossie of humiliating her with perverted suspicions and blackening the name of a man who had only been good to them. After a day or two of this treatment, Jossie felt her conviction wavering, wondering if she was making a mistake.

What if Sergio really is about to make Aline's record? Jossie thought. What if I'm derailing her future, this great opportunity before her? What if I'm just imagining things?

After all, who was Gloria Trevi until Sergio came along? Where was Crystal before Sergio stepped in? And look at Lucerito—before Sergio, who knew she could actually sing and not just look pretty standing next to a piano? So didn't it make sense that Mr. Midas might have seen something in Aline that was invisible to the untrained eye? Otherwise, why would he bother?

Jossie didn't know what to believe anymore.

Which was exactly Sergio's plan.

Sergio had never gone back to Mexico at all. The entire time Jossie was fretting at the Best Western, Aline claims, Sergio was hiding out in a nearby apartment he'd rented, then slipping into the studio by night to work with Gloria.

He coached the girls on how to handle Jossie, giving them each specific assignments: polite bewilderment from Gloria and Mary, self-righteous anger from Aline, all part of his strategy to sap her confidence and blur her moral certainty. Sergio figured that if Jossie was isolated in a foreign country with no one to offer advice or support, she'd eventually begin questioning herself instead of him.

But Sergio was nowhere near as calm when it came to dealing with Aline. He was furious about being ambushed and made sure that Aline paid for it. When Gloria and Mary took Aline to see Sergio in his new hideaway, Aline would recall that Sergio slid off his belt and whipped her. He kept lashing at her, Aline says, even though she wept and pleaded that it wasn't her fault. But rather than driving her away from Sergio, the whipping only hardened Aline against Jossie. "I hated her more than ever," she'd say.

Three days after his sudden disappearance, Sergio reappeared at the Best Western to meet with Jossie. Finally, she had a chance to recover her daughter's passport and take her home, not to mention give Sergio a piece of her mind. When Sergio appeared at her door, Jossie let him in and immediately—

Crumbled.

By the time they were face-to-face, Jossie would say, her anger had melted into confusion and a general sense that something wasn't right, but she couldn't even tell anymore if Sergio was to blame for that feeling or her own paranoia. Sergio, for his part, acted the exact opposite of a man with something to hide. He listened to Jossie's complaints with a stony expression and answered with courteous condescension: If the señora is dissatisfied with the free professional training her daughter is receiving, then by all means, take her home. It would be a pity, he sighed, since Gloria was nearly done with her album and Aline's would be next, but if the señora had some kind of problem . . . What was the problem again, that Aline forgot to leave a phone number? I see. But she did call, correct? So what exactly is the problem, since she called as promised?

By the time Sergio finished, Jossie found herself apologizing. Seeing his advantage, Sergio pushed further. Now Jossie could remain in Los Angeles or return to Mexico, it was all the same to him, but under no circumstances could he allow her in the studio. It would make the girls far too self-conscious. Work hours were off-limits.

Jossie agreed. But work hours, she soon discovered, were unpredictable, never-ending, and usually nocturnal. Aline was disappearing from their room in the middle of the night and often not turning up again until the next evening for a shower and change of clothes before heading right out again. Jossie sat there, brooding and uncertain.

"I was sick of such a miserable, humiliating experience," Jossie would say. "More than intimidated or angry, I just felt sad, lonely, and uncertain." Maybe, Jossie started to think, maybe Aline was angry because she was right. Maybe Jossie really was blowing things out of proportion.

One evening, though, Aline seemed to soften and appreciate her mom's situation.

"*Mamá*, if you don't believe me, why don't you just talk to Sergio's girlfriend?" Aline said.

"Girlfriend?" Jossie had never seen Sergio with any adults at all, let alone a romantic partner. "Who is she?"

Aline looked astonished. "You don't know? It's Gloria's cousin."

Jossie didn't know what to make of this girlfriend *ex machina* suddenly dropping into the situation. How come no one had ever mentioned her before? She eyed her daughter skeptically, wondering if this was just another ploy to get her to leave. She decided to call Aline's bluff.

"Yes, of course I'd like to speak with her. Can you get me her phone number?"

Aline shrugged. "Just go to her room. She's been here with us the whole time."

Brandy Ruiz, who changed her name from Mariana to pursue her singing career, had lived nearly all her life in McAllen, Texas. Even though Brandy felt more American than Mexican and spoke only broken Spanish, Gloria assured her young cousin that with Sergio's help, she could become a Latin American sensation just like her.

"Such a gorgeous girl!" Aline would recall. "The prettiest face I had seen in my entire life. Very pale, with dark hair and a tiny nose. Like a model!" Aline wasn't alone in this opinion; a *Dateline NBC* reporter who would later interview Brandy about her time with the Gloria Trevi clan called her "the most beautiful non-celebrity I've ever seen."

Brandy was sixteen when Gloria encouraged her to come to Mexico City and attend Sergio's star school. Brandy's parents agreed, and after traveling down from Texas and dropping her off at the Adolfo Prieto studio, they soon heard back from their daughter that Sergio's school was "very real, very legit." Brandy said she was thrilled with the instruction she was getting. Sergio was turning her into a better singer than she'd dreamed possible, and her gorgeous, glamorous cousin Gloria kept telling Brandy that a face like hers, with those lovely hazel eyes framed by silky black hair and a spray of freckles across her nose, was just made for album covers.

Brandy had been at Adolfo Prieto for a few months when one night she woke up to the sound of her door creaking open. She saw Sergio looming over her. She didn't like what she saw in his eyes, she'd later say, and squirmed away. Sergio grabbed her. When she resisted, she said, he smacked her across the face and threw her down, heaving his heavy body on top of hers. She cried for help as he tore at her nightclothes, and soon her rescue appeared in the open doorway: her cousin, Gloria.

But Gloria just stood and watched. Then she silently walked away.

The next morning, Brandy left Adolfo Prieto at dawn. She called her parents from the bus station and told them she had to come home right away, without giving a reason. They bought her a ticket over the phone and Brandy caught the very next bus for the border. When she arrived in McAllen, she was too confused and ashamed to tell her parents what had happened. It was all so horrible and unbelievable, and she knew her parents would never believe it. So rather than torture herself by playing it back again and again in her mind, Brandy tried to shut it all out and get on with her life. She told her family that singing wasn't for her after all.

A few months later, Brandy overheard her mother chatting excitedly with someone on the phone. She froze as she heard her mother say, "Yes, yes. She's right here. You can tell her yourself!" Brandy's mother passed her the phone and watched, ecstatic, as Brandy slowly lifted it to her ear. It was Gloria. *Prima*, your dream just came true, Gloria gushed. Sergio landed you a record deal! We start recording next week!

Brandy listened, dumbfounded. What was Gloria talking about? A record deal? Brandy had never even recorded a demo. Why on earth would any record company be interested in some unknown teenager they'd never heard sing, even if she was La Trevi's cousin? Did Sergio have that much power? And if so, why use it for her?

"I didn't want to go," Brandy would later tell NBC's *Dateline*. "But my father made me." Because she still hadn't told her family what had happened at Adolfo Prieto, they assumed her reluctance was just nerves. "Trust your cousin," her parents urged. "She knows what she's doing!" The more Brandy mumbled out excuses, the more she began to question herself. Gloria had seemed so carefree on the phone, so happy and warm. Was Gloria faking all that? But why? Why would they bother bringing her back . . . unless by some miracle, she really did have a record deal?

Brandy had done such a good job of blocking out her last night on Adolfo Prieto that now she struggled to remember the details. It was all so dark, so sudden. Maybe it was just a bad misunderstanding? Maybe she'd accidentally done something to lead Sergio on and give Gloria the wrong idea? Maybe it was actually her fault . . . ?

The next day, Brandy packed a bag and boarded a plane for Los Angeles.

Sergio greeted her with polite indifference. On recording nights, she trailed along behind Mary, Aline, and the other girls, never really sure what she was supposed to be doing. In the studio, Sergio focused all his attention on Gloria. Out of the studio, he disappeared, leaving the girls to mostly eat supermarket food in their hotel rooms before getting some sleep before another all-night session.

Brandy had no idea why she was there, until out of the blue one night, Sergio pivoted from the control panel and turned to her. "Tomorrow," he said. "Tomorrow is your night. Get your songs ready."

Startled, Brandy scrambled to prepare her best two songs. She rehearsed them quietly with Aline and Mary in their hotel room the following day while Gloria slept. At the studio that evening, Gloria led Brandy into the recording booth and showed her how to adjust the microphone height and headphone volume. She gave Brandy a kiss on the cheek and left her to it. For the rest of the night, Sergio worked patiently on take after take while Mary and Gloria flashed thumbs-ups and beamed encouragement through the control booth window.

At daybreak, Sergio called it a session. Two very solid songs were in the can. "Very nice work," Sergio said, while Gloria, Mary, and Aline clustered around, congratulating her.

Brandy's head was spinning with exhaustion and amazement as they approached the Best Western. Sergio took her by the arm and pulled her aside. Have you met Aline's mother? he asked.

I've seen her, Brandy replied. But I haven't met her.

She's been hanging around, Sergio said, driving Gloria and Mary crazy. Typical out-of-control stage mom.

Brandy didn't know about Sergio and Aline, so this didn't mean much to her. Poor Aline, she murmured.

It's becoming a real problem, Sergio went on. She's been very disruptive, butting into things she doesn't understand. In fact, we may have to close down and head back to Mexico. She's wasting too much of my studio time. But, Sergio suggested, maybe you can help. Why don't you meet with Aline's mom and listen to whatever craziness comes out of her mouth? Just nod along. For instance, she's under the impression that you're my girlfriend. Crazy, right? But, whatever. Let her think what she thinks, and maybe she'll calm down and go home.

"I don't know if Mariana ever really was involved with Sergio," Aline would later say, referring to Brandy by her birth name. But from that moment on, Brandy had her assignment: whenever Jossie was around, Brandy was to rush up and hang on Sergio's arm. Gloria couldn't do it, because for months she'd been denying to the world at large, and Jossie directly, that she had any relationship with Sergio. Backtracking now and claiming she was lying would only make Jossie more suspicious. Mary Boquitas wasn't an option; first, she'd been posing all along as Sergo's strictly professional office manager, but worse, she tended to stammer and clam up under pressure.

Instead, Sergio shrewdly chose the one girl in his clan who looked older than sixteen, spoke limited Spanish, and believed she was just within reach of her own solo album. Brandy agreed to play along.

And it worked. Within a few days, Jossie packed up and returned to Mexico. She left just hours before Brandy, shaken and weeping, begged her father from a pay phone to come to L.A. and please, please bring her home.

"Mariana didn't say anything to me," Gloria would later say. "I felt bad for her after I heard some tracks from the album she had abandoned. It would have been a hit." But if anyone was to blame, Gloria said, she knew who it was: Jossie.

"Ever since *la señora* Jocelyn showed up in Los Angeles, Mariana had been in a tailspin, eating more and more and getting fatter by the day," Gloria would contend. "Sergio was working on Mariana's album, he'd talked to her about what she should wear and gave her money to buy clothes. Mariana's personality was getting worse by the day, and her attitude was strange and dark."

The same day that Jossie left, Brandy would later say, Sergio and Gloria brought her up to his hotel room. As they entered, Sergio suddenly grabbed her and threw her down on the bed. Terrified, she tried to get to her feet. Sergio bashed her across the face, knocking her back down.

"He beat me up and abused me, and I saw my cousin standing there watching." Gloria remained in the room, Brandy says, while Sergio climbed on top of her. "Sergio Andrade is the most evil man I've ever seen in my life. He began to rape me and I couldn't get away. He hit me, I screamed, and my cousin Gloria heard me. But she let him do what he wanted."

When she arrived back home in McAllen, Brandy sat down with her parents and grandmother and told them what had happened. Before anyone else could speak, her grandmother shook her head. No one will believe you, her grandmother said. They'll call you a liar and you'll ruin the family. Whatever happened, it's over now. Live with it.

"After that, I contemplated suicide many times," Brandy says. When she finally did break from her parents and go to the police, they told her too much time had passed and there was nothing they could do. With nowhere else to turn, she went public and told her story on *Dateline NBC*. To this day, she can still hear the last words Gloria spoke to her echoing in her mind:

"This is your fault. If you say anything, I will defend Sergio."

24

THE UGLY GIRL

For the second time, Sergio woke up to discover that a young woman who could destroy him had vanished.

Just like before, he had no idea where Brandy had gone but he did have a sickening idea of what she could be saying. And just like before, he knew exactly what to do. He had Gloria make some casual "just-checking-in" phone calls to various aunts and cousins, and through that family grapevine, she discovered that Brandy was back home in McAllen. As far as Gloria could make out, there was no mention of any kind of fuss. So Sergio shrugged it off and went back to work.

Because despite all the turmoil around him—the gaslighting of Jossie, the juggling of a half-dozen young women constantly at his side, the clandestine liaisons with Aline in his secret apartment, and now the looming catastrophe of Brandy's disappearance—Sergio was still on pace to complete Gloria's brilliantly named second album, *Your Guardian Angel* (*Tu Angel de La Guarda*), right on schedule.

In less than two weeks, Gloria had recorded clean takes on the ten original songs she had written for the album, plus two more that Sergio had commissioned. As usual, Sergio's ear for his singers' material was flawless—and absolutely ruthless. Sergio believed that even if audiences didn't know the story behind the lyrics, they could still feel the truth in what they were hearing. That was one great secret behind Gloria's appeal: Sergio made sure that despite her sexy-punk public image, she also gave hints of very real pain.

For *Your Guardian Angel,* Sergio found two songwriters with a gift for channeling Sergio's thoughts into Gloria's language. The first song, "Wild Hair" ("Pelo Suelto"), is a girl-power anthem calling for all those "nice" Mexican schoolgirls to follow Gloria's lead and unknot their braids, shake out their hair, and let the wind swirl their locks like a flag of freedom. But the second song is the one that really has something to say. "You Had It Good with Me" ("Las Pasabas Bien Conmigo") is shadowy and a little sinister. It's a love-gone-wrong song, but loaded with so much spite, obsession, and self-loathing that it feels one step removed from a suicide note.

"I know I'm uglier than the girls you date now," Gloria sings, while her backup singers chant "Nadie, nadie, nadie" in a heartbroken chorus of rejection.

With Gloria's album nearly finished, Aline's mother out of the way, and Brandy apparently silent, Sergio could now focus on payback. A parent had once again forced him to go into hiding, just like with Lucerito, and for a man who insisted on absolute obedience and control, this was infuriating. It was time to show those teenage girls who was boss.

On the same morning that Brandy disappeared, an exhausted Aline accidentally dozed off after another endless night in the studio while Sergio was off talking to Gloria. When she woke up, she knew she was in trouble.

Sergio dragged her to the bathroom and ordered her to strip naked, Aline would later say. Sergio pointed to the floor. If you can't control yourself better than a dog, he said, I'll have to treat you like one. Lie down there, next to the toilet. That's your new bed. Aline curled up on the cold tiles and cried herself to sleep.

"That became sort of a habit with us," Aline would say. From then on, Sergio would send her to the floor whenever he was displeased.

This story instantly jangled someone's memory. Rubén Aviña, Sergio's publicist, had heard a nearly identical version from another of Sergio's singers, right down to the detail of being "trained to behave like a dog." The account of sadism always bothered Rubén, not only for its cruelty but also because he could never shake the feeling that for some weird reason, the singer was telling him the complete truth except for one key detail.

The detail? The name of the sadist.

And the singer: Gloria Trevi.

According to Rubén, he'd fallen out of touch with Gloria after the Boquitas Pintadas disbanded and Sergio dropped out of sight. He was delighted to see her again once Sergio launched his new Adolfo Prieto Street academy and found Gloria to be the same compulsive oversharer as ever. Gloria caught Rubén up on her life, telling him that during her time as a panhandler and penniless aerobics teacher, she'd moved in with an older man, a "doctor who specialized in female function, like a gynecologist." Gloria was vague about the mystery doctor's identity, referring to him only as "Alejandro," but very specific about his age. He was thirty-four while she was seventeen—exactly the age difference, Rubén noted to himself, between Gloria and Sergio.

One evening, she told Rubén, "Alejandro" erupted in anger over something she'd done. She tried to apologize but only made things worse because she didn't really know what she'd done wrong. Alejandro shoved her into the bathroom and demanded she strip off her clothes. "Entire days locked in the bathroom!" Gloria would say. "My God! I'd spend the time crying, sleeping on the floor like a dog. Alejandro would bring me food, then lock me up again like I was in a cell."

When he finally freed her, Alejandro would bathe her in affection, taking Gloria out for a fine meal and telling her, over and over, how much he adored her. "Many times, I made up my mind to walk out on him, because as deeply in love as I was, at the same time I was really afraid of him." Finally, Alejandro made the decision for her. "He said he was sick of me," Gloria told Rubén. "He told me to hit the road."

There's no way she's making this up, Rubén thought. The details, the raw emotion, the compulsion to get it off her chest—nobody could fake all that, not even a natural performer like Gloria. Rubén was sickened by the story and frightened for Gloria. He could guess the true identity of "Alejandro," but he could also see that no matter how viciously Gloria says she was tortured, she was still willing to cover up for her torturer.

Aline had been sleeping on the floor for a few days when Sergio stunned her again. This time, by keeping his promise.

As soon as the last track of Gloria's *Your Guardian Angel* was locked, Sergio told Aline that the recording studio now belonged to her. He began working with her full-time, prepping her exactly as he had with Gloria, and Crystal, and Lucerito, coaching her with precise instructions on how to hit her notes, carry her melodies, and articulate her lyrics. He assembled eight songs he believed would suit her style and reworked two she'd written herself.

Aline's rehearsals were shaky. After weeks of being whipped and insulted and disciplined, she'd say, her confidence was shattered and her most recognizable trait—her warm, eager, joyful spark—was gone, replaced by self-doubt and sullen watchfulness. Sergio's solution was simple: You don't have to believe in your talent, he told Aline. You only need to believe in mine. El Maestro knew what he was doing, so Aline should leave the thinking to him and do what she was told.

He sent Aline into the recording booth, and as she began to sing, her doubts melted away. Her voice through the headphones sounded lovely in her ears so she leaned in, throwing back her head and cutting loose with power and volume. Through the control booth window, Sergio was nodding along and guiding the beat with his hands like an orchestra conductor. Aline's day had finally arrived, and it was more glorious than she'd ever dreamed. The shame and pain she'd endured for months was replaced by a flood of gratitude. It was the price an artist had to pay, she reasoned.

"During this unforgettable process of recording, with Sergio signaling me directions for how to interpret the verses, I felt more love for him than ever before," she'd say.

Only when Sergio revealed the title did Aline suddenly feel sick to her stomach. Sergio had decided to call her album *Ugly Girls* (*Chicas Feas*). Mary and Gloria thought it was a scream, especially when Sergio kept popping his head into their hotel room and calling, "Anyone seen the ugly girl?" Aline was embarrassed and bewildered. Why would Sergio work so hard to create a gorgeously mastered album, laboring hours a day for nearly two weeks in the studio, only to turn it into a punch line? Maybe for Sergio, she was just a toy, a living doll he could dress beautifully one day and kick around the next, depending on his mood. The night before her album cover shoot, Aline claims, Sergio made her spend another cold night on the hard floor, guaranteeing that with her puffy eyes and tear-streaked face, the camera would truly see *la chica fea*.

Los Angeles, Sergio decided, had been a game changer.

A month earlier, he'd been dealing with a suicidal superstar, an increasingly suspicious mother, and a hungry Mexican press that, only by some miracle, hadn't begun probing what was going on with all the young girls in the house on Adolfo Prieto Street. Now, Gloria was feeling better and Sergio had remedies to keep his other problems at bay:

A new release by Mexico's favorite daughter!

A new singer to prove Sergio's star school was legit!

And a ready-to-release album that would shut Jossie up once and for all.

He was safe. It was time to go home. And besides, in a few days Aline was due to begin tenth grade.

Aline burst through the door, electrified to tell her mother all about her album. But Jossie didn't want to hear it. She was armed with new determination—and new locks on the door. "This is it," Jossie told Aline, locking them both inside the house and pocketing the key. "This thing with Sergio is over."

By the time Jossie had gotten back to Mexico from L.A., she'd already begun to regret leaving Aline behind. Being alone in a strange country, surrounded by people who made her feel stupid and unsure of herself, she'd lost her grasp on reality. Now that she was home she felt her confidence return, along with the nagging sense that Sergio and Gloria were manipulating her. She didn't know what they were lying about, but she was sure they were lying about something.

Jossie laid down the law. From that moment on, Aline would not leave the house unless Jossie was with her. There would be no more star school, no visits from Gloria, no phone calls from Sergio. Once school began, Jossie would drop Aline off in the morning and pick her up in the afternoon. If Sergio still wanted to release Aline's album, fine—but Josse would personally accompany her to every rehearsal and every public appearance and bring her home afterward. Aline wouldn't even be allowed to answer the phone.

Aline couldn't believe it. Here she was on the brink of stardom, and she was grounded? She screamed insults at her mother, flying into a rage that abruptly only ended with a slap. Aline then reversed tactics. She apologized. She negotiated. She pleaded. But Jossie was unbending. This time, she wouldn't allow herself to be fooled.

Early the next morning, the phone rang. It was Gloria. Jossie hung up on her. A few hours later, there was a knock on their front door. Jossie opened it to find Gloria standing there. That was the moment, Jossie would say, when a stab of certainty pierced her heart. Everything she'd gone through in L.A. had been a game to deceive her, she now knew for sure, and anything that was about to come out of Gloria's mouth would be a flat-out lie. Because there were only two possible explanations for why Mexico's biggest pop sensation was running around the city carrying messages between a high school sophomore and her middle-aged manager:

Either they were terrified of something Aline would say . . .

Or they'd trained her to say nothing.

"The two of you can go to hell!" Jossie shouted, and slammed the door in Gloria's face.

For three days, Jossie kept Aline under lock and key. On day 4, Jossie allowed her out for an hour to walk to the grocery store with their housekeeper. On day 5, Jossie had to drive her husband to work. She locked the door behind her, dropped her husband off at the office, and was back in plenty of time to make breakfast for Aline before she woke up.

Except Aline was gone.

25

ALINE'S ESCAPE

At the exact moment Jossie was pulling up in front of her house, Aline was running desperately down a side street toward a taxi. Waiting inside was Mary Boquitas. Aline tumbled in, breathless, and the cab squealed away.

Aline had engineered her escape the day before during her visit to the grocery store with the housekeeper. Aline watched, waiting, until the housekeeper was busy counting out money to pay for the groceries. Then she quickly slipped off to a pay phone and called Sergio. Sergio promised she'd be picked up the following morning during the only thirty minutes that Jossie would be out of the house.

The next problem was the locks. As soon as her mother and stepfather pulled out of the driveway the next morning, Aline began tearing through the house looking for keys. She found one that looked shiny and new hidden in the kitchen. Hoping it was a spare for the new locks, she slipped it into the door and gave it a turn. It clicked. With just minutes to spare before her mother arrived, Aline slipped out the door and took off at a sprint.

Sergio has a hideout for you, Mary told Aline as the cab

sped away. Nora, Sergio's ex-girlfriend whom he'd paid to keep an eye on Crystal, had agreed to stash Aline in her house while Sergio figured out what to do next. Soon after they arrived at Nora's place, Sergio appeared. There, he found his current teenage wife and his former teenage baby mama giving romantic advice to his runaway teenage girlfriend.

"We have to deal with this intelligently," Sergio announced. If we're not careful, Aline would recall him saying, your mother will have me charged with kidnapping. And once police and TV cameras were involved, not even Sergio's famous, silver-tongued big brother Lalo could get him out of a jam like that. So on the car ride over to Nora's house, Sergio had whipped together a three-part plan:

Step 1: Jossie would be absolutely ballistic, so Sergio's first line of defense was to enlist his elderly mother to go to Jossie's house and plead for mercy.

Step 2: Jossie knew Sergio would disappear again, just as he had in L.A. So Sergio would throw her off-balance by stepping into the lion's den and appearing at her door to take the heat, face-to-face.

Step 3: The Bombshell.

Standing in Jossie's living room, surrounded by the stormy faces of Aline's stepfather, cousins, and mother, Sergio dropped the bomb that stunned them all into silence.

"I was shocked," Jossie said later. So shocked, she doubted her own hearing. Did Sergio really just say . . .

Señora Jocelyn. Please allow me the honor of marrying your daughter.

"I was completely against it," Jossie would say. Aline was

only fifteen, and Sergio, to her knowledge, was at least thirty-six. But privately, Jossie knew her hands were tied. Sergio was very, very smart. Since Jossie couldn't locate Aline, she couldn't prove he was involved with her disappearance. And if Jossie went ahead and had him arrested anyway, Sergio's best defense was to clam up. As long as Aline remained invisible, Sergio could shrug and play victim and Aline would remain in whatever bolt-hole she'd disappeared into. Even if Sergio caved and Aline was brought back home, what would stop her from running off again? Jossie didn't even know how she'd escaped in the first place.

So several weeks later, on November 19, 1990, Jossie arrived at the small restaurant where Aline was preparing to step before a municipal justice to become the second Mrs. Sergio Andrade. Luckily, Mary Boquitas hadn't objected when Sergio asked to fast-track their divorce; he managed to become single again just days before the wedding. Aline was sipping from a champagne glass of Coca-Cola; she was still too young to drink. One observer said she looked less like a bride and more like a girl receiving First Communion.

"Are you aware of what you're doing, marrying a man twice your age?" Jossie pleaded with her for the last time.

"Mamá, you have to understand," Aline replied. "I'm in love."

Gloria and Mary were there but could only stay a few minutes before leaving for rehearsal. Somehow in the midst of plotting Aline's escape, cajoling her family, finalizing his divorce, and planning his second wedding, Sergio still managed to keep an eye on his day job. *Your Guardian Angel* was due to drop that week, and Sergio had a feeling it could be the biggest hit of his career.

With the release of Gloria's second album, Mexico became a nation of Trevi-maniacs. Within a week, "Your Guardian Angel" was at the top of the charts and blasting through Gloria's previous sales records, forcing Sergio to rescramble the concert tour. Those 5,000-seat auditoriums wouldn't do it anymore; tickets sold out in a matter of hours, delighting scalpers who were soon enjoying a 500 percent markup from fans who were desperate to shout out the words of "Pelo Suelto" at the feet of their idol.

Concert promoters across Latin America and the U.S. began booking Gloria into 20,000-seat arenas and jacking up ticket prices. "We insisted they pay us in cash, before the show," Gloria would say. "Suitcases full of money were showing up all the time, to the point where the sight of them used to crack me up."

Even though Aline was now the wife of El Maestro and about to become a solo artist herself, Sergio ordered her to slip back into her hot pants and resume her position behind Gloria as part of the backup troupe. Aline was bewildered and a little humiliated. Wasn't she supposed to be Sergio's Next Big Discovery? Then why was she still stuck in the background, shaking a tambourine and shouting out the letters of another singer's name? She wasn't even allowed to call herself "Aline." Sergio insisted she perform as "Erika," the first name she hated, as long as she remained a backup performer.

Aline didn't get it—so Sergio opened her eyes.

"He said he couldn't pull me out of Gloria's band until someone was found to replace me," Aline says. They couldn't sabotage Gloria, right? That wouldn't be fair. So Aline's own record release would have to wait for, what . . . months, a year? Longer? It was 100 percent in Aline's control because it simply depended on how long it took her to bring in a fresh girl. Recruiting was a woman's job, Sergio added. Not a man's.

Aline caught her breath. Oh my god! In her mind's eye, she saw a white car pulling up at a radio station with a mysterious silhouette inside, the door swinging open, a wild-haired goddess emerging, striding across the street, cutting through the crowd of teenage girls, ignoring everyone else and heading directly toward Aline . . .

Suddenly, it all made sense.

That was exactly the time when Gloria was waiting for her own first album to be released. Sergio must have made her the same deal: Bring a new girl to Adolfo Prieto Street, then we'll see about getting your record out. Aline's thoughts flashed to Mary Boquitas. As long as Aline had known her, Mary had been toiling away in purgatory, serving as Gloria's backup and Sergio's top lieutenant while waiting for her own shot at the big time. All the Adolfo Prieto girls must be part of a secret pact, Aline realized, whether they knew it or not: You don't get what you want until Sergio gets what he wants.

And what Sergio wanted was . . .

Well, Sergio never really explained. It wasn't his way to be explicit. "Find someone appropriate," was all he said, but those three words were enough to tell Aline exactly what she was supposed to do: Find someone who looks like Gloria, hungers for fame like Gloria, and, most of all, obeys like Gloria. And if Aline refused, what could she do? Sergio could threaten to kill Aline's album with nothing to fear. The danger of her running home and telling her mother ended the day she said "I do."

So just a few weeks after her marriage, Aline began scouring the country for Sergio's next girlfriend. Gloria would even confirm this years later, although she suggests Aline was the instigator. "Aline was proposing backup singers left and right," Gloria would state. "She was urging him (Sergio) to choose one to take her place in my band, so he could make definite plans to launch her as a soloist." Gloria also verified that Aline knew exactly the kind of girl to hunt: "The requirements," Gloria would say, "were youth, good looks, and voice. That's why Aline was inviting every halfway-decent-looking girl that crossed her path to come audition."

Gloria was a skilled songwriter and the veteran of thousands of high-profile interviews by the time she made those comments. She knows precisely how to say exactly what she means, so when she rattles off the priorities for her backup singers, it's hard to believe the order is random. Being young was the #1 factor, followed by beauty at #2. The ability to actually sing came dead last. Creativity and experience didn't even make the rankings.

And youth was something Aline was dangerously close to losing herself. It might not have dawned on her yet, but Gloria and Mary knew from personal experience just how close Aline was to the far side of the hill. Even though Sergio and Aline had just been married a few weeks earlier, Aline was fast approaching her sixteenth birthday: exactly the age when Gloria and Mary had both been cut loose by Sergio.

Sergio met Mary Boquitas at fourteen, married her at fifteen, and demoted her to a secondary sex object and a sofa in the basement at sixteen. Likewise, Gloria beat out dozens of competitors for that last spot in the Boquitas Pintadas at age thirteen, then later held a special place in Sergio's heart—not to mention his bed—until she, too, was sent to the basement.

Aline didn't have Gloria's street smarts or brazen self-confidence to succeed as a recruiter. But she could rely on one tool that Gloria never had: a comic book. Sergio had begun a magazine called "The Amazing, Incredible, Scarcely Believable Adventures of Gloria Trevi" (*Las Insólitas, Increibles e Inverosimiles Aventuras de Gloria Trevi*). *Las Aventuras* was mostly photos and cartoons, clearly aimed at preteens. Gloria drew the comics herself, typically of baby-faced girls with big round eyes getting in trouble in school, or flirting with boys while strings of red hearts floated around their heads. There were some song lyrics ("Play 'Pelo Suelto' yourself!"), plus lots of glam shots of Gloria singing, modeling outfits, and posing with fans. These fans were always girls, and they always looked about twelve years old.

But even for devoted young Trevolutionaries, *Las Aventuras* was a little . . . creepy. In several issues, there appeared a full-page drawing of a naked woman (with hands strategically placed) alongside this quiz:

- Have you had sexual relations?
- If your answer is "No," write and tell us the reason.
- How often do you make love?
- How old were you when you first had sex?
- With whom?
- How did it feel?
- We've received very few answers, so listen up! Get moving and send us your responses!

To any parents flipping through their tween daughter's magazine and freaking out by this point, *Las Aventuras* offered something of an explanation:

> You might be asking yourself, "Why are they doing this?" Well, because we want to do a complete survey of real sexual practices among the young people of our country and that way be able to help answer any questions they might have.

For a public service, the quiz was weirdly bossy ("Listen up!") and offered zero indication of what Sergio and Gloria intended to do with the letters they received. Were they going to publish the results? Fund research? Start a sex advice column? And why, exactly, did a nineteen-year-old pop singer turned amateur sexologist and her middle-aged manager feel the need to know "With whom?" and "How did it feel?"

By the time Aline was deployed as Sergio's new recruiter, she had the full force of *Las Aventuras* behind her. Sergio even put Aline on the cover of Issue #6, with a special, full-page announcement inside:

AMIGA!
THIS IS THE OPPORTUNITY
YOU'VE BEEN WAITING FOR!
GLORIA TREVI IS INVITING YOU
TO JOIN HER BACKUP BRIGADE.
INTERESTED?

Girls were encouraged to apply by mailing in two photos (headshot and full body) plus a video or audio sample of their singing. The lucky girl (or girls, since there was no cap mentioned) would rehearse, travel, and appear onstage with Gloria. They'd also enjoy "a good salary, a magnificent working environment, and the possibility of launching their own careers as professional singers."

But that was just the teaser. The real bait was two concert photos of Mary and "Erika" (Aline's backup-singer stage name) with this offer:

Remember Erika and Mary?
They're part of Gloria's backup brigade.
Now they're beginning a career as solo artists
You can take their place!

You're not just meeting Gloria. You're two steps from *being* Gloria. Which is why, to anyone who knew Sergio Andrade as a musician, the whole thing was super weird bordering on super fishy. This was Mr. Midas, the classically trained composer at the center of the Mexican pop music universe. Performers across Latin America would open a vein for five minutes of his attention. But instead, he was going to plop on headphones and listen to 50,000 hours of scratchy homemade audition tapes from an army of adolescent randos?

Sergio could leave the initial screening to someone else, of course, except El Maestro never left anything to anyone else. As a control freak, Sergio was relentless. He approved or rejected all of his artists' songs, rewrote their lyrics, selected studio musicians, mixed and arranged every track, orchestrated their photo shoots, and even selected concert-tour hotels. Aline wasn't even allowed to write her own "personal letter" for her album sleeve because Sergio insisted on penning it himself ("Ever since I was a little girl," Sergio wrote, "I felt the need to write little stories and sing, sing, sing").

Maybe Sergio would sign off on a contest like that if it was a dinky radio station promo, with the winning girl hopping onstage for one song and right back off again. But to bypass the deep pool of experienced backup talent available for a star of Gloria's caliber and, instead, choose some kid off the street to live, rehearse, and travel with Mexico's hottest pop act based on nothing except a two-minute tape and a couple of selfies seemed impossible—

Unless the selfies were the only thing Sergio really cared about.

26

GLORIA'S BACKUP BRIGADE

Polaroids and cassette tapes came pouring in by the hundreds.

And after her concerts, Gloria began hearing a new kind of teen scream as she was hustled out to her limo: instead of autographs, girls along the rope lines were now begging for an audition. From town to town, the crowds grew larger and more frantic as rumors spread that some girls actually had been plucked off the street and brought to Adolfo Prieto.

But Sergio's recruiters didn't just wait for volunteers. Gloria brought in Andrea, her childhood friend from Monterrey. Mary Boquitas found Gaby in remote Tamaulipas, but Sergio sent her home after learning she was twenty years old. No one knew where the de la Cuesta sisters came from; teenagers Karola, Karla, and Katia just seemed to appear in the studio one day and never left.

Surprisingly, it was awkward Aline who landed Sergio's favorite new recruit. Marlene Calderón approached Aline for an autograph after a talent show in Los Mochis. She blurted out how much she'd dreamed of becoming famous, and while she was talking, Aline sized her up. Tall, lanky, thirteen years old—perfect. "I thought Sergio would really like this girl,"

Aline would say, so she briefed her husband about Marlene as soon as she got back to Mexico City. "Well, send for her!" Aline recalls him responding. Sergio told Aline to return to Los Mochis at once, with Gloria's friend Andrea along for support, and bring Marlene back for an audition.

Sergio auditioned Marlene without Aline in the room, so Aline would always wonder afterward if Marlene was also pressured to strip naked. But Aline was there when Sergio congratulated Marlene's mother on the scholarship Marlene had won to Sergio's studio—assuming, of course, that Marlene was permitted to drop out of school, leave home, and come live at 108 Adolfo Prieto Street.

"He repeated exactly what he'd told my mother, years ago," Aline would say. "The exact same story." One week later, Aline and Andrea returned to Los Mochis to help Marlene pack for her move to Mexico City. Marlene's mother clung to Aline, begging her to take care of her baby. That moment seared itself in Aline's memory and would become one of the most shameful and painful episodes of her life.

"If that poor woman had only known it was all a trick, or had any idea what was awaiting her daughter," Aline would lament, her voice trailing off. "And it was my fault."

Marlene turned out to be a much better Aline than Aline. At least that's how Sergio saw it.

"Everything was the same as with me, except she fell more quickly," Aline would explain. Marlene didn't need to be coerced or eased into the program; right from the get-go, she followed Sergio's every command. And unlike Aline, who never knew that Sergio was still sleeping with Mary and Gloria until after she'd fallen for him, Marlene didn't seem to care that Sergio was married to Aline.

"Within one month, she was completely installed in 'The System,'" Aline would say. "Meaning, she knew who was who, what her obligations were, and what her role was in 'The Game.' He had her in his office all day, and she was by his side at all times. She began sleeping with Sergio—that was obvious. And he'd begun to punish her, just like me."

According to Gloria's own reckoning, Marlene was one of at least eight of the studio girls that Sergio was regularly pulling into his office for sex. Besides Aline and Marlene, Gloria would say, there was also longtime clan member Sonia Ríos; new recruits Wendy Castelo and Katia de la Cuesta; Gloria's childhood buddy Andrea; and Gloria herself, at least on her twentieth birthday. "He caressed me . . . with force and ownership," Gloria would relate. "Then we made love until we fell asleep." Of course, those were only the girls she was certain about. "I suspected he was having other little adventures," Gloria adds, "though I couldn't be sure."

Aline was no longer shocked by anything she saw or was asked to do. She had lured a thirteen-year-old girl into a sexual relationship with her middle-aged husband, but her guilt would only catch up to her much later. In the present, Aline had accepted Sergio's world as her new normal. Gloria recalled spying Aline in bed with Sergio and fourteen-year-old Katia de la Cuesta, and by Aline's own admission, she wasn't bothered anymore by Sergio's punishments or his demands for fresh young recruits.

"This was much more than I had even dreamed of," Aline would say. "The other thing, the ugly part, didn't bother me that much anymore. Everything has a price in life, I figured—and I'd paid for what I'd gotten."

Sergio kept his end of the bargain. A few months before her sixteenth birthday in September 1991, Aline's debut album was released. Critics weren't kind. The gentlest of them pointed out that Aline was just a kid, so no wonder her lyrics were bland and her range was "purely adolescent," as one reviewer put it.

But so what? *Ugly Girls* was inching its way up the charts, due in no small part to Gloria's fame and Sergio's string-pulling. First, Sergio put Aline on the cover of Gloria's fan magazine. Then, according to Gloria, he began using her to strong-arm radio stations. If Aline's title track didn't appear among their Top 5 Most Requested, well . . . maybe Gloria wouldn't be available for that station promo after all. And had Sergio mentioned that Gloria had just recorded a new single that was only available for limited release? Limited, it went without saying, to stations who played ball for *Ugly Girls*.

Sergio's strategy worked like a dream, Gloria would claim. Astonishingly, Sergio even managed to defy impossible odds (not to mention years of bitterness and vows of "Never again!") and persuade Raúl Velasco to put Aline on *Siempre en Domingo*. Despite Don Raúl's dread that he was doomed to once again find himself on the humiliating end of another Sergio Andrade escapade, the only thing that shocked him as he watched from the wings was that Aline's performance was so bad.

Gloria Trevi's protégée she might be, but Gloria Trevi she was not. Unlike her mentor, who "ate the stage" when she got her chance at live TV, Aline was so overwrought with emotion that she barely managed to warble her way through "Ugly Girls" before she began weeping. Despite two years of coaching from Mexico's hottest starmaker and Mexico's hottest star, Aline sounded just like every other old-school, overwrought, sob-choking balladeer—exactly the kind of singer that Gloria was making it her mission to blow away with her punk-rock ballistics. Without Gloria's inventive genius and raw talent to draw on, the best that Sergio could do was play it safe and make Aline sound like every other ham performer.

For once, Don Raúl felt it was his turn to apologize. He burst out of the wings to join Aline at the end of her song, blustering joyfully into the cameras to draw attention from her cringey awkwardness. But the damage was done. *Ugly Girls* sank like a stone after that *Siempre en Domingo* fiasco, and not even Sergio could turn it around. Sales were so dismal that Polygram Records soon canceled Aline's contract.

"How about BMG?" Aline asked Sergio, hopefully. "They took a chance on Gloria!"

But wife or not, Sergio had no time to stage a comeback for a singer who'd barely even launched. If he wanted to continue attracting young women to Adolfo Prieto and persuade their parents and any snoopy reporters that it was a legitimate school, he had to keep coming up with ways to showcase his students. Sergio had a ton of promises to fulfill, and they were pulling him in a million directions.

While dealing with the *Ugly Girls* meltdown, he was also—

- Masterminding Gloria's first feature film, a glamorized biopic based on her hit "Pelo Suelto"
- Commissioning original songs and hiring musicians for Gloria's third album, due for release in less than a year
- Arranging photo shoots and nationwide distribution for Gloria's first pin-up calendar
- Signing off on every issue of Gloria's fan magazine
- Vetting all media requests and supervising every interview
- Rehearsing Mary Boquitas for her long-promised solo album
- Coaching Marlene Calderón and Wendy Castelo as backup vocalists for Mary Boquitas

- Training Katia and Karla de la Cuesta to join Gloria's new stage act
- Auditioning new recruits for Adolfo Prieto Street. Because, yes, Sergio was still bringing in more young women.

But the blunt truth is this: even if Sergio did have the time to lobby for Aline, would he? Mr. Midas knew better than to double down on his mistakes, as he'd once warned Gloria. As the man with the golden touch, he had to protect his reputation as a flawless eye for talent. The faster his rare misfires disappeared, the better. So rather than whipping up any press by demoting Aline back into Gloria's entourage, Sergio quietly began repositioning her from singer into model. Now that she was taller and more mature looking—taller, in fact, than Sergio himself—it wasn't hard to land her some magazine work and TV commercials.

Sergio rarely accompanied her on these assignments, however, instead deploying Andrea or Katia, the oldest and most loyal de la Cuesta sister. And just after her seventeenth birthday, Aline was stung when Sergio told her that he needed "more time alone with his thoughts." From then on, he said, he'd be sleeping alone and his young wife would be sharing a bed with Andrea and Katia. Aline dutifully gathered her things and moved downstairs.

Shortly before Christmas, Aline was lying in bed with the other two girls, staring at the ceiling. Sergio and Gloria were out of town, appearing at a music festival in Chile. Aline hadn't seen her family in nearly a year, because Sergio kept warning that her mother was toxically jealous and intent on poisoning her success. Aline had thrown that accusation in her mother's face the last time they spoke, and now, she couldn't stop thinking about her mother's reply.

"*Cariña*," her mother had said. "Someday you'll see this differently. And when you do, call me. No matter where you are or what time it is. We never have to talk about it. But I'll come get you."

About two o'clock in the morning, Aline eased her way out of bed, taking care not to awaken the other girls. She slipped out of the house and made her way to a pay phone. By the time dawn was breaking over Mexico City, she was wrapped in a blanket in her mother's kitchen, sipping warm milk with egg and cinnamon, talking about the family Christmas party ahead and all the foods Aline was craving.

They never mentioned Adolfo Prieto Street, or Sergio, or the note she'd left behind:

I promise I won't say anything

And she never did—until the day she realized that if anyone was going to save the rest of those girls, it would have to be her.

27

MISS WICKED

"The next part is really amazing," Pati Chapoy is telling me. "Truly astounding. So after Aline runs off in the middle of the night and never returns, do you know who finally caught up to Sergio?"

She pauses, giving me a beat to guess.

"*La policí—*" I begin, but she's already shaking her head, lips tight.

"Na. Dee. Ay," she says, spitting out each syllable. "*Nadie*. No one even asked him about it, as far as I could tell. His teenage wife—this famous girl who's been on TV shows and magazine covers and has a major record deal—suddenly vanishes into thin air and no one goes 'Hmmmm. What about that? Is she okay?'"

Pati and I are back in her office at TV Azteca. I'd circled around to see her again with another notebook full of questions after I'd spent nearly all of the past two days spellbound by Aline's story. Keeping track of the bizarre twists and secrets in the Gloria Trevi saga would typically fall to a full team of law enforcement officers, but as Aline's midnight run made clear, for a long time the only one paying any attention to the mysterious goings-on at 108 Adolfo Prieto Street was Pati Chapoy. Likewise, she knows more than almost anyone about Sergio and Gloria's professional life during that time, and for a simple reason: several chapters took place in the same chair I'm sitting in at that moment. The first time Pati seriously began to wonder about Gloria, in fact, was the day they sat down together in this room.

It was 1996, four years after Aline's escape, and since then, Gloria had skyrocketed to superstardom while Aline had kept her promise and remained silent. As far as the outside world could tell, Gloria was a strong, enormously talented, truth-telling feminist hero, guided by a legitimate and hardworking manager who just happened to specialize in young female performers.

The gritty panhandler who'd once begged for food truck scraps was now an entertainment colossus. Gloria dominated everything she tried, and she tried everything. She had platinum records, a top-rated TV show, plus two hit movies with a third on the way. Her first three albums sold more than five million copies. And her most recent had smashed sales records, thanks in part to accidental publicity by protesting Catholics who were scandalized by the title: *Mas Turbada que Nunca*, a naughty-wink pun which means "Crazier Than Ever" but also "Masturbating Like Crazy."

U.S. fans were also climbing aboard the Trevi train. Gloria sold out two concerts at Madison Square Garden and then turned Los Angeles's Hollywood Park into a one-woman Woodstock, packing in an astounding 40,000 fans. American reporters were crazy about her, too:

Variety: "La Trevi is a genuine political and cultural phenomenon."

People: "A powerhouse, with a mind as compelling as her voice."

The *Chicago Tribune* made Gloria sound like a Nobel laureate:

> Gloria Trevi, who has often been called the "Madonna of Mexico," may well be the most important Spanish-language female singer of her generation. Not because of the Madonna comparison—which she rejects by saying that Madonna is the Gloria Trevi of North America—but because of her subversive, and very particular, mix of art and politics. Trevi's influence on Latin American popular culture is no passing fancy. Before Trevi, there were no real female rock singers in Latin America. Before Trevi, there were no rebellious, spit-in-your-eye female singers in any genre in the Spanish-speaking world. The boys in the audience may drool over her saucy image, but the girls feel empowered—and for young Latinas, that's a rare and extraordinary experience.

So if you weren't a fan of La Atrevida—aka Miss Wicked—you had to endure some daily torture because Gloria's face, voice, and bare butt were everywhere. Radio stations played Gloria's hits on rotation, garage mechanics plastered up her million-selling pin-up calendars, and serious academics even brought the Trevolución into college classes.

When Gloria gave away a pair of used panties as a record promo, she was applauded by Dr. Carlos Monsiváis, one of Mexico's most celebrated cultural critics. She wasn't selling sex, he argued; she was "subverting through satire." Elena Poniatowska, his fellow thought leader, dubbed Gloria "one of our most authentic artists." Hosannas even emerged from the depths of the jungle, where a Zapatista guerrilla leader was quoted as saying "A woman that brave is a sister to our struggle."

So naturally, when a reporter like Pati Chapoy got the chance to meet Miss Wicked face-to-face and find out what really made her tick, she had a million questions. But before long, she was left with only one: *What the hell is wrong with her?*

Pati watched Gloria out of the corner of her eye from across her desk while pretending to give Sergio her full attention. She could barely make sense of what he was saying because her mind kept screaming *Why is this woman zonked out like a zombie?*

The three of them—Sergio, Gloria, and Pati—were supposed to be hammering out the details of a blockbuster deal, a secret negotiation that would pay Gloria a fortune to flip from Televisa to rival upstart TV Azteca. A plan like this was tricky work. It involved dozens of contingencies and tens of millions of dollars, and one mistake could damage all of their careers.

But every time they met, the same thing happened: Sergio talked and talked while Gloria sat with her head down, eyes on the floor.

This is the great crusading feminist? The wisecracking, rule-breaking rebel? As a TV executive, Pati was annoyed that the star she was hiring was so disengaged. But as a journalist, she was intensely curious. Something very strange was going on with Gloria, and no one else in the world seemed to know.

Years had passed since Pati was a young music critic covering Sergio's arrival on the Latin American pop scene. Since then, she had rocketed through the ranks to become production director for TV Azteca. But Pati was still so addicted to the Thrill of First—the first to spot a hot trend, a breaking story, an undiscovered talent—that she continued hosting her own current events show, making her one of the very few executives in the business to work both sides of the camera.

And at that moment, as she sat across from Gloria and Sergio, Pati's nose for news was twitching. She couldn't stop wondering what was going on with this woman. In public, she was a human fireworks display. Here at Sergio's side, she was so lifeless she seemed drugged.

Sergio, on the other hand, was bursting with ideas. Like a telenovela! He wanted to create a soap opera about Gloria's life on the streets, he said, with Gloria starring and Sergio directing.

"And what do *you* want to do?" Pati asked, staring pointedly at Gloria. "Are there any projects you're dying to try? You have the creative power of an entire network at your disposal. Dream big!"

Gloria said . . .

Nothing.

An awkward silence filled the room. Finally, Sergio piped up and began prattling again.

Afterward, Pati pulled Sergio aside to ask what was wrong. Was Gloria angry at her?

Sergio simply smiled. "Gloria is just shy," he said.

Twice, Pati tried to connect with Gloria by inviting her over for dinner. "She'd be exactly the same. Sergio would bring Gloria and Mary Boquitas, and the two girls wouldn't talk the entire evening. Sometimes they'd whisper a little bit to each other. Otherwise, they didn't say a word."

Was it an act? Could Gloria's strange silence around Sergio be a bargaining ploy to throw Pati off balancc? Pati couldn't get a read on Gloria, but she knew exactly what Sergio was capable of. "He's been a liar all his life," Pati says. "[The singer] César Costa once told me that Sergio was supposed to fly with him to Los Angeles to record César's new album. After they boarded the plane, Sergio said he was going to get off and grab a newspaper. He never came back. The plane took off, and César Costa never saw him again. That's Sergio Andrade."

Pati had to consider another possibility: maybe Gloria was the one calling the shots. Pati had just seen a new film, *The Usual Suspects*, about a criminal genius named Keyser Söze who secretly pulled the puppet strings while posing as a shy underling. Could Gloria be the brains behind this operation while Sergio was just a big, blustering smokescreen?

No, Pati decided after watching Gloria closely during their next meeting. This was no act. "In a two-hour period, she was silent. If I asked Gloria something directly, if I said, 'What do you think about this, Gloria?,' Sergio would say, 'Gloria, Mrs. Chapoy is asking you something. Answer her.' Only then would Gloria lift her face and speak. Otherwise, she was staring at the floor, silent. She didn't say a word unless Sergio said so."

By this point, Pati was getting concerned. Was Gloria going to slip into one of these stupors on camera? She decided to drop by Adolfo Prieto Street to see if she could find out what was going on.

"How did you get inside?" I asked her, since of course Sergio's compound had to be locked down, hard to find, and ultra-guarded.

"I knocked." Pati shrugged. "And when no one answered, I walked in. The front door wasn't even closed all the way." She stared, bewildered. Pati expected to find a humming warren of offices with a crisply efficient receptionist at the front desk, just like all the other management agencies she'd seen over the years. Instead, she had to make sure she hadn't wandered into a middle-school lunchroom.

"All I saw were these thirteen-year-old girls," Pati told me. "He said he was preparing to launch their musical careers, but they looked very young to me. Unless you're already a star, like Lucerito, that's very uncommon in music."

"Don't other producers have similar training schools?" I asked.

Pati shook her head. "No. I never saw anything like it anywhere else. Other producers would come to me with a boy or a girl they'd discovered, but not with a singular group of girls like Sergio's."

The singular group began trailing along every time Sergio and Gloria had an appointment with Pati. "Gloria was never by herself, and she never looked anything like what you see onstage," Pati would note. "Gloria never had bodyguards, only these young girls who looked after her. They were ten-, eleven-, twelve-year-old girls, all of them dressed in old jeans and hats."

Suddenly, Pati felt a pang of doubt about her own role in this plan. Was she a businesswoman first and a journalist second? Because if she asked Gloria and Sergio too many questions, they might walk out on the biggest deal of her career. But if she ignored all this weirdness right under her nose, she might miss scoring a major scoop—not to mention, helping a young woman who might be in trouble. Which of her two jobs was she supposed to be doing?

Turns out, it wasn't up to Pati. Sergio took the decision right out of her hands. On the day of their next meeting, Sergio and Gloria never showed up. Hours later, Pati discovered they'd just signed with her Televisa rivals. Sergio had been playing a game after all; he'd been using Pati to drive up Gloria's market price.

Okay, Pati thought. Like it or not, one of her jobs was over. Now it was time to lean into the other one—and find out what was really going on behind the walls of Adolfo Prieto Street.

First, Pati wanted to test whether her instincts were on target. At an entertainment industry function one night, she eased Gloria's name as casually as she could into a conversation. Gustavo Adolfo Infante, host of a competing news show and Pati's nemesis each year in voting for Mexico's Best Interviewer, instantly lit up.

You know, it's peculiar, he would say. Remember that special I did on Gloria's show in Chicago? Well, I was boarding the plane when I realized Gloria was on the same flight, sitting next to Mary Boquitas and some other girl. As I'm passing their seats I go, '*¡Que onda!* How cool we're all flying together!' All three of them kept staring down at their feet. So I go, 'Okay, well . . . maybe we can get together for dinner in Chicago.' Now, keep in mind I've met her many times. I'm there to *film a special on her*! And all three of them totally ignored me. They didn't say one word. *Ni sí, ni no, ni nada*—not yes, not no, nothing."

But at the event, Gustavo continued, "she was on fire! We got her in front of the cameras for my interview, and she was a riot. Electrifying! But the second we stop rolling, she goes right back to the way she acted on the plane. Shut down. Silent. Like a light switching off."

"Strange things were happening," agreed Maritza Lopez, Sergio's favorite photographer.

Maritza had worked with Gloria from the beginning, starting with Gloria's first albums and then every year after for her pinup calendars. The two women always had a blast, brainstorming new looks and pushing each other to get wilder and more creative. Gloria thrived on the attention, and Maritza loved a model who would try any pose, wear any outfit, and offer a thousand fresh suggestions of her own.

But by 1995, all that had changed. Maritza stared in bewilderment as two vans pulled up for the photo shoot and a gang of young teens piled out. Who are all these girls? Until then, the calendars always had one subject—Gloria—and one goal: get as close to frontal nudity and sexual suggestion as possible without being slapped with a pornography sticker. Each year, Sergio pushed a little further, so Maritza knew 1995 was going to be a doozy, basically a *Playboy* spread . . .

So why all these kids?

The backdrop of the photos was supposed to be a sexy pool party, with Gloria splashing around with friends in tiny bikinis, then setting off for bed in sheer panties and nighties. Not only were these girls uncomfortably young, but they looked terrible, with dirty clothes and greasy hair like a bunch of teenage runaways. Maritza had them shampooed and styled, a process they all sat through without a smile. Usually, that's the best part of the day, with lots of excited laughter as looks are transformed and outfits are sampled, but not with these girls. They were all cowed and quiet—

"And *starving*!" Maritza would add. Sergio wouldn't allow them to eat, so during lunch, the girls all sat in silence until Gloria snuck over to them with potato chips and snack cakes, which they devoured. Maritza didn't know how she was supposed to get decent shots with this crew, but she was in for another surprise: when it came time to hop into the pool and prance around, the girls erupted, laughing and playing and performing. So was Gloria, as fun and outgoing as ever.

When Maritza said, "Got it! That's good," they immediately shut down again. So did Gloria. "She turned into someone else," Maritza would say. "Gloria talked to no one but Sergio and it was all 'Yes sir, No sir,' with her eyes down."

There was no more excited brainstorming, no more happy camaraderie. As soon as the last frame was shot, Gloria and the girls climbed back into the vans and disappeared.

28

KARINA

Pati was on the hunt, but so was Sergio.

While Pati was searching for information about Sergio's gang, Sergio was searching for more girls. Recruitment had gotten a lot easier because he didn't have to wait for Gloria's fan magazine to hit their mailboxes anymore. Now, all he had to do was put Gloria onstage and take his pick from thousands of young women waiting outside, hoping for stardom.

In Chihuahua, Gloria was so idolized that fans would mob the airport whenever she came to town. On October 8, 1994, a twelve-year-old named Karina Yapor was at the front of the crowd as Gloria and her entourage arrived. It was a Saturday, and Karina's mother, Teresa, had taken time away from caring for her wheelchair-bound husband to make the long drive to Chihuahua International, but she didn't mind: adoring Gloria was one way she and Karina bonded.

Karina had been a Gloria diehard for nearly half her life, ever since she was a seven-year-old rocking out with her mom in the living room to Gloria's first big hit, "Dr. Psiquiatra." Since then, Teresa and Karina rarely missed any of Gloria's Chihuahua shows. Sometimes, they'd even drop by the front desk of Gloria's hotel to drop off homemade treats, like Teresa's special pineapple cake.

And that Saturday at the airport, Karina could swear that as Gloria was breezing past thc throng of fans, she looked Karina right in the eyes and smiled. Thrilled, Karina fought her way back to share this with her mother. As she did, she spotted Gloria in a side room being interviewed by a crush of reporters. Karina felt a burst of wild confidence based entirely on her idol's smile, so she grabbed her mother's hand and tried to sneak the two of them into the press pack.

She got nowhere, of course. A security guard was on them in a heartbeat. *Por favor*, a very familiar voice called out. *¡Déjalas entrar!* Let them come in, please! Karina could see Gloria smiling and waving to them above the heads of the reporters.

The security guard stood down, allowing the Yapors to squeeze into a corner and watch the rest of the press conference. As it ended, Karina and her mom found themselves alone with Gloria and four members of her clan: Mary Boquitas, Marlene Calderón, Katia de la Cuesta, and another new girl, Gabriela Holguín.

"Look how big you've gotten!" Karina recalls Gloria telling her. "You've grown so much, you're almost taller than me."

Karina was sure Gloria couldn't possibly recognize her and was just being polite, but Gloria wasn't finished.

"I'm going back to Mexico City in a few days," Gloria went on, "and I'd like to bring some photos of you to my manager. I can always use more girls in my group, and my manager is looking for fresh talent to launch as soloists. If El Maestro likes what he sees, perhaps he'll invite you to come audition." The audition is a very big deal, Gloria stressed. "If you're accepted, you'll train with us and your parents will get a salary of $2,000 a month on your behalf."

Karina and her mom were speechless. Gloria was still talking, something about a part for Karina in Gloria's new movie, but the Yapors were too stunned to listen. Two thousand dollars . . . *a month!* Karina's father had a degenerative spinal disease, forcing Teresa to support the family on her own meager salary. A windfall like that would be a miracle.

But, Gloria added, there were requirements. Karina would have to move to Mexico City and live with the other girls. She'd be on the road a lot. And no parents were allowed to observe rehearsals in Sergio's studio. El Maestro found they interfered too much with the girls' focus.

So—were they interested?

Four days later, as Karina would later testify under oath, she and her mother were on a flight to Mexico City.

They were met at the airport by Mary Boquitas and Katia de la Cuesta, the eldest of the three de la Cuesta sisters and now one of Sergio's top lieutenants. They escorted the Yapors to the luxurious Hotel del Bosque, near Chapultepec Park, and showed them to their suite. Karina was overwhelmed by the extravagant surroundings but a little regretful: she hadn't packed her Barbies and wasn't used to sleeping without them.

Early the following morning, Mary came by to pick Karina up for her audition. Karina's mother trailed along, but Mary stopped her. No parents allowed. Teresa watched from the lobby as Mary and her daughter disappeared into a cab. With a jolt, it dawned on her: She had no idea where they were taking her daughter or when she'd return. No one had told her the address of Sergio's school.

Mary wasn't taking Karina to Adolfo Prieto Street, anyway.

A while back, Sergio had decided to keep his whereabouts as below the radar as possible. Even though he now owned splendid homes in Cuernavaca, Texas, Los Angeles, Spain, and Mexico City, he often slept in a battered RV. "That was so no one would know where he was," Aline would explain. "He'd park the camper near his house so he could be close to home, but anyone passing by would see the lights off in the house and think he was out of town." For auditions, he'd switch up various hotels, never using the same one too often. Girls were only allowed to enter Adolfo Prieto Street if they passed Sergio's hotel screening, and sent directly home if they did not.

Karina was driven to a hotel only a few blocks from where she and her mother were staying. Mary led her upstairs to a master suite, then left her alone. Karina was waiting nervously when Gloria popped in. "Do everything he asks, and don't let anything stop you," Gloria urged her. "Please, don't disappoint me."

As Gloria was talking, the door creaked open behind her. Gloria suddenly fell silent, mid-sentence, as Sergio entered the room. Gloria slid back out—leaving Mexico's most powerful and predatory producer alone with a twelve-year-old who still slept with her dolls.

Karina froze. Somehow, she'd gotten the impression that Gloria's manager was as young, hip, and fun as Gloria. Instead—

He's very fat, and old, very serious, she thought.

Sergio sat down. Karina remained standing. How close are you to your family? Sergio asked. Do you go to church? Do you have a boyfriend?

A boyfriend?! Karina giggled. "No," she said. "I'm only twelve."

"Hm," Sergio grunted. Abruptly, he shifted gears. We have an outfit for you, he said. Go change and come back.

In the bathroom, Karina found a crop-top blouse, a miniskirt, and a pair of white boots. But the skirt was too small! Karina tried to make it work, struggling to pull it down far enough to cover her backside without exposing too much in front. Gabriela Holguín came in while Karina was still struggling.

"Hurry up," Gabriela commanded. "Everyone is waiting."

Karina began to panic, but then recalled what Gloria had said: "Don't let anything stop you." She gave the too-tiny skirt a final tug and walked back into the suite.

Sergio was stone-faced as ever. Profile right, he ordered Karina. Now left. Turn around. Can you dance? Let me see.

Karina swayed and swirled until Sergio grunted again.

"Do you act?" he asked.

"Not really."

"Well, try a little now. Try acting like a 'fresh girl.' Do you know what that is?"

"I don't think so . . ."

"It's like a wild girl. A girl who's boy crazy. Let yourself go wild."

Wild? Karina was confused but did her best. Her cheeks crimson with embarrassment, she flounced around like the slutty villains she'd seen in telenovelas. That won her a laugh from Sergio.

"Thank you," Sergio said. "I'll decide shortly."

He turned to leave and instantly a door popped open. Katia de la Cuesta appeared. Karina wondered if she'd been spying through the keyhole the entire time.

Katia returned Karina to her mother, who was still waiting anxiously back at the hotel. Karina was bursting to fill her in, but as she began talking, she saw her mother's gaze lock on something behind her. Karina turned to see Sergio approaching. For some reason, he must have followed right behind Karina and Katia in a separate cab.

Sergio introduced himself to Teresa. "I have some wonderful news," he said. "Karina has passed her audition."

Karina was ready to shriek with joy, but she held it in while Sergio sat down with her mother to go over a few points of business. First, Karina would have to leave school and her family in Chihuahua and move to Mexico City immediately. She would need a passport, a U.S. visa, her birth certificate, and a notarized letter from both parents granting legal guardianship to Sergio. Those documents were necessary, he explained, so Karina could travel out of the country on tour with Gloria. As soon as Karina's paperwork was in order and she passed a three-month trial period, Sergio promised, the Yapors would start receiving her monthly salary.

Karina's mother wept the entire flight back to Chihuahua. There would be no more family parties, no more after-school snacks, no more bedtime chats in Karina's room. It broke her heart, but how could Karina turn down the opportunity of a lifetime? At age twelve, her childhood was over.

Miguel Yapor, Karina's father, hadn't met this Sergio Andrade and he had next to zero confidence in putting his daughter in the care of Miss Wicked. Still, he couldn't ignore the breathtaking future it could mean for Karina and the immediate financial rescue for the family. Troubled and uncertain, he went to the parish priest for advice.

To Miguel's surprise, the priest was all for it. Don't think of it as losing a daughter, the priest counseled. Think of it as gaining a missionary. Keep in mind, good Catholics have always been fearless about spreading the Word to those who need to hear it. Karina might have a calling; it could very well be that her mission in life is to immerse herself in this world as a living guide of Christian faith.

And so, convinced that God was on his side, Miguel Yapor sent his twelve-year-old daughter into the lion's den.

29

TREMBLING IN THE DARK

Karina Yapor arrived back in Mexico City with the packet of legal documents that Sergio had requested. At the airport, she was picked up by Mary Boquitas and Katia de la Cuesta. The three girls caught a bus into the city and made their way to a small house on a side street. Karina entered Sergio's star school and saw—

Nothing.

No furniture. No instruments. No students.

"Um . . . where are the classes?" Karina stammered. "And the teachers?"

"Right here," Katia said. "I'm your instructor."

Katia handed Karina a pair of shorts and a T-shirt to put on. "Okay, now on the floor," Katia commanded. "Sit-ups! *Vamos. Uno . . . dos . . . tres . . .*"

When Karina's stomach cramped so badly she could no longer get her back off the floor, they switched to push-ups. Then leg lifts, squat thrusts, jumping jacks . . . until Karina felt ready to faint. Finally, Katia allowed Karina to stop. She opened a can of tuna for the two of them to share, then pointed Karina toward a cot and told her to get some rest. The real work, she said, would begin the next morning.

At dawn, the two girls were up and at it again. "You have to lose weight," Katia said, even though Karina was already tall and slim for her age. "Only very fit girls can go onstage with Gloria." They exercised all morning, took a break, and started again in the afternoon. For dinner, their only meal of the day, they shared another can of tuna.

Day 3 was the same. On day 4, Mary Boquitas showed up in an unmarked white van. "Get in," Mary said. "It's time for the next part of your training."

Mary drove them out of Mexico City, through the forest of a massive national park, to a house in Cuernavaca she called "Casa Blanca." There, Karina was given two tiny bikinis, red high heels, and a see-through minidress. "Put them on in there," Mary said, pointing to a bathroom, "and come out." When Karina emerged in the first bikini, Sergio was there.

"Turn," he ordered.

Karina heard a click and whirr. Sergio was taking Polaroids. Karina tottered out of the room, awkward on the unfamiliar heels, and changed into the other outfits. Sergio snapped shots of her in each, then gathered the photos and left without a word. As soon as the door closed behind him, girls began materializing like ghosts from other rooms. It was eerie; a second earlier, Karina thought she was in an empty house and suddenly she was surrounded by strangers.

Mary made introductions, but not by name. Sergio insisted that all the girls use whatever alias he gave them. It's like a christening, Mary explained brightly. You're turning into someone new, and your name should reflect that. When you join the clan, you become whoever Sergio decides you are.

Mary clapped her hands, calling the girls to order. It was dance and vocals day, but first—sit-ups, push-ups, squats, and leg lifts. Mary then had the girls sing scales and practice dance steps, over and over, before finishing with a final round of calisthenics. When they were done, the girls all drifted off to various rooms.

"Is it dinner now?" Karina asked. She hadn't eaten since the previous evening.

"Not today," Mary said. "We're getting ready for Gloria's calendar shoot so we really need to get in shape."

There would be no half can of tuna that night, or the next. There wouldn't be much sleep either. Mattresses were scarce and crowded with two or three girls at a time now that the clan had grown to ten: Mary Boquitas, Wendy Castelo, Marlene Calderón, Sonia Ríos, Gabriela Holguín, the three de la Cuesta sisters, Karina, and Edith Zúñiga, another new arrival who'd somehow been recruited from Chile.

By her third morning in Casa Blanca, Karina was feeling woozy and desperate. She didn't want to disappoint Gloria and her parents, but she didn't think she could go on much longer. The one hope was that if she pushed herself a little harder, she might be rewarded like the other girls with a special meal at the main house. At least, that's what she assumed was happening. As she had the previous few nights, an exhausted Karina dropped into the bed she shared with Wendy Castelo only to have Wendy—who was then about fifteen—get up a little later and head out the door.

"El Señor sometimes likes to talk with girls in private. It's a real privilege if El Señor shows that much interest in you," Mary Boquitas explained. Sergio had so much esteem for Wendy, Karina noticed, that she didn't get back until the next morning.

Finally, it was Karina's turn. Sergio came by the house and said he was taking her out to eat. He drove her to a Burger King, where Karina devoured a hamburger. She began to feel better.

"So tell me about your values, your way of thinking," Sergio asked. "What do you think about lying, and people who tell lies? I think they're the worst."

Karina agreed; lies were certainly very bad. Sergio seemed happy with her answer because he then suggested they go to the movies. Karina was delighted but confused; since she'd arrived in Mexico City, Sergio had barely spoken to her, even when he was snapping Polaroids while she modeled her bikinis. Sergio took her to see *The Specialist*, which turned out to be another grown-up adventure for Karina because back home in Chihuahua, her parents would never allow her to see a movie in which Sharon Stone's breasts and Sylvester Stallone's bare butt were on display.

Embarrassed by the nudity, Karina clamped her eyes shut.

Big mistake.

Sergio was silent and simmering as he drove Karina back to the house after the film. Karina didn't know what she'd done wrong until Wendy Castelo returned from one of her visits to the main house and clued her in.

"Sergio is very upset. He doesn't believe you're really a virgin, so all this pretending to be shocked by some little nude scene really offends him. He just hates hypocrites."

Karina was in a panic. "But I am a virgin!"

"Well, you'll have to prove it. Otherwise, Sergio is probably going to send you home."

"Prove it? How can I prove it?"

Wendy had an idea. "All you have to do is confess to Sergio that you're in love with him. Then when you have sex with him, he'll find out you're telling the truth about being a virgin." Problem solved!

While Wendy was sketching out this plan to a horrified Karina, Mary Boquitas appeared. She'd just come from Sergio's house, and yes, Karina's time was up. First thing in the morning, Mary was supposed to put her on the next plane back to Chihuahua. Karina's scholarship was revoked, and because she hadn't finished her probationary period, her parents would get none of the money.

Honesty is very important in an artist, Mary lectured Karina. Sergio can't turn you into a true interpreter of passion and poetry if you're not honest with yourself, because then you won't be honest with your audience. If Sergio suspects a singer is a liar, that's it. He won't waste his time on her.

"Isn't there anything I can do?" Karina pleaded. "I'm telling the truth, I swear."

Mary sighed. "I don't think so. I've never seen him this enraged."

"She can go see him," Wendy suggested again.

Mary appeared to think it over. Well, it's late and he's already made up his mind, Mary ventured. But it might be worth a try. You'd better go right this minute.

Karina hesitated. She'd never seen Sergio lose his temper, but she'd heard frightening stories from the other girls. "Let's go," Mary urged. "I'll drive you." Karina followed her outside to the white van. When they got to Sergio's place, all the lights were off. Mary led Karina into the dark house and down the hall to a door. Mary pushed it open, nudged Karina inside, and shut the door behind her.

Karina stood trembling in the dark, waiting.

Sergio's voice spoke from the gloom. "Come here." Karina saw the glow of a luminous watch and moved toward it. Karina approached and found Sergio lying in bed. She began to cry and say she was so, so sorry, she really was a truthful person and would never, ever—

Sergio silenced Karina by pulling her onto the bed in a hug. He kissed her on the forehead.

"Thank you, Sergio! Thank you so—"

"Quiet," Sergio said, but Karina was too keyed up from nerves and relief to stop. She continued chattering out apologies and explanations until Sergio locked her in a tighter embrace and kissed her, hard, on the lips.

Karina was in shock. Sergio went straight from kissing to groping, she would later say, pushing one hand into her blouse and another down her pants. Instinctively, she twisted away and reached for his wrists, but Sergio used the momentum of her parry to tug her hands onto his crotch.

Karina jerked free. She got to her feet and stood there, paralyzed by confusion.

"MARY!" Sergio bellowed.

The door opened instantly as if Mary had been there all along.

"Bring Karina back to Casa Blanca," he ordered. Karina staggered out behind Mary. They got into the van. Neither said a word.

¡Muy buenos días, muchachas! Sergio called as he breezed into the girls' house the next morning. "Where is our new friend? Where's Karina?"

Karina hurried out of her room. "Sit down," Sergio invited. "Let's talk about your progress." He began chatting with Karina as if nothing had happened, quizzing her about her musical preferences and how she was adjusting to the dance lessons. Karina kept her eyes on his feet while they talked, unable to look him in the face.

But Sergio was so warm and friendly that after a while, she began to relax and lift her gaze. The whole episode must have been some kind of mistake. She didn't know what kind of a mistake, since no middle-aged man had ever groped her before, but she wanted to believe that Sergio was the benevolent genius who would make her a star, so she decided a misunderstanding had led to a blind impulse. It was over; she would forget about it.

"Let's go to lunch," Sergio offered, and her spirits rose even higher at the decadent pleasure of two actual meals in two days. They chatted as they ate, and Karina felt a glow of gratitude. This was what she'd been hoping for all along, a real mentorship relationship and some feedback after so many punishing hours of classes. Sergio seemed genuinely interested and gave no hint of any discomfort. He dropped her off at Casa Blanca that afternoon with a big, friendly wave and a promise they'd speak again soon.

Several days later, Karina was just finishing her evening calisthenics when Mary beckoned. Sergio is free tonight for your next private session, she said. Mary drove Karina to Sergio's house and dropped her off at the front door. Karina knocked, and when Sergio answered, he immediately pulled her inside and began caressing her. This time, Karina went blank. She didn't decide, she didn't resist, she just . . . went. "I don't remember how it happened," Karina says, "but I woke up the following morning in his bed, naked and covered with a sheet."

She got up and dressed, and when she came downstairs, Gloria was in the kitchen making breakfast. "I'm so happy for you both," Gloria said. "I haven't seen Sergio this content in a long time." And she proposed exactly how twelve-year-old Karina should celebrate:

"Let's go get you some birth control."

30

KARINA, DELUGED

Later—much later, after she'd gone on the run with Sergio and Gloria and abandoned her newborn baby in Spain while fleeing from the police—Karina was finally brought before a judge to tell her story under oath. There, she struggled to answer a simple question:

Why?

Why, after you were sexually assaulted, didn't you call your parents and go home? Why did you remain in a house that was more like a prison camp than a music school, where you were starved, threatened, and exhausted with endless exercise? It obviously wasn't the high-powered star academy you were promised, and the classes, led by a pair of second-rate twenty-year-old singers, were worse than the dance lessons you'd gotten in a strip mall ballet studio in Chihuahua. The doors were unlocked. Pay phones were on every street corner. The bus station was a walk away.

So why did you stay?

"I honestly don't know," Karina would testify. "I felt absolutely confused. I didn't understand what was going on."

It's a crucial question. It was just pointed in the wrong direction. If you know anything about psychological manipulation, Karina Yapor is the last person you'd expect to have any clue about what happened to Karina Yapor. You'd have as much luck looking for answers from a frog slowly being boiled in a pot, with the heat eased up so artfully that the victim never detects what's happening. And in Karina's case, the recipe was followed perfectly.

Take that half can of tuna. Maybe it was dumb luck, maybe he picked it up from all those psychology books he studied during his Boquitas Pintadas period, or maybe it was the result of lots of human experimentation, but somehow, Sergio had landed on just the right amount of food to bend someone's mind without breaking it. Any prisoner-of-war interrogator would be very intrigued to know more about the Adolfo Prieto Street meal plan—and there was a lot to discover.

That was exactly the kind of research the CIA performed in the decades following the war in Vietnam. What they wanted to know was how the Vietcong were so effective at taking the toughest, best-trained, most patriotic American fighting men and, in a matter of weeks, turning them into Ho Chi Minh supporters and Communist true believers.

The answer had to be torture, right?

But the more they interviewed released American prisoners, the less they heard about fear and the more they heard about . . . reverence. Okay, in one sense that had a certain logic. It's always easier to gain someone's trust if they adore you, that's obvious. But how do you become besties with someone you're holding prisoner? Starving them and holding them against their will should make the victims bitter and vengeful . . . and yet something very different was going on.

It took a while but eventually CIA researchers cracked the code. The best Vietnamese brainwashers, they realized, relied on four cunningly simple techniques. To test their conclusions, the research team broadened their scope, examining North American religious cults, South American jungle hostages, and African child soldier regiments. Again and again, to the point where it became ridiculously predictable, they kept finding the same four tactics at work.

When they wrote up their findings, the analysts couldn't resist adding one quirky detail. Typically, you don't get a lot of human sentiment in CIA white papers. But in this case, they had to highlight a bitterly ironic story: this brainwashing protocol that was causing so much misery in so many places actually had its start with a hero trying to save a bunch of drowning dogs.

The dogs were in the laboratory of Russian scientist Ivan Pavlov. Everyone knows the famous account of how Pavlov trained his dogs to salivate at the sound of a bell, but not many know how close he came to losing them. 1924 was the year of "the Deluge," the great Leningrad flood that swept through the city when a massive rainstorm caused the Neva River to rise nearly ten feet overnight. Residents fled for their lives, evacuating the city in a panic. One of Pavlov's lab assistants, however, suddenly remembered the dogs were still locked in their cages. He turned back, wading through the submerged streets. When he plunged into the flooded basement, only the dogs' muzzles were still reaching for air.

He freed them and got them to safety, but the dogs weren't the same. Even weeks after that trauma, they were listless and less active, nearly numb. But Pavlov found they also obeyed better and were more trainable. It was as if staring death in the face had taught the dogs they had no control over their own lives. They didn't have the will or inclination anymore to follow their own instincts. Instead, they did as Pavlov commanded.

Pavlov dubbed this effect "Cortical Inhibition of the Higher Cerebral Function." In simpler terms, you could call it the brain's automatic sleep mode. When we're faced with something so frightening and stressful that it threatens to permanently damage our sanity, a shutdown mechanism is triggered. It's the same reason we plug our computers into surge protectors instead of directly into the outlet: if a blast of excessive energy hits the electrical grid, the surge protector acts as a buffer and automatically switches off, saving your laptop from frying out. But sleep mode comes at a cost: once it's triggered, we stop being captains of our own ship. We have diminished control of our own decision-making, allowing someone else to step in and order us around.

Pavlov was curious about the operator's manual for sleep mode, so he kept experimenting until he made a crucial discovery. He didn't have to nearly drown his dogs, he realized: instead, he could get the same effect by breaking that one big stressful experience into four smaller ones. That was a huge breakthrough. Trying to stage near-deadly events over and over again was dangerously tricky, and the outcomes were always uncertain. How close to drowning is too close? How do you factor in dogs who are manically afraid of water versus dogs with a higher fear threshold?

But by microdosing the trauma, Pavlov could create a formula that lowered the risks to the dogs while increasing his own control over the process. All he had to do was make his dogs tired, sleepy, hungry, and disoriented. Those were the four magical microstresses:

- Physical exhaustion
- Emotional tension
- Chronic discomfort
- General confusion

It was simple. Pavlov worked them out, kept them cold and awake, cut back their food, and confused them with bewildering tasks. Soon, the dogs were desperate for rest, warmth, and a decent meal. But here's what really surprised him: instead of resenting their handlers for mistreating them, the dogs became more attentive and affectionate. The more tired and uncertain the dogs became, the more they looked to the trainers to tell them what to do. It was as if the relief of finally being allowed to rest and eat was so great that it blanked out the memory of who had starved and exhausted them in the first place.

So, the Soviet experts asked, what's your goal with these American prisoners you're interrogating?

To make them talk, the Vietnamese officers replied.

No, the Soviets corrected them. It's no use making prisoners talk if you're not sure they're telling the truth. Your goal isn't to make them speak. It's to make them *want* to speak.

According to the CIA's study, captured U.S. servicemen were subjected to the same four stresses that Pavlov used on his dogs: harsh work details, meager rice portions, constant sleeplessness, and confusing interrogations.

Keeping prisoners awake seems pretty mild after all those movies we've watched with brutal interrogation scenes, but it's actually extraordinarily effective. "Deprivation of sleep," the CIA white paper points out, "results in more intense psychological debilitation than any other method of engendering fatigue." With that, layer on the constant gnawing of an empty stomach and weakening body. The Vietcong captors would starve prisoners for a few days, then suddenly provide them with a solid meal. Irresistibly, the prisoners would then obsess over their own behavior, trying to figure out what they'd done to earn it. That was enough to alter their perception: their captors transformed from enemies they swore to resist into guardians they had to please.

"Studies of controlled starvation indicate that the whole value system of the subjects underwent a change," the CIA found.

But the most cunning tool of all was the fine art of . . .

Chatting.

Instead of grilling the prisoners, the Vietcong captors asked friendly questions about their families, favorite foods, hobbies, and childhoods. Feigning genuine interest, the interrogators asked for more and more detail, taxing the prisoners to recall, for instance, the kind of car their dad first drove, whether it was new or used, and whatever happened to it anyway? The more a prisoner struggled to remember his own past, the more he began to question his own memory.

Naturally, the conversation segued from there into other everyday subjects—nothing classified or war-related, of course, just grade-school stuff like culture and history. *Tell us about your Constitution. You know we borrowed from it ourselves, right? Yes, because the French colonized us the same way the British colonized you . . .*

Almost invariably, the interrogators would know more about American laws than the American prisoner, making him once again strain his memory and question his convictions. A few days of chitchat like this, and a tired, hungry, homesick prisoner's head would be spinning. Was he sure that waging war in a faraway land was the best thing for his country? How confident was he that back home, he'd really been told the truth about the people he'd been ordered to kill? Was he actually that much different than his captors? "Friendliness of the interrogator, when least expected, upsets the prisoner's ability to maintain a critical attitude," the CIA study found.

And that's the moment everything changes. A warm blanket and a bowl of soup appear, and a few reassuring remarks are made. Nothing else needs to be said. You're so hungry, the simple broth tastes magnificent. At this point, your animal brain takes over. Your educated mind may be grittily holding on to higher principles like loyalty, humanity, and personal guilt, but those are all things you were taught. Your natural instincts—the ones you were born with—aren't interested in lofty ideals. You're alive today because, for thousands of years, our natural instincts evolved to keep us alive in a brutally harsh world.

So when something comes along that's good for survival (like eating, or exercising, or giving birth) your animal brain is quick to let you know. It releases into your bloodstream a burst of serotonin and oxytocin, the "love hormones," to reward you with a sense of joy and peace. Your subconscious automatically connects this wonderful feeling with the person who made it happen. It's not questioning why you were hungry; it's focused on the immediate issue of who handed you a bowl of soup—or the can of tuna.

The prisoner no longer sees a tormentor. He sees a savior.

31

KARINA, WENDY, MARLENE

"You have to learn what love means," Sergio told Karina. "You can't keep acting like a little girl."

Karina had hurt Sergio's feelings. She didn't understand how at first, but Sergio was kind enough to yell at her until it all made sense. See, Karina hadn't managed to memorize all the lyrics to a new song by the end of the day, and when Sergio swung back his arm to slap her face, she'd cringed.

That's not love, Sergio fumed. That's not maturity. That's not trust.

Maestro, I'm so sorry, Karina pleaded. I won't move next time.

The other girls all get it, Sergio raged. Why are they more loving than you? Perfect example, he went on. There's another girl who's in love with me, and even though she knows you're my favorite, she accepts it. She loves me just the same! Now *that's* someone who understands honesty and human emotion. That is a girl who will become a great artist.

Who did he mean—Gloria? Karina felt herself sinking into the same fog she often felt when Sergio was scolding her. She couldn't quite make sense of what he was saying and found herself repeating, "Yes, sir. Yes, Sergio. Yes, maestro."

"Marlene!" Sergio shouted.

Marlene appeared instantly. She was naked. She seemed to know exactly what Sergio intended. She approached Sergio and began caressing him.

Karina was more bewildered than embarrassed. Was this her signal to beat it? No, he was beckoning her closer. *If you love me, prove it*, he commanded. He pointed to Marlene. *Love those who love me.* Karina obeyed. She climbed into bed with Marlene and Sergio and did everything he asked. Afterward, he reminded her that she was still in trouble. That was simply a learning experience. Her real punishment was yet to come.

Two days later, it arrived. Sergio announced he was displeased with three of the girls: Marlene, Wendy, and Karina. They were told to assemble outside Sergio's bedroom door. Marlene was summoned inside first. The other two girls could hear the murmur of Sergio's voice and then, suddenly, the horrifying swish of a cord whistling through the air and smacking into flesh. Marlene whimpered. *Uno*, Sergio counted. The cord whisked again and *crack! Dos . . . tres . . .*

Wendy and Karina clutched each other. *Diez*, Sergio concluded. Marlene staggered through the door, covering her face with her hands to choke back her sobs. "WENDY!" Sergio shouted. Wendy shot Karina a doomed look and entered the bedroom. Another ten blows.

"KARINA!"

She almost fainted when she saw the extension cord in his hand. Sergio ordered Karina to lower her shorts. He showed her where to kneel next to the bed. Karina buried her face in a pillow; she knew screaming would only make him angrier. But Sergio made her move it aside.

You're acting like an infant, he scoffed. Could she do herself the favor of accepting punishment like a real woman? Karina bent over and bit her lip.

When he finished, Karina's back and bottom were aflame with throbbing welts. Sergio put away the extension cord and called Wendy and Marlene back into the room. "We all began to have sexual relations with him," Karina would later report. This kind of scene was repeated often, Karina says, the only difference being the viciousness of the beatings and the combination of girls. In a matter of weeks, she'd spiraled from things she thought were sinful to things she'd never imagined.

Despite her own fear and pain, Karina felt worse for Gloria.

Sergio would fly into titanic rages, ordering the other girls to wait upstairs in a bedroom while he tore into his wealthiest and most willful disciple. "He would scream at her for being rebellious, for disobeying his orders, and go on for hours," Karina would say. "We could hear his shouting and her sobbing, sometimes all day or through the night."

"One day, I saw her leaving Sergio's room in tears," Karina went on. "She came up to me, weeping, and asked me to promise her that I would never do what she had done. Since I was currently being punished by not being allowed to speak, I couldn't ask her what she had done and could only nod in agreement."

And even though Sergio's entire empire was based on Gloria's ability to look sensational in a bikini and project untamable independence, Karina said he would beat her as savagely as any of the other girls. Once, when Sergio called Karina in for sex with him, along with Gloria and a new girl, Liliana, Karina found it strange that Sergio wouldn't let Gloria take off her shirt, even holding it down himself when it began to ride up. Only later did it register that he must have been hiding lash marks.

All it would take was one paparazzi photo of those welts and instantly, the entire multimillion-dollar Gloria Trevi entertainment operation would come crashing down. But perversely, Sergio's savagery also helped keep it alive. The more Sergio abused Gloria in private, the more outrageous she behaved in public; the more outrageous she was onstage, the more popular she became; and the more popular she became, the more Sergio felt compelled to bring her to her knees.

And so the cycle continued—year by year, girl by girl—until, finally, a crack of light broke through the wall of secrecy.

32

"THE MENNONITES"

Over at TV Azteca, Pati Chapoy felt a knot of dread in her gut.

Everything she could see convinced her that something very strange and potentially dangerous was going on with Sergio's girls—but she still couldn't see very much. All she knew for sure were her Three Nevers:

1. *Never* had she seen a talent mogul surround himself with so many random girls with zero experience or parental involvement. From a professional standpoint alone, it seemed insane. The girls hardly spoke or bathed—how could Sergio possibly imagine he was going to put them onstage?
2. *Never* had she seen a star as publicly celibate as Gloria. The whole point of show business is to Show. Your. Business. To make yourself relatable by sharing little glimpses of your normal life. But no one, ever, had caught so much as a glimpse of a possible Gloria love interest. Her secrecy was downright fanatical.

3. *Never* had she heard of a millionaire superstar who lived in a group home with a gang of teenagers. Despite her wealth, Gloria was still bunking down the way she had in Sergio's basement, with girls piled in every room. Gloria had no domestic staff—no cook, no gardener, no cleaning woman—which meant no one else ever entered. "We washed our clothes at the laundromat, and I took my turn washing the dishes, vacuuming, or dusting," she would say. "I didn't want outsiders inside my house."

Pati was also hearing bizarre stories from behind the scenes of Gloria's new TV show. Pati may have lost the bidding war for Gloria's contract, but not her information pipeline. She had plenty of friends at rival Televisa who passed along whispered updates.

"We called them 'The Mennonites,' since they all lived together and dressed alike and didn't talk to anyone except each other," said a female producer who worked closely with Gloria. "It was the strangest sight. You'd see these young girls marching in, all of them silent, never doing anything unless Sergio told them to.

"You knew they were staying at the most expensive hotels in Mexico City," the Televisa producer went on, "but they always wore cheap, dirty clothes and shared them—even Gloria. One of the girls would be wearing a pair of shoes, and the next day Gloria has them on. Do you know any other boss who wears her employees' clothes?"

On the first day of rehearsal, Sergio pulled the producer aside. You know how men are, Sergio told her. Especially with a beautiful woman like Gloria. So let's keep them away.

Okay, the producer agreed. Which men do you mean?

All of them, Sergio replied.

The producer looked around the set. That was going to be tricky.

"All the technicians were men," the producer would later explain. "So Sergio had his girls do their job for them. When Gloria needed a microphone, Karla de la Cuesta was the one who put it on her. Sergio wouldn't even let Gloria speak directly with Bernardo López Valdés, the director of the show. Instead, everything had to go through me."

Whenever they weren't needed in the studio, Sergio made the girls wait outside in his big black Lincoln. Once, while Sergio and the girls were busy consulting with the makeup artists, the Televisa producer and several crew members sidled over to peek inside.

"It was a mess!" the producer said. "I swear, it looked like they must have been living out of that car. They had clothes, underwear, and hairbrushes all over the place. I don't know how Sergio could stand riding in there with all that clutter."

Sergio caught the Televisa crew peering into the car but laughed it off. No, no, they weren't living out of the car, he said; they were just moving between hotels and hadn't checked in yet. "None of us knew what was going on, but none of us believed him," the producer said. "His clothes were filthy, too."

Gloria's dressing room was equally strange in exactly the opposite way. "Gloria was a weird girl," the producer said. "I've been working at Televisa for a long time, and I can tell you in the dressing room of every other star, they have perfume, antiperspirant, and a picture of a loved one, because they spend all day in there. Gloria didn't have any of that. You didn't even see a toothbrush."

Gloria never fraternized with the crew, like the rest of the cast. Instead, she shut herself inside that empty room for hours at a time. Whenever she was called to set, she'd be flanked by two of the sisters de la Cuesta. "Gloria was never alone," the producer marveled. "She was always escorted by those two, short girls but very strong. I'm telling you, it was very weird."

During lunch breaks, Gloria's girl gang would pile out of Sergio's Lincoln and wait silently by the food table until Sergio decided if they'd be allowed to eat. "Diets," Sergio would explain to the Televisa crew. "Girls blow up at that age."

If he gave the go-ahead, the girls went nuts. They devoured everything they could lay their hands on and stuffed the rest into their pockets and handbags. They didn't just scavenge food, the producer would add. "They took everything that wasn't locked up. The toilet paper from the bathrooms, creamers and sugar packs from the break room—they were like a pack of starving mice."

Gloria seemed just as impoverished. Whenever she had her period, she begged for sanitary napkins from female crew members. "We never knew why she didn't have any," the producer said. "At first I thought it was because she was such a big star, so she was used to people giving her everything. But after seeing her so much in those dirty old clothes, I started wondering what Sergio was doing with her money. She was a millionaire, but she acted like a beggar."

Privately, the producers and director were getting nervous. Televisa was gambling a fortune on this show, paying Gloria a staggering $8 million and flying in designers from New York and Los Angeles to devise high-concept backdrops sketched to Sergio's specifications. "Everyone expected a huge hit," the producer said. "We had Gloria at her peak, and that's all the newspapers could talk about, how Gloria had come back to Televisa. Everyone was dying to see what she'd do."

But instead of bringing the thunder, Gloria trudged around like a sleepwalker. "In our planning meetings, everyone has to give their opinion, but she never did," the exec says. "And she was emcee of the show!" If she ever said anything, it was only about how she agreed with Sergio.

"Was she going to ruin the show by being so flat? At the end of every meeting, everyone said, 'Where's the explosive Gloria? Where's that strong woman?' She wasn't that tough and sexy girl."

For the first live run-through, Gloria marched on set as usual—stony-faced, eyes down, a silent de la Cuesta over either shoulder—and suddenly, it was like a switch was flipped. "My God, you couldn't believe it was the same person," the Televisa producer marveled. "We were amazed! Even next to beauty queens, she looked magnificent, and she was so smart and funny!"

But as soon as the session ended, Gloria shut down and returned to her empty dressing room. "We always felt there were two Glorias, and we started calling them by different names," the producer said. "On camera, she was 'Gloria Trevi,' offstage she was 'Gloria Treviño.' Anytime a reporter showed up, she'd immediately start talking and moving differently. After the reporter left, she went back to taking orders as Gloria Treviño. If we asked her what she wanted for lunch, Sergio answered. If someone wanted an autograph, she looked at Sergio first."

Several Televisa executives were so unnerved by Sergio that they did their best to avoid him. "He was always looking for your eyes, to dominate you," the producer explained. "Once you looked into his eyes, you were in his hands." Those few Televisa crew members who thought about disagreeing with Sergio gave it up after witnessing the way he treated his own star. "One time Gloria tried to make a suggestion, and Sergio just snapped at her. 'I'm the one who makes the decisions,' he said. 'So please shut up.'"

Typically, an entertainment manager's job is to live behind

the scenes, shopping for new projects, supervising contracts, and then getting out of the way. Not Sergio. He was front and center on every move Gloria made. Gloria still wrote most of her own songs, but Sergio was the ultimate authority who decided which would be recorded, and when, and how, and what she'd eat for lunch in between. When Gloria started making movies, Sergio closely supervised the first and then took over to write and direct the next two. Subordinating himself to anyone was out of the question.

"Even though he wasn't the director of the TV show, things had to be the way he wanted, or else he got very mad," said another Televisa executive who worked with Gloria on a separate special. "He was very dominating. Sometimes he wouldn't even speak, just turning that glare on you like he was trying to shrink you down to nothing with his eyes."

That same stare flashed into the exec's mind years later, once the horrors of Sergio and Gloria's clan were revealed. Suddenly, it all made sense. "Gloria was always making noise about the rights of women when secretly, she was just as abused as the worst of them," the Televisa exec explained. "She was never the strong woman. The girl with power. She could never speak up because those two eyes were burning on her back all the time, ready to cut her down. It was only onstage that Gloria could be the woman she wanted to be."

So all that time, the Televisa exec suspects, Gloria wasn't performing at all. Every time she whipped some boy with his belt or hurled her own body onto the floor, she was acting out something she'd experienced herself.

"Deep inside," the exec said, "her mind is screaming, *Help me!*"

33

THE HUNTRESS

"I've never encountered a trickier challenge," Pati told me.

As a journalist, she wasn't driven; she was obsessive. She'd covered many scandals and cover-ups in the past, but she'd learned that if she kept pressing her contacts and scouring public records, someone on the inside would eventually relent and give her the hard facts and firsthand information she needed. No matter how deep and dark the secret was, there was always one person ready to talk. She just had to stay on the hunt long enough to find them.

But with Sergio and Gloria, the hunt led her straight to a brick wall. Pati could never get any of the girls to step away from the group for even a moment for a private chat. Gloria's silent entourage kept growing, with more and more new faces appearing all the time, but as soon as they joined the clan, they sealed their lips and never seemed to leave.

Wait! Suddenly an old face sprang to mind. Whatever happened to what's her name . . . Erika? Aline? Wasn't she supposed to be Sergio's Next Big Sensation? Aline was constantly by Gloria's side and vice versa, with the superstar helping her former backup singer launch a solo career. That was about five or six years ago, but since then—nothing. Pati couldn't remember the last time she'd seen any sign of Aline. Was it possible she'd left the clan? If so, would she be willing to talk?

Looking back, Pati can pinpoint that moment as the first time she ever bothered looking into Aline. Until then, Aline was just another of Gloria's semi-anonymous clan members. Pati had no idea how to locate the girl, or whether her real name was actually Aline, Erika, or None of the Above. Court records are the surest way to track down legal identities and addresses, and that's where Pati discovered a bombshell: a divorce decree between Sergio Gustavo Andrade Sánchez and one Érika Aline Hernández Ponce de León. Good god! Did Sergio actually marry that girl? There was one way to find out: listed beneath Aline's name was a street address and phone number right there in Mexico City.

Back at her office, Pati immediately began dialing. After a few rings, she was elated when a tentative voice answered. Pati introduced herself and got right to it: she believed something dangerous was going on inside the house on Adolfo Prieto Street. She was looking for someone to either prove she was right or convince her she was wrong. Aline listened, mostly in silence, before quietly saying goodbye and hanging up.

Pati slumped back in her chair, defeated. That was her best shot, and she'd blown it. Now that Aline knew a reporter was on the hunt, she'd probably alert Sergio and go underground.

A few hours later, the front desk buzzed her office phone. A young woman was downstairs and wanted to see her. "She came and started telling me her story," Pati told me. "And I almost fainted, because I'd never heard anything like it before." As Aline talked, her face and arms broke out in angry red hives. "Just by remembering what she had been through, her whole body reacted," Pati said. Pati was horrified, but she'd been in the entertainment business long enough to know how convincing a professional performer could be. "It took three hours for her to tell me the whole story, and by the end, I frankly didn't believe it. It was just too shocking."

Pati was sympathetic but firm. As far as she knew, Aline could just be another ex with a score to settle after a bitter divorce. Yes, everything Aline was saying matched the rumors that Pati had heard, but at this point, they were still just rumors. "Is there anyone who can back up these allegations?" Pati asked.

Aline returned a few days later with her mother. Aline told her story all over again, this time with her mother correcting her on dates and chipping in additional details. Both women answered every question that Pati threw at them. Still, Pati insisted on more. Was there anyone outside Aline's own family who might speak up?

Aline nodded. "I know two people who've left the clan." One was Marina, Gloria's teenage cousin who'd fled back to Texas. The other, she said, was right inside these offices. Rubén Aviña had quit working as Sergio's publicist and was now a writer for TV Azteca. Aline told Pati that Rubén had seen a lot and heard even more. He was there when Gloria first appeared to audition for Boquitas Pintadas and was still with the clan when Aline left.

"Aline's information gave me the chance to start investigating this case," Pati said. "I got right on it and stayed with it." At first, Rubén was reluctant to talk. But when Pati got him into a conference room with Aline, something changed. For the sake of his career, he'd done his best to downplay what Sergio was up to. Now, as he looked Aline in the eyes, he was pierced by the fact that everything she'd suffered could have ended—instantly—if he'd only spoken up. He'd failed Aline back then. He wouldn't fail her again.

"Let's get a tape recorder," he told Pati. "I've got a lot to say."

Gloria's show was going to be the next jewel in her entertainment crown. She'd already struck gold with music, movies, and her own magazine. Now, she was poised to become the Queen of Mexican Television.

That was the consensus inside Televisa, at least, where the excitement was running high despite Sergio's meddling, Gloria's unpredictability, and the weird backstage presence of their clan of tweens. Televisa had decided to reboot its most popular variety show, *XE-TU Remix*, with Gloria at the helm. As a programming idea, it was genius: Mexico's top show would now be hosted by Mexico's top star, with plenty of comedians, celebrities, and bikini models to back her up. Best of all, it wasn't just Gloria, but Gloria live. Who knew what kind of wild stunt La Atrevida might pull next? Gloria on the loose was must-see TV.

"She was as crazy as Sergio," the Televisa producer recalled. "On one show, Gloria brought in this homeless boy named Marcelo. She'd found him living on the streets. Right there on national TV, she adopted him. She said, 'You're going to be my kid. Let the entire country bear witness! You are now Marcelo Trevi. I'll take care of you from now on as my own son.' Seriously, that was the kind of stuff that was happening. You never knew what she might do."

Marcelo was never heard about again. Televisa producers were appalled by the way he'd been exploited and abandoned, and they complained enough for the network's legal department to arrange a financial settlement that would cover Marcelo's living expenses for a few years, not to mention short-circuit any potential lawsuits.

Sergio was just as volatile. He'd become so powerful that the Tiger only reined him in when Sergio submitted a request for giant buckets of human feces. How would we procure this, Sergio wanted to know. Real shit, he specified. Not fake. And lots of it. It took some back and forth between Sergio and the bewildered showrunners before they understood that:

(A) Yes, he was serious. Because

(B) Swimming-in-Human-Shit was actually a plot point in a new script he was developing for Gloria. The way Sergio saw it, subjecting game-show contestants to the real thing on live TV would somehow be a terrific movie tie-in for whatever Gloria was going to do in the film.

Televisa replied with a hard no, but the fact that Sergio's nutty request traveled all the way up the chain of command to the Tiger before it was finally shot down demonstrated just how much creative control Sergio had over *XE-TU Remix*. To him, the wilder Gloria behaved the better—and Gloria didn't let him down.

During one show, Gloria declared that if more people didn't tune in and watch, she would kill herself right there on live TV. The following week, she broke down in sobs, pulled out a knife, and slashed her wrists. She collapsed to the floor, blood gushing from her arms, as frenzied stagehands raced over to save her.

"She had faked the whole thing," the Televisa producer said. "It was a dummy knife and fake blood, but she hadn't told anyone she was going to do it. That kind of thing is absolutely forbidden on TV, so the government threatened to ban the program."

The *XE-TU Remix* director freaked out. What the hell was wrong with these people? It was one thing to be pushy about Gloria's outfits or whether another of the clan girls should get a minute or two on camera; it was another thing to jeopardize all their careers by staging a fake suicide. Bernardo López Valdés let loose with everything he'd been holding back, ripping into Sergio so brutally that Sergio turned and walked away, yelling over his shoulder that he was leaving for good and never returning.

After that, Gloria and the girls were impossible. "When I would go to her dressing room to tell her she had ten minutes to go onstage, they would shut the door in my face," the Televisa producer reported. "She said we had insulted the man she loves, and she would never forgive us." On one of the live show days, Gloria was nowhere to be found. Frantic, the Tiger himself tried to call Sergio, but no one seemed to know where he was.

"With minutes to go before airtime, Gloria came breezing in and walked straight onstage, like a diva," the producer would say. "She hadn't rehearsed, she hadn't told us what she planned to do for an hour of live TV, and the audience could tell. It was chaos. You can't run a show like that."

The Tiger wasn't going to. Halfway into the season, he canceled *XE-TU Remix*. Gloria's debut as the new Queen of Mexican Television had flamed out in three months.

To hell with Televisa. Sergio had his screenplay ready to go. Within months, cameras were rolling on Gloria's third feature film, "French Fry with No Ketchup" (*Una Papa sin Catsup*).

For his plot, Sergio returned once again to his favorite subject: ninth-grade girls. Although Gloria was now twenty-six and busty enough to sell millions of pin-up calendars, Sergio had her playing a thirteen-year-old who looks just like the criminal mastermind known as—no surprise—"Crazy Hair" (*Las Greñas*). The film is a series of silly gags about switched identities, but one scene is unforgettable. As a punishment, Gloria's character has to unclog a school toilet. For nearly five full minutes of a ninety-minute film—just as Sergio had forecast—Mexico's sweetheart is shown swimming through a sea of diarrhea and stained toilet paper. As the pipes strain, foul water leaks on to the heads of children in the classrooms below and into a sandwich that the school's principal is eating.

It's impossible to watch this scene without cringing for Gloria and recoiling at Sergio's subtle-as-a-sledgehammer metaphor: Sergio believed he was so superior that he could shit on anyone he pleased—including the megastar who obeyed his most humiliating commands.

Papa was a box-office disaster. Gloria's fans mostly ignored the film while critics tore it apart, calling it "preposterously unfunny" and "a money-grab built on Gloria Trevi's bizarre personality—half spoiled brat, half sexpot." Even the kindest reviewers were left scratching their heads about why Gloria kept making rom-coms without any rom. It was already strange enough that no one had ever seen her with a romantic partner in ten years of public life, but if she was going to make movies about her sex appeal, couldn't she at least pretend to have a love interest? How come none of her films ever had a male lead?

But none of that mattered to a pair of *Papa* superfans in Chihuahua. Karina Yapor's parents had barely heard from their daughter since she'd left nearly a year earlier for Sergio's star school. They had no idea if she was actually in *Una Papa sin Catsup* and were thrilled when she suddenly appeared as the young daughter of a suburban family. Karina's parents relished those few minutes with their daughter and kept going back as if replaying a home movie. In the film, thirteen-year-old Karina is pimply and bony, looking more boy than girl.

By its release, she was also pregnant.

34

THE ZÚÑIGA SISTERS

Gloria stood in front of the microphone, sobbing. She covered her face in her hands. It was May 1997, at the end of a concert in Mexico City. Thousands of her fans fell silent, waiting for her to speak.

"My dear friend, El Maestro Sergio Andrade, is dying," Gloria finally announced. "He has prostate cancer. So this will be my last performance. As of today, I'm retiring from the stage to care for him, the way he has always cared for me." Gloria made the sign of the cross, then lifted her face and hands to the heavens, Madonna-like.

"I offer myself to our blessed Virgin of Guadalupe so she might heal him."

Aline was the first to call bullshit. She had seen Sergio on a late-night talk show a few weeks earlier promoting *Una Papa sin Catsup*. He was very plump and talkative, she told Pati Chapoy. "That's not consistent with a person who's wasting away from cancer, as far as I know," Aline said. And what about Gloria—if she's so dedicated to nursing Sergio, why didn't she just cancel the show instead of putting on that big weep-fest at the end?

Pati had been working with Aline for several months by that point to prepare her sex-clan investigation to go on the air. Aline had been instrumental in connecting Pati with Gloria's teenage cousin in Texas, and everything Pati heard during that interview aligned with Aline's story. Pati found Aline to be bright, poised, and very believable, so she paid close attention to what she was saying now.

Something fishy is going on, Aline warned Pati, and she could guess what it was: word had spread that she and Rubén Aviña were about to go public.

Aline was right: Sergio was freaking out.

Not necessarily because of her, though, or even Karina. He'd dealt plenty of times before with both situations—bad publicity and babies—but he'd never gone to the extent of staging his own death. Even during the worst of the Lucerito crisis, back when angry uncles were hunting him in the streets and the national media were calling for his head, Sergio just hung out at his ex-girlfriend's house for a while before popping back up on his own radio show.

And by 1997, Sergio was used to dealing with the consequences of his habitual unprotected sex. At least half the girls, Karina would say, had lost or terminated pregnancies. Sergio's preferred method was to make the girls lift heavy stones in the back garden in hopes of triggering a miscarriage. If that failed, he'd fly them to Houston for an appointment at his regular abortion clinic. Karina would later testify that Sergio had already gone this route with Gloria, Wendy Castelo, thirteen-year-old Marlene Calderón, and two of the de la Cuesta sisters, fifteen-year-old Karola and sixteen-year-old Karla.

As a final fail-safe, Sergio had Option #3: marriage. He'd already used a wedding license as cover after it was discovered he was sleeping with Mary Boquitas and Aline when they were young teens. Now that he was divorced again, there was nothing stopping him from making Karina the fourth Mrs. Sergio Andrade. Sergio was shrewd enough to know that forming a pretty little family with Karina, with lots of cute baby photos with their newborn, had a short-term downside of sparking lots of stories about his strange-but-legal relationship, and a major upside of defanging any embarrassing accusations from his "vindictive" ex-wife.

So if he had nothing to worry about, why was Sergio so worried? What was rattling him so badly?

Failure.

Ever since his miserable childhood under a demanding father and brother-worshipping mother, Sergio had built his sense of self-worth on his string of successes—on being "*lo maximo*," "the boy genius," "Mr. Midas." Sergio's Midas touch was the reason his clan existed in the first place; once he lost it, he'd no longer have any way to attract the controllable young women he craved. If there was one thing Sergio feared more than scandal, it was scorn. And if the girls in his clan started whispering about his series of flops—the canceled TV show, the failed movie, the media ridicule over the title of Gloria's latest album (*Mas Turbado que Nunca*, that raunchy pun meaning "Crazier Than Ever" and "Masturbating like Crazy")—they might start having serious doubts about his ability to deliver on his promise of launching them all to stardom.

Sergio was worried less about what his former wife was saying and more about what his current girls were hearing. If he was going to keep the illusion of stardom alive in his girls' minds, he had to get them out of town.

A few days after Gloria's announcement, Karina Yapor suddenly appeared at home, her arms loaded with gifts. Her parents were thrilled but also a little confused. Why hadn't Karina called to let them know? And who was this silent young woman by her side?

Sergio had sent Karina back to Chihuahua with one of his most trusted lieutenants, Marlene Calderón. Their orders were to keep the visit short and remain on message. "I was supposed to tell them that a book was coming out by Aline," Karina would later say. "And they shouldn't believe anything in it, that Aline was a liar and part of a defamation campaign orchestrated by TV Azteca."

But Karina's parents couldn't focus on what she was saying because they were so disturbed by her appearance. Their baby had lost so much weight, her eyes looked haggard, her skin was a mess, and half her face was veiled behind oily, stringy hair as if she didn't want to look them in the eyes. The Karina they knew was silly and loving; the Karina who came home was cold and serious, barely saying a word to her brother.

Don't worry about it, Karina told them as Marlene listened carefully, I'm just tired from all our rehearsals and concert tours. But Sergio is taking us on a long vacation. He's selected the best girls in the school for a special training seminar in Spain, at the Manuel de Falla Academy. Karina said she'd be away for a few months but promised to write weekly.

And with that, they were gone. Before Karina's parents could even put dinner on the table, the two girls called a taxi and left. "After that," Karina would say, "we traveled to Los Mochis so Marlene could see her family and carry out the same mission."

That was Karina's big chance. She didn't even have to run away to escape: for several hours, she was safe in her childhood home, her worried parents by her side, Sergio and Gloria a distant city away.

But she still chose to return to Sergio.

To explain why, Karina would later tell her story about bath time.

When she first arrived at Adolfo Prieto Street, she was consumed with trying to avoid punishment by obeying Sergio's rules. But Sergio's rules were so random and unpredictable ("Sergio says you only pretended to like your dinner") that Karina often didn't know a rule existed until after she'd broken it.

That's when she had her big breakthrough. "You can only become an artist if you learn to think like an artist," Sergio constantly lectured the girls, and thinking like an artist, of course, meant thinking like Sergio. So that's what Karina did: instead of obeying, she began anticipating. Every move she made, she put to the Sergio Test: Would Sergio want her to have another bite of tuna fish? Would he want her to smile back at the TV showrunner who greeted her on set? Would he be happier if she asked what she'd done wrong or just accept her punishment? Sergio's desires became her desires: "I'm hungry" turned into "Would Sergio want me to be hungry?" If not, then she wasn't.

Living life by the Sergio Test made things much easier. When Sergio said it was time for her to take a bath, she agreed. "That meant he was going to punish me, and then we'd have sexual relations." Instead of crying or racking her mind about what she'd done wrong, the way she used to, Karina would simply strip, shower, and wait by his door until beckoned to enter.

She actually got a little too good at anticipating Sergio's needs. "In the room next to the bathroom was Tamara Zúñiga, who'd recently joined the group," Karina would later say, referring to Edith Zúñiga's younger sister. "When I came out wrapped in a towel and headed toward the recording studio for my beating, Sergio got really angry, since Tamara wasn't supposed to know what was going on."

Sergio's face twisted into such a mask of rage that Karina believed this was the moment he'd finally kill her. She fainted. When she came to, Katia de la Cuesta was holding a bottle of rubbing alcohol under her nose and Sergio was standing behind her, wrapping an extension cord around his fist. Are you feeling better? he asked. Yes, Karina answered. Then bend over the soundboard, he commanded. He whipped her while Katia de la Cuesta watched and then told Katia to strip and join them.

"Sexual relations and punishments took place almost every day," Karina would say. "That was our way of life."

Tamara Zúñiga was terrified. Despite Sergio's intent to bring her along slowly, there was no way to hide the sounds of whimpering and grunting in the rooms around her.

What's going on? Tamara asked her older sister, Edith.

Just do what Sergio says, Edith told her.

I don't want him to hit me. Tamara trembled.

Just do what Sergio says, Edith repeated.

Tamara and Edith were both from Chile. Gloria was performing there when she recruited thirteen-year-old Edith from a crowd of fans, and it was Edith, two years later, who told Sergio that her pretty little sister had just turned thirteen. Soon after, an excited but bewildered Tamara was seated between Edith and Mary Boquitas on a flight to Mexico City.

At first, Sergio barely paid her any attention. Just when Tamara thought she was invisible enough to escape the treatment the other girls seemed to be getting, Gloria appeared at her door one evening.

"Do you know about Sergio's sadness?" she asked Tamara.

As Tamara would later testify, Gloria gave her the same story she'd been telling new clan girls for years: Sergio had his heart broken by Lucerito, his one true love, and never really recovered. Because he's such a sensitive artist, Gloria went on, regular people like us will never understand the pain he suffers. All we can do is try to help—by, say, joining him in the Jacuzzi? To show him he's loved and lift his spirits? That's not such a big deal, right?

Tamara was petrified. She stammered out, *No, no, I can't*, until Gloria gave up. Later that night, Tamara would say, Sergio came into her room, tore off her clothes, and raped her. After that, he attacked her regularly and kept her locked inside the house by day, only giving her limited outdoor privileges after she became more submissive. Tamara was desperate to escape, but as a thirteen-year-old in a strange country with no money, no access to a phone, and a passport locked inside her molester's wall safe, she was powerless.

The Karina-Marlene operation was Sergio's first big experiment in sending the girls off on their own to placate their parents. It was risky, but the last thing he wanted was for some nosy mom to send Mexico City police over to Adolfo Prieto Street on a wellness check and find the place abandoned. Buying some breathing space in advance could save him a lot of headaches.

Karina followed Sergio's instructions precisely, so soon after she returned, Sergio dispatched Tamara and Edith Zúñiga back to Chile under the watchful eye of Mary Boquitas. He modified their script a little: it was doubtful the Zúñiga family would hear any Mexican news reports about Aline, but just in case, the girls were to tell their parents that Sergio was taking them away to prepare for their own albums to launch, so they might not be in touch for a while.

While they were all lunching together in the Zúñiga house, however, the phone rang. It was Gloria, calling for Mary. Mary excused herself and took the call in a back bedroom. As soon as she was out of earshot, Tamara poured out everything she and Edith had been through to her parents.

Her parents stared at her, paralyzed. When Mary finished her call and returned to the table, the girls hushed up and everyone finished their meal as if nothing had been said. As Mary rose and said it was time to return to the airport, however, Tamara's parents said they just needed a little more family time alone with their girls. Mary could go on ahead, they said, and Tamara and Edith would follow shortly. Reluctantly, Mary left. She wasn't happy, and neither were mom and dad Zúñiga.

"My parents thought I was making it up," Tamara Zúñiga would later testify under oath. The girls offered to tell their story to the police, but that didn't help. "The police didn't buy our story either."

Mary, sitting in the airport lobby, was getting nervous. Now it was her turn to be the stranger in a foreign country, and she became increasingly anxious about what the Zúñiga girls were up to. She scanned the lobby for police, and when her flight was called, she didn't hesitate. She boarded alone and got the hell out of Chile.

35

THE MASTER MAGICIAN

Sergio was shaken by the defections but couldn't dwell on them. There wasn't time. Once the remaining twelve girls had assembled back in Mexico City, he issued new orders: pack two bags of essentials and leave everything else behind. They had one hour.

The girls scattered to their rooms. When they reassembled fifty-nine minutes later, Sergio herded them into a pair of waiting vans with blacked-out windows and together they headed to the airport.

Put yourself in Sergio's shoes: where on earth do you hide a gang of twelve young women and Mexico's most famous face?

All of Latin America was out. There was no city, mountain town, or resort area where Gloria, Mary Boquitas, or even Sergio himself wouldn't be recognized in minutes.

The United States? Forget about it. If a middle-aged man with a dozen Mexican girls tried to cross the border, he'd be red-flagged as a sex trafficker and pulled aside for grilling. The only possible exception was Los Angeles, where Sergio owned a home and could tell a plausible story about making a film or recording an album, but that would plunk him right in a hotbed of Latin performers and music reporters. He'd be spotted in a day.

Asia, Africa, Eastern Europe: no, no, and no. Language barriers were too high, transferring money was too risky, and their complexions were too noticeable. That left Western Europe, which was likewise a no-go for the same sex-trafficking red flags, except for—

Spain.

Spain was perfect. Armies of tourists pour into Spain each year, including plenty of celebrities heading toward raves on Ibiza, bullfights in Pamplona, and yachts off the Mallorcan coast. No one would raise an eyebrow at a dozen young backpackers or give a second glance at a beautiful woman they vaguely recognized as famous but couldn't quite place. Sergio had been to Madrid many times and knew exactly where to find the kind of big, bustling hotels in the heart of the city where a clatter of Spanish-speaking girls would go unnoticed.

After landing at Madrid's Barajas Airport, Sergio loaded his band-on-the-run into a fleet of taxis and headed downtown. Once he had everyone checked into their rooms, Sergio discovered he still had one problem left to deal with.

"On the first day we arrived in Spain, something incredible happened to me," Karina, thirteen years old at the time, would say. "While I was having group sex with Sergio, Wendy, and Marlene, Sergio felt something strange in my abdomen, and he told me to get a pregnancy test that he himself would administer. The result was positive."

Mary Boquitas had warned Sergio months earlier that Karina might be pregnant, but he was too focused on getting the girls out of Mexico and covering his tracks with their parents to do anything about it. There was no ignoring it now, though. A few days later, Karina was flying back across the Atlantic, this time heading to Houston with Mary Boquitas. At the clinic, however, Karina was told she was too far advanced for an abortion. They turned right around and returned to Houston airport. There, they split up: Karina on a flight to Madrid, Mary to Mexico for the second part of her mission.

Sergio didn't want to leave a traceable trail of bank withdrawals and credit card statements, so he'd left Mexico with all the money he could safely carry. Because Mary was authorized to withdraw from his personal account, he sent her back for more. Mary exited the bank that afternoon with a suitcase stuffed with cash, enough for her to live on for months, and nothing stopping her from going back for more. This was her chance. If she'd ever been tempted to flee the clan, her moment had arrived. By the time Sergio figured out what was going on and froze his account, Mary would be long gone on Sergio's dime.

Instead, she walked into a travel agency and booked herself on the next flight to Madrid.

In September 1997, Karina's parents received a thick envelope plastered with Spanish postage stamps. Inside were snapshots of Karina's smiling face—and only her face—in front of Madrid's Prado Museum, the pond in Retiro Park, and the towering Roman aqueduct in nearby Segovia. They loved the photos (Karina is putting on some weight again!), but the letter—that was another story.

The penmanship was hers but the voice was someone else's. They knew their daughter had changed in many ways over the past year but becoming a thirteen-year-old existentialist philosopher wasn't one of them. "I have learned the secrets of life, something very few people ever master," Karina had written. "And it is, 'Patience above all things,' one has to be calm because no matter how difficult things appear, those things that make you suffer will make you king of the heavens."

It sounded like Karina was frantically scrawling down someone else's stream of consciousness with no real idea what she was writing. "You can't imagine how much work they give me in school, right now I have, besides everything else, to transcribe songs from one tone to another, for example from G major to C major, which means from 'so!' major to 'Jo' major, and first, I also have to write from memory the songs that I am playing. This scholarship is really a great opportunity to increase my knowledge and for that reason, I am really happy."

In reality, Karina was seven months pregnant and living in a cold and nearly empty rental house on the dismal outskirts of Madrid. Instead of music classes at the "Manuel de Falla Academy," she spent most of each day in a straight-back chair in front of a typewriter, clattering out Sergio's musings. Sergio had set himself up as a sort of pasha and poet-in-residence, dictating song lyrics and poems to the girls by day and climbing into bed with several of them at night, including an increasingly anxious Karina.

Karina hadn't seen a doctor or had any training in childbirth. At thirteen, she had no idea what to expect. She was terrified when furious contractions woke her up in the middle of the night on December 12, 1997. She stumbled from room to room in the dark house, searching for Sergio and finally finding him in one of the back bedrooms with Liliana Regueiro, a young Argentinian who had joined the clan shortly before they decamped to Spain.

"I think the baby is coming!" she cried.

"Don't interrupt," Sergio snapped, and continued berating Liliana about something.

When he finished, he called for Katia de la Cuesta. Sergio and the two young women squeezed into Sergio's tiny car for the two-hour drive to Madrid. Karina barely made it into the emergency room before giving birth to a five-pound baby boy. Sergio chose his son's name, Francisco Ariel, but refused to touch him. The next morning, Karina bundled up her newborn and cradled him in the back of Sergio's car on the trip back to Toledo.

Sergio fretted as he drove. He hadn't liked the way the nurses in the hospital kept glancing back and forth between him and Karina, *twice* asking if Sergio was Karina's father. What if they started talking and got the Spanish police involved?

That meant it was time to get out of Toledo. Sergio gave Karina a few days to rest, then ordered everyone to pack their bags. He took Karina and the baby in his car and sent the rest of the girls to the bus station, with directions to meet him a few hundred miles south in the beachy tourist town of Málaga. There, the floppy hats and sunglasses the girls were all wearing as disguises would look more natural among the hordes of Christmas vacation sun-seekers on the Costa del Sol.

The clan settled into a few rooms in a cheap Málaga vacation rental, but not for long. After barely two months, they were headed back to Madrid.

Spanish police who later retraced the clan's movements concluded that during this period, Sergio was pimping out his clan as prostitutes. Their theory matched a number of known facts:

- Small packs of young Mexican women who matched the clan's description were reported soliciting strangers at truck stops and along Madrid's Gran Via.

- The clan had begun living in neighborhoods near red-light districts.
- Sergio had to be running low on cash since it had been months since he'd gotten a resupply from Mexico.

Police discovered that Sergio shuttled his clan between two houses in San Agustin del Guadalix, a village of six thousand about a half hour's drive from Madrid. Sergio had rented one of the homes in the name of a Spanish singer he'd once managed a few years earlier. Neighbors told police that they constantly saw young girls coming and going in vans and keeping to themselves. The windows were always covered, and a high trellis surrounded the backyard. "They were very strange people, very secretive," one neighbor reported. Those witness statements, plus unusual newspaper advertisements that appeared in Madrid at that time, reinforced investigators' belief that Sergio was trafficking the girls.

Not true, several of the clan girls would later claim. They insisted they made good money by busking on street corners and begging for change. Gloria was amazing at it, Karina would add, a true Artful Dodger who taught the rest of them the best way to separate old ladies from their pocket money. Gloria's strategy was to ambush elderly shoppers on their way home from the supermarket when their little grocery wagons slowed them down too much to brush by. She would then launch into a sweet-faced lie about how she and her friends were Latin American students who'd run out of money and were saving for a flight home.

At night, Gloria would pull on her floppy hat and sunglasses and park herself outside a bustling bar with a sketch pad and crayons, selling caricatures to half-drunk partiers who had no idea they were buying an original work from one of Latin America's most celebrated recording artists. Perched on her stool, with millions in her bank account back home, La Trevi was right back to where she'd started ten years earlier: hustling on the streets for Sergio.

"Miss Wicked: Vanished?"
(La Atrevida: Desaparecida?)

As soon as one newspaper blasted out that headline, the rest were quick to follow. The onslaught had begun.

It was March 1998, and no one had seen Gloria since the previous summer, back when she'd made that bizarre announcement about Sergio's supposed cancer. Something very strange was going on. For the first time in years, Gloria hadn't released her Christmas pin-up calendar. Valentine's Day, usually Gloria's biggest blow-out holiday with a TV special and sexy-Cupid photo spread, came and went with no sign of her.

Reporters checked with studios and discovered that Gloria had zero projects in the works: no movies in development, no concerts scheduled, no albums being recorded. The Trevi entertainment empire hadn't just ground to a halt; it had disappeared entirely. No one was even answering phones in Sergio's studio. Gloria's mother tried to quell the media speculation by holding a press conference.

"It's just because of wild talk like this that Gloria decided to go on an artistic retreat," her mother scolded. Gloria had phoned her that morning, in fact, and she sounded great, having fun and working hard. And Sergio was writing his first novel. Wasn't that exciting?

The tabloids went wild. Gloria Ruiz had only convinced the press that someone was covering up *something*. A stream of anonymously sourced stories began appearing nearly every day about Gloria Trevi dying from a drug overdose . . . being held for ransom by drug cartels . . . recovering from a mental breakdown in an American psychiatric institution . . . and, of course, the most plausible of all: giving birth to Sergio's baby. ("Thereby ending years of intrigue about why this woman who constantly talks about sex never seems to have any," commented one tabloid but echoing them all.)

TV Azteca issued an all-hands-on-deck order to every one of its affiliates in the United States and Europe: if you hear the slightest Gloria Trevi rumor, drop whatever else you're doing and track it down. Mexican newspaper reporters began staking out restaurants in McAllen, Texas, where Sergio had a home, and showing photos of Sergio to diners and servers to see if anyone had spotted him recently.

The result: nothing.

As the search grew more frenzied, the speculation grew darker. *It's quite possible we're dealing with murder*, TV gossip hosts conjectured. They kept bringing up *Star 80*, the movie about the world-famous Playboy model, Dorothy Stratten, who was shot to death by her domineering boyfriend when her stardom outgrew his control. The warning signs were there all along, the TV hosts lamented. Now it's time for the police to get involved.

But in a flash, everything made sense. Suddenly everyone understood exactly why Gloria had become a ghost.

36

BATTLESTAR ALINE

The title was a grim pun.

Aline: La Gloria por el Infierno means Aline: "Going Through Hell for Glory." But also Aline: "Gloria Put Me Through Hell."

Aline's exposé hit the bookshelves on Wednesday, April 15, 1998, three days after Easter. She was still too observant a Catholic to make the comparison herself, but the symbolism wasn't lost on the news media: after being entombed for years, Aline was roaring back to life.

And wow, did she have a story to tell. All those painful memories she'd shared during her sessions with Rubén Aviña were now spilling off the page, with Rubén as her co-author. Aline's account of her years with Sergio was shocking and explicit, and she left no doubt that Sergio's #1 enabler was Mexico's greatest champion of female rights, using her star power to lure adolescents into Sergio's house of horrors.

In response, Sergio didn't say a word. He had a better idea.

"*Por favor!*" Gloria Trevi laughed in mock amazement, shaking her wild curls and throwing herself back in her chair. "I've heard some crazy ones before but nothing like this." She opened her palms and beseeched the heavens above. "If I'm lying, let lightning strike me right now!"

Twelve days after Aline's book came out, on April 27, 1998, Gloria suddenly appeared in public for the first time in half a year. Cristina Saralegui, a popular and respected daytime talk show host, had gotten a call from Sergio offering Gloria for an exclusive appearance, all questions on the table and nothing off-limits. Cristina agreed, but then she and her team heard nothing more from Sergio or Gloria—until, thirty minutes before the scheduled interview time, a dark SUV rolled up to the studio and the missing pop star stepped out, as radiant as ever.

So, Cristina asked once the cameras were rolling, where have you been?

"Italy," Gloria replied, working in seclusion on her next record and a movie script. She was also studying politics, she said; she wasn't kidding back when she talked about running for president of Mexico, and she was now about ready to launch her political career. She wouldn't have interrupted her creative sabbatical for this nonsense except out of loyalty to Sergio and concern for her fans and family.

"I have not been kidnapped," Gloria declared. "I am sane, I do not belong to any Satanic cult, I am a Roman Catholic, Apostolic Christian. Can you imagine how my mother must have felt to come home and hear that Gloria Trevi committed suicide? Thank God she didn't have a heart attack!"

Cristina held up a copy of Aline's book. "Are you denying these allegations?" she asked.

"I don't know much about it." Gloria shrugged. "I hear it's all lies."

Cristina began ticking off Aline's claims: orgies, whipping, sexual abuse—

"Anyone with a scrap of brains in their heads should be able to tell that's not true," Gloria erupted. "Sergio Andrade has a heart of gold. I've seen him help the poor, I've seen him help people in need!"

"Did he ever beat you?"

Gloria scoffed. "If he's guilty of anything, it's being overprotective. After news spread of fans killing artists, he got nervous if anyone came near me. That's why I don't understand how anyone can say he hit me." Gloria jumped to her feet, unbuttoned her blouse, and pulled it open. She stood there in her skirt and white bra. "You've all seen me in much shorter shorts, in my calendars and during my shows. But here, take a good look—there are no bruises on my body."

Gloria was off and running. This whole slanderous mess, she went on, is a revenge plot cooked up by TV Azteca and Pati Chapoy! Pati was one of Sergio's lovers, Gloria claimed. She cheated with Sergio behind her husband's back! She is so in love with Sergio that she would rather see him destroyed than in love with anyone else. Look at her, Gloria scoffed, in her prissy salmon suits and her little shoulder shawls, using little Aline as her pawn to whip up a witch hunt of greedy, lying teenagers to tell phony stories of sex and sadomasochism in exchange for TV time and book deals.

"I want to tell everyone, if you really like being hooked like that, you must really like science fiction. In that case," Gloria continued, "I'd strongly recommend you buy something by Stephen King, who writes extraordinary fiction and is a person with a great deal of talent."

But despite all the nonsense, Gloria added, she was happy to be back in Mexico. "I'm sick of Italian food," she laughed. "Ravioli here, ravioli there—I couldn't wait to get home and eat tortillas and chili!"

Ravioli? Italy? Miguel Yapor, watching the program from his wheelchair alongside his wife at their home in Chihuahua, was at first bewildered, then worried. What was Gloria talking about?

In all her letters, Karina told them she and Gloria were in Spain. And now Gloria was going on and on about Italy? And everyone on TV was saying Sergio was abusive? Maybe it was time to go to the police, Miguel thought. He hesitated, not sure if he was overreacting. Before he made up his mind, Sergio appeared at his door.

Miguel was dumbfounded. It was May 1998, three weeks after Aline's book came out, when Sergio arrived at the Yapors with a gift box of Spanish *turrón* in his hand. Standing behind him were Gloria and their own little girl. "I had a feeling you'd be worried because of all this chatter," Sergio explained, as they entered and got comfortable in the Yapors' living room. They'd traveled all the way back from Spain, he said, to ease their minds.

It was a pity and rather embarrassing, Sergio said, but the truth of the matter was, Aline wanted to punish Sergio for her own failure. She's a talented girl who lacks the heart and discipline of a true artist, Sergio went on. Gloria nodded vigorously while Karina stared down at the floor, as oddly silent as she'd been on her last visit.

I don't understand, Miguel said. Were you in Italy?

Gloria jumped in for that one. Oh no, she replied. We were at the Manuel de Falla Academy in Spain. I just had to tell a little story so the media won't follow us. They can be very annoying, you know. If we don't lead them astray, we'll be pestered by reporters night and day and won't have a moment's peace to work.

Gloria hopped to her feet, cutting off any further questions. *Come on, everyone!* she chirped. *Group photo time!* Gloria squeezed in next to Miguel, draping herself across him so flirtatiously that he actually relaxed his usual stone-face stare and blushed. Not Sergio, though. He looked none too happy when the camera came out and quickly reached for it, appointing himself family photographer so he could take all the pictures—and appear in none of them.

As he handed the camera back to Karina's mother, Sergio checked his watch. We have a few matters we need to deal with in Chihuahua, he said. It was a lovely visit, but they really must run. And before the Yapors could speak alone with their daughter, she was gone.

Gloria returned later, just her and Karina.

I wanted to share a few things while Sergio isn't here, Gloria began. You can see how shy he is. He'd squirm if he heard me tell you what a fantastic job he's doing with Karina at the Manuel de Falla Academy! Sergio thinks she's nearly ready to debut as a solo artist.

"I'm a little worried!" Gloria said. "Once Karina gets onstage, everyone will forget about me."

Really? The Yapors couldn't see it. How was their daughter supposed to perform in front of an audience when she was too withdrawn to speak to her own family? Every time they tried to ask Karina a question, Gloria would yelp out some wacky answer, then double up in laughter at her own joke and prattle on, filling in the awkward pauses left by Karina's one-word responses.

But abruptly, Gloria grew serious. Sergio puts on a brave face but it's been so hard for him lately, she lamented. Aline is spreading the worst lies! The problem is, Sergio is a true artist and doesn't want to take time from his creative work to respond. I do everything I can to speak up for him. Everything. You've seen that.

The Yapors nodded along until Gloria added: Maybe you can, too.

Us? The Yapors were baffled. Why would anyone listen to some disabled electrician and his wife in Chihuahua?

It's very easy, Gloria assured them. All you have to do is—

"Gloria asked us for a letter they could use to defend themselves against the defamation that she said Aline was publishing about them," Teresa Yapor, Karina's mother, would later testify. They just needed a little note, Gloria urged, saying the Yapors had no problem with Sergio. "We never managed to talk to Karina alone, but I felt okay because she assured us they were taking good care of her."

Teresa wasn't sure what to make of Aline's accusations because she only knew what she'd heard on TV, and a bunch of people were saying Aline was just making it up. "None of us had read the book yet," Teresa would recall. To her, it was a choice between some young woman she'd never heard of calling a legendary producer a sicko . . .

. . . versus the legend himself lounging on her own sofa next to a world-famous celebrity, the two of them lavishing praise on her daughter and praising the Virgin of Guadalupe and swearing that all the rumors were jealous lies.

That same afternoon, Teresa and Miguel Yapor sat down before a notary public. Gloria, it turned out, needed a little more than a personal note. She got the Yapors to sign a legal document, witnessed and stamped, declaring that as the lawful guardians of Karina Yapor, they were pleased with the professional and ethical manner in which Sergio Andrade was overseeing their daughter.

As soon as Gloria had it in her hand, she and Karina kiss-kissed the Yapors and headed straight back to the airport.

Three weeks later, Miguel received a baffling phone call. The line hissed and crackled before a stern voice came on. It was the Mexican consulate in Madrid.

An infant boy, badly malnourished and close to death, had

been abandoned at La Paz Hospital in Spain. The woman who brought the baby in had disappeared. Birth records showed the mother was a fourteen-year-old Mexican citizen by the name of Karina Yapor Gómez.

But that's impossible, Miguel stammered. I just saw my daughter a few weeks ago, right here in Chihuahua! She doesn't even have a boyfriend! She is in the care of Gloria Trevi, studying under very strict conditions at the Manuel de Falla Music Academy.

Sir, the Mexican consul responded. There is no such thing as the "Manuel de Falla" music school. The police believe your daughter is involved in a prostitution ring. You need to come to Spain immediately.

37

CLAN ON THE RUN

When Sergio left the Yapors, time was running out and the law was closing in.

He'd gotten word that the criminal investigation sparked by Aline was gathering speed. As far as he knew, other girls could be stepping forward at that very moment with accusations of their own. How long till Gloria's cousin spoke up? And the Zúñiga sisters? What would prevent dozens of girls from his past, now a little older and realizing they weren't alone, from banding into a movement that could bring him down?

And once a warrant for his arrest was issued, there would be nowhere in Mexico he could hide. Fleeing back to Spain wouldn't help: Spanish cops had a proud history of coming to their sister country's aid whenever fugitive druglords thought they could hide out on the Mediterranean coast, so a request from Mexico to capture a suspected sex-trafficking pedophile would surely launch an instant manhunt.

That was the bad news. Then came worse.

Before traveling to Chihuahua to visit the Yapors, Sergio had secretly stopped off in Mexico City for a few days with

Gloria and Karina to withdraw more money. Hiding out in his hometown was risky, but he needed to get his hands on all the cash he could before he became a wanted man. While there, he called back to Madrid to check in with Mary Boquitas.

Sonia Ríos has something to tell you, Mary said, and passed her the phone.

Sergio, Sonia whispered. *I'm pregnant.*

Before Sergio could react, Karla de la Cuesta got on the line.

Me too.

Sergio must have been fighting to hold himself together as they flew to Chihuahua later that day to see the Yapors. It had been hard enough getting all the girls into Spain in the first place, and now they not only had to go on the run again, but this time they'd have a newborn on their hands and two more on the way. It was impossible.

Two more on the way . . . Sergio could feel an idea tickling at the edge of his mind. Then it hit him. *Yes! That could totally work.* In a flash, Sergio saw his escape route opening ahead of him. Those two babies aren't a setback, he realized. They're a solution. They're going to be the miracle children who part the seas and lead him to freedom.

Sergio's brain was still buzzing with his scheme when they pulled up at the Yapors' house. He did his best to focus on the job at hand—projecting calm and instilling confidence—but when he told the Yapors he had to leave to take care of some urgent business, he wasn't lying. He couldn't wait to put his scheme in motion. It would take some fancy footwork, but if he pulled it off, there was nothing the Mexican police could do to him for the rest of his life.

Everyone would have their own special assignments, he decided:

GLORIA

- Circle back to the Yapors and get them to write The Letter. Mary Boquitas was going to need it.
- Go to Mexico City and sanitize Sergio's house of incriminating evidence.
- Ask BMG Records for cash and a work visa.

KARINA

- Remain in Mexico and help clean Sergio's house.
- Stay out of sight by sleeping at Sergio's mother's house.
- Return to Madrid with The Letter for Mary Boquitas.

DE LA CUESTA SISTERS

- Care for Karina's baby until she returned.
- Clean out the rental house in Madrid.
- Pack lightly, be prepared to move fast.

MARY BOQUITAS

- Buy three plane tickets for Argentina.
- Buy one plane ticket for Mexico City.
- Meet Karina's arrival at Madrid airport and retrieve The Letter.

LILIANA, WENDY, AND MARLENE

- Fly to Argentina and meet up with Sergio.

SONIA RÍOS

- Fly to Mexico City and meet up with Gloria.

Later, none of the girls would remember if Sergio ever bothered to share his master plan with them. All these odd tasks must have seemed baffling and random, but they knew better than to question El Maestro. They kept quiet and got to work.

Gloria and Karina eased into Sergio's house, being careful to avoid being spotted by the neighbors. They hit the desk drawers first, pulling out stacks of Polaroids. Among them were nude photos of Gloria and Mary, Karina would say, from back when they were barely teenagers as members of Boquitas Pintadas. Stacked in boxes around the office were hundreds of letters in high-school handwriting: one of Sergio's punishments was to make the girls write adoring, apologetic letters to him asking forgiveness for their misdeeds. Karina even found some of the fabled sheets of paper that Aline had talked about on TV, when she said she'd been forced to huddle under Sergio's desk and scrawl "I will never lie to Sergio Andrade" one million times.

Sergio had ordered them to burn it all in the back garden, but Gloria thought that would attract too much attention. Instead, she called one of her brothers and persuaded him to drive down from Monterrey—twenty hours round trip—and help them secretly haul everything to a home that Sergio owned in McAllen, Texas. Days later, on June 19, the house went up in flames. Firefighters burst through the door to find smoldering piles of documents and Gloria's pinup calendars . . . but no Gloria.

Because by then, Gloria had already moved on to her next task: BMG Records.

One of Sergio's thorniest problems was getting travel documents for Karina. Karina couldn't leave Spain without a passport for her baby, but she also couldn't stay in Spain without adding him to her tourist visa. Either way, as a minor she would need parental consent.

Unless—

Gloria and Karina arrived together at the Mexico City offices of Gloria's longtime record label. Exciting things were happening, Gloria told her BMG team. She and Sergio were writing up a storm and absorbing all kinds of useful new influences during their time overseas. Her next album was going to be a monster, Gloria promised. She handed over a demo of a new track, "I'm Not Made of Money" ("No Soy Monedita de Oro").

But, Gloria said, to finish recording the album we could use an advance of, say . . . $100,000?

Sure, the BMG execs were quick to agree. Gloria's records were a blue-chip stock, proven winners that always paid off millions of dollars more than the initial investment. But Gloria wasn't done.

Plus, we'll need that payable in Spanish pesetas, not pesos. And for Karina here, we'd like you to make her an honorary BMG employee. You don't need to pay her anything, Gloria hastened to explain. She just needs documents from you stating she's on staff at BMG International so she can get a Spanish work visa.

The BMG team considered Gloria's request—a six-figure cash advance in a foreign currency and fake work records for a fourteen-year-old girl—and correctly assumed it was—

(a) a shady and possibly illegal attempt to sidestep international banking laws, and

(b) an even shadier and definitely illegal attempt at some combination of fraud, human trafficking, and/or corruption of minors.

Everyone at BMG was aware of Aline's allegations, and while they were still willing to chalk it up as a he said/she said and give their superstar the benefit of the doubt, that benefit did not stretch to willful collusion and accessory after the fact. We're going to have to check with legal, they told Gloria, and that was enough to make her reverse course, chatter out a word storm of never-minds, and back her way out the door. The last thing Gloria wanted was for anyone with a law degree to get involved.

That was the last time anyone at BMG would see Gloria until her face showed up alongside Sergio's on an international WANTED poster. Seeing an opportunity in the media firestorm, BMG quickly released Gloria's new single. When asked how a recording from a woman not even the police could find turned up at BMG, a spokesman would shrug and claim that "a plain white envelope appeared at the reception desk."

Sergio, meanwhile, was hunting vacation rentals in Argentina.

He needed something with a lot of beds, of course, preferably in a bustling corner of Buenos Aires near a hospital with a good maternity ward. Also, a month-by-month lease: he wouldn't need it for long and wanted to exit at a moment's notice. As soon as he found what he was looking for, he called Mary Boquitas: *Start sending the girls.*

Buenos Aires was a terrible place to disappear. Argentinians speak a very different kind of Spanish, heavily accented with undertones of Italian, so the girls would give themselves away as soon as they opened their mouths in a grocery store. Even worse, Argentina *loved* Gloria. La Atrevida had performed so many stadium concerts in Buenos Aires, and Sergio had been such a vocal supporter of Argentinian musicians, that there was no place they were probably more famous outside of Mexico.

But that was okay. Argentina wasn't a hideout. It was a springboard. Looking at his road map, Sergio traced a long, diagonal route out of Buenos Aires and straight up to São Paulo, Brazil. Overland, it wasn't bad at all: about 1,400 miles, less than the drive from Boston to Miami. Plus, there was only one border crossing: right at Iguazu Falls, the stunningly beautiful and—more importantly—*heavily touristed* natural attraction with a constant stream of visitor traffic. Split the girls up on a couple of tour buses and in no time they'd be in Brazil, with its beautiful beaches, its magnificent cuisine, and best of all—a lovely legal loophole that made newborn babies a Get-Out-of-Jail-Free card.

38

THE GREAT TRAIN ROBBER

The real mastermind of Sergio's plan was a British crook named Ronnie Biggs. Ronnie was a lousy criminal who would have died in prison if he hadn't discovered his one special talent: a flair for escape.

Ronnie began thieving at age thirteen but was caught so often that after cycling in and out of jail for nearly twenty years, he resolved at age thirty-one to give up the life for good. He'd learned painting and carpentry behind bars, and it wasn't long before he had steady work, a loving wife, two young sons, and a comfy house in the London suburbs. But home-repair jobs began drying up during England's recession in the 1960s and Ronnie found himself a little light on cash. He went to see an old friend who was rolling in it: Bruce Reynolds, whom he'd known since their youth detention days.

Bruce spent his time behind bars pursuing a much more ambitious plan for release than Ronnie's. Anyone can apprentice with a carpenter, he reasoned, but how often do you get the chance to pick the brain of a great burglar? And here he was, locked up with dozens of them! Bruce put himself through a felony PhD program. He soaked up tips from the old masters, focusing especially on the mistakes that got them busted, and walked through the prison gates as a master cracksman. Crime has always been a recession-proof industry, so when Ronnie showed up later looking for a handout, Bruce was able to offer him something much tastier. Bruce was in the midst of finalizing plans for the greatest heist of his career, an operation he called his "Sistine Chapel": the Great Train Robbery.

Bruce had learned that after long holiday weekends, the Royal Mail train from Glasgow to London carried up to five times the normal amount of bank cash. Bruce came up with a scheme, but he needed one last guy to fill out his gang. He was afraid the conductor might trip some kind of secret alarm, so he wanted someone he could trust to drive the train to the getaway spot after they stopped it mid-route. If Ronnie could find an experienced engineer, Bruce offered, the two of them would each get a full share of the haul.

Ronnie agreed—and as usual, he blew it.

On the day of the Great Train Robbery, the gang discovered that Ronnie's recruit had only operated old locomotives and had no clue how to operate modern controls. Despite Ronnie's blunder, the bandits got away with an absolute mountain of cash: 2.6 million British pounds, worth more than *$60 million* today.

They'd pulled off the perfect crime. Or would have, if they hadn't left fingerprints at their farmhouse hideout which police quickly traced to ex-cons Bruce and Ronnie. Bruce managed to slip off in time and flee to Mexico. There, he could have lived free and happy for the rest of his days if he hadn't gotten restless five years later and returned to England for an ill-fated encore caper. Ronnie, on the other hand, was scooped up right away and sentenced to thirty years in prison. It was a crushing setback, but it also set the stage for his hidden greatness to emerge.

On a warm July evening in 1965 at Wandsworth Prison, fourteen notorious convicts on the "Escape Watch" list were taken out to the yard for exercise time. Suddenly, a masked man appeared above the wall, holding what appeared to be a shotgun. A rope ladder tumbled down and four prisoners ran for it, while the remaining ten formed a human shield blocking out the guards. The escapees made it over the wall and onto the roof of a delivery truck, where they slipped through a top hatch, changed out of their striped uniforms, and disappeared into the night.

Unlike his previous escapades, Ronnie had planned and executed this one brilliantly. Long before the jailbreak, he'd instructed his wife and sons to leave the country with no forwarding address, making it seem as if they were making a fresh start far away. Once free, Ronnie was smuggled by boat across the English Channel to France. There, a gangland doctor did plastic surgery on his face and an underworld contact from the old days provided a fake passport. Ronnie waited for his incisions to heal, then made his way to Marseille to join the mob of emigrants departing every day on steamships. On board, he remained below deck in the crowded dormitories for the entire passage, only emerging two weeks later to find his family waiting for him in Australia.

That's where his story might have ended, if not for a pair of obsessive British detectives who began closing in after four years of searching. Just in time, Ronnie got a tip from a crony that British police were heading to Melbourne. With hours to spare, he left his family behind and set sail once again, this time for Brazil. When the British detectives finally cornered him in Rio, it was too late: Ronnie had used his head start to outwit them once and for all.

Ronnie always knew that Brazil had a soft spot for outlaws, but it was only after he got there that he discovered this crush was actually court protected, thanks in part to a real-life Robin Hood couple called Maria Bonita and Lampião—Pretty Mary and the Lantern.

The Lantern was a shepherd whose father had been murdered by corrupt policemen in the 1920s. He took to the mountains, vowing revenge, and earned his nickname by learning to fire a rifle so quickly the flashes looked like a lantern's glow. Many other impoverished Brazilians had been abused by police, and before long, lone-wolf Lampião found himself at the head of a renegade army.

The Lantern and his desperados wandered the country, robbing rich landowners and sharing the loot with poor farmers. The Lantern was so strict about protecting the downtrodden that once, after he'd stolen a mule to escape a police ambush, he circled back to return it. He was already a legend by the time his band passed through the village where Pretty Mary was living with her abusive alcoholic husband. Mary was reportedly so enchanted by this gentle-looking outlaw, with his round professor's spectacles and boyish face, that she ran up to him as he was about to ride off and impulsively asked to join his gang.

The Lantern and Pretty Mary fell in love, and for more than a decade they reigned side by side as the bandit king and queen, beloved and protected by villagers everywhere, until they were machine-gunned to death in a police raid in 1938 and transformed from avenging superheroes into immortal legends. Brazil's affection for outlaws like Lampião and reputation for sheltering them is one reason that "running off to Rio" has become a euphemism for escaping the law. And the other reason?

Ronnie Biggs.

When the British detectives tried to arrest Ronnie in Rio in 1971, the Great Train Robber wasn't alone. He'd been dating a Brazilian showgirl, who came forward to say she was pregnant. Scotland Yard didn't care, but the Brazilian government did: according to legal custom, Brazil would not extradite the parent of a Brazilian child, even a child yet to be born. Britain's most-wanted fugitive was untouchable.

The British detectives went home empty-handed and furious, while Ronnie became a celebrity. He was so popular that his son was given a role on a hit children's TV show, and Ronnie himself found a surprising second act in entertainment. He achieved cult hero status among punk musicians, who revered his ability to spit in the face of the law. The Sex Pistols even collaborated with the aging criminal on their 1978 hit "No One Here Is Innocent." That same year, twenty-three-year-old Sergio Andrade was immersing himself in all things punk as he pivoted from classical music to rock. He would have known the Ronnie Biggs story very well, and remember this final, shouted line from Ronnie's greatest hit:

"God save the worthless creep!"

39

NEW PLAN: *RUN!*

If you're Sergio, the arithmetic is easy:

> 1 ticket to Brazil + 1 newborn baby = a lifetime of freedom.

As he understood it, any child born on Brazilian soil was automatically a Brazilian citizen, so he just had to get there before Sonia Ríos and Karla de la Cuesta gave birth and *poof*—all his problems would disappear. Granted, that didn't help Gloria and the rest of the girls, but as usual, Sergio had another scheme up his sleeve.

He also had tremendous luck—or tremendous connections. By the fall of 1998, Aline had been cooperating with the police for nearly six months. She'd laid out all her accusations against Sergio and Gloria, giving specific dates, locations, and events. Other girls were coming forward as well. But for some mysterious reason—maybe creaky police bureaucracy, or Gloria's fame, or the long shadow of Sergio's powerful brother—no arrest warrant had yet been issued.

That was a happy surprise for Sergio, who now had time to

quietly slip back into Mexico and take care of one last piece of personal business. If he had to spend the rest of his life in Brazil, Sergio knew he needed someone who could travel to Mexico on his behalf and, if possible, never be forced to testify against him. Karina would have been perfect, but Sergio was up against the same hitch as ever: Karina was still a minor.

So he called Mary Boquitas in Madrid and told her to put Sonia Ríos on a flight to Mexico City. Gloria met Sonia at the airport and before she knew it, the pregnant eighteen-year-old who'd been recruited from her mother's fruit stall in Pachuca was suddenly standing in front of a municipal judge on the outskirts of town and making a vow to love, honor, and obey as the latest Mrs. Sergio Andrade.

With that mission accomplished, Sergio hurried to catch the next flight for Argentina with Gloria, Karina, and Sonia, touching down just as most of the other clan girls were arriving from Madrid.

Remaining behind were two young women and one loose end.

Karina's baby was still a problem. Mary Boquitas had taken over as designated caregiver, since she was the last clan member still in Madrid, but it quickly became clear that she had neither taste nor talent for the job of surrogate mommy. Little Francisco Ariel was nine months old but so underfed and sickly he'd shriveled to the size of a newborn. Mary couldn't wait for Karina to take him off her hands. Karina was supposed to be arriving any day now with The Letter, the notarized guardianship statement from her parents that should authorize the baby's passport. As soon she had it, all three of them would be able to get out of Spain and join the clan in Argentina.

Karina was exhausted when she stepped off the plane in Madrid's Barajas Airport at dawn after the eleven-hour red-eye flight. At immigration control, she handed over her passport and the letter from her parents, just in case anyone wondered why a fifteen-year-old was traveling overseas by herself.

The customs and immigration officer flipped through her passport, then paused. Karina's tourist visa had expired.

A few hours later, she was marched onto a flight back to Mexico.

Mary was growing frantic. Another day had passed with no word from Karina or Sergio. Francisco Ariel was looking bad. Really bad. The color had drained from his face and he kept getting skinnier. Mary was terrified. *Where the hell was Karina?!*

In desperation, Mary bundled the baby and caught a taxi to the hospital. Still believing that Karina was on the way, Mary registered the baby under Karina's name instead of her own. Otherwise, Karina wouldn't be able to visit Francisco Ariel or check him out when he was healthy. Mary then slipped out of the hospital, leaving the baby in intensive care. Back at the apartment, she waited by the phone until Sergio finally called.

New plan, he said. Karina won't be coming. She's been deported. So get the baby, pretend it's yours, and tell the Mexican consulate you need a passport urgently. As soon as you have it, Sergio went on, head to the airport. We'll meet you and Karina in Argentina.

To an outsider, it would seem insane that Mary Boquitas would sign on to a crackpot scheme like trying to smuggle a desperately ill infant out of the country under orders from her sexually abusive, viciously tempered, wildly self-absorbed ex-husband who had divorced her to marry a series of progressively younger teenagers. But Mary Boquitas was now twenty-nine years old, which meant she'd been obeying Sergio's commands for more than half her life. She'd been isolated in his world since middle-school age, meaning her entire education was based on one principle: Sergio is godlike and never to be doubted.

That said, Sergio never did explain to Mary exactly how she was supposed to kidnap a baby from a closely monitored intensive care unit and persuade Mexican government officials to blindly issue a passport for a very ill child with zero proof of maternity. Mary's likeliest approach would be to sit patiently by the baby's side, acting motherly, until the nurses were distracted and she could sidle for the exit, exactly as she'd done before. But when she arrived back at the hospital, any chance she had of getting her hands on Francisco Ariel quickly blew up in her face: because she'd registered "Karina Yapor" as the baby's mother, Mary wasn't even allowed to enter the baby's room.

Who are you again? hospital staff asked. *And where is this baby's mom?*

Mary had a feeling someone was about to call the police. As soon as she saw a chance, she made an excuse and bolted. Francisco Ariel was left to fight for his life, alone, as Mary boarded the next flight to Argentina.

Karina did likewise. After she was sent back to Mexico, she managed to reach Sergio, who told her that Mary would bring Francisco Ariel to Argentina. Karina returned once again to the airport, where Sergio had arranged yet another flight for her.

Somehow, Sergio was pulling it off: he'd secretly moved his entire clan from Mexico to Spain and now, despite all the chaos of pregnancies, cash smuggling, deceived parents, crisscrossing international flights, evidence destruction, and deportation, he was on the verge of sneaking them all into Brazil without losing a single follower.

His one big worry was whether Karina was going to freak out when she learned that Mary Boquitas had left her baby in a hospital six thousand miles away. When Sergio broke the news, he promised her that the Mexican authorities would take good care of her son and deliver him to her parents—even though no one in Karina's family or the Mexican consulate had any idea the baby even existed. Karina just nodded. Then she joined the rest of the clan as they embarked on the next leg of their journey.

Crossing the border from Argentina into Brazil was as trouble-free as Sergio had hoped. But cash, as always, was tight. Once they arrived in São Paulo, Sergio picked up where he'd left off in Spain by fanning the girls out as his spare-change collection team, sending them off to sell sandwiches on the beach and beg outside supermarkets, relying on Gloria—his multimillionaire megastar—to take point as scrounger-in-chief.

He also resumed his strategy of keeping the girls in constant motion, moving them from house to house and city to city, packing up and disappearing whenever he suspected the new neighbors might be getting a little curious about the middle-aged Mexican man next door who was always surrounded by ten silent women, two of them very young and very pregnant.

Cramming all eleven of them together wasn't so bad—at first. Sergio was extraordinarily resourceful when it came to sniffing out short-term, cash-only, no-questions-asked accommodations. In São Paulo, he found a vacant house in a dying suburb surrounded by lots of helpfully overgrown bushes. According to Karina, it was bleak and cold and so echoey it seemed haunted, but she and the rest of the clan loved it. After more than a year on the run, they'd become used to the harshness of urban camping, and even though this old dump was empty except for mattresses jammed side by side on the bedroom floors, it was a relief after months spent bouncing between small apartments and tiny vacation rentals in Spain and Argentina.

But that little luxury didn't last for long. Soon, Sergio got anxious again and headed for Rio de Janeiro, where he settled for a two-bedroom apartment in a walk-up building. Space was so tight, Karina would recall, that at night the girls had to pick one sleeping position and stick with it because there wasn't enough room to roll over. Karina slept with Marlene, Liliana, Mary Boquitas, and two of the de la Cuesta sisters. Gloria and Sergio shared the smaller bedroom with Sonia Ríos, while Wendy Castelo and the youngest de la Cuesta bunked out in the kitchenette.

Living on top of each other caused the girls to squabble like never before, to the point where even the most docile began to rebel. One night, mom-to-be Karla de la Cuesta stormed out of the house and vanished into the streets. Sergio and the other girls searched the city night after night, staking out the airport and the entrance to the Mexican embassy. Finally, after three scary days, Liliana finally spotted her. Sergio immediately pulled her into a bedroom and closed the door. After they came out, the incident was never mentioned again. The other girls never did find out where she'd been.

A few weeks later, it was Karola's turn; after she'd been screamed at by Sergio, the teenager climbed out the apartment window and startled the neighbors by climbing into the unit next door. The neighbors called the police, but before they arrived, Sergio hustled the rest of the girls off to a shopping mall in the care of Mary Boquitas, while he and Gloria cowered in the back bedroom and waited for the police to stop pounding on the door. Karola apparently had a change of heart, because she refused to file a complaint or even tell the police who she was living with. Apparently assuming she was a pouty teenager in a spat with her parents, the officers shrugged and left. A repentant Karola softly called through the door until Sergio let her back in.

But he sure as hell wasn't going to hang around that apartment. Sergio ordered the girls to pack and checked them into a hotel across town, but they'd no sooner arrived than Marlene disappeared. A day later, she walked into a police station and said she'd like an airline ticket back to Mexico, please. After being told she'd have to pay for it herself, Marlene said never mind and returned to the hotel.

Marlene's timing was off by a few days. If she'd waited a little longer before approaching the police, she'd have gotten a much different reception. Later that week, a bombshell announcement in Mexico City would spark banner headlines across Latin America:

Superstar Gloria Trevi and her manager, famed impresario Sergio Andrade, were wanted on suspicion of rape, kidnapping, and corruption of minors.

The manhunt had begun.

40

"I NEVER THOUGHT I'D BE HIDING A CORPSE"

Karina Yapor's parents were frightened but firm:

There's no way that baby is Karina's.

During two months of phone calls from the Mexican consulate in Spain in the autumn of 1998, they insisted over and over there must be some mistake. They refused to believe that their daughter—whom they'd just seen a few weeks ago!—had birthed a baby at age thirteen and abandoned it somewhere in Madrid.

Señores, the Mexican consul replied. We have your daughter's travel visa. You yourself say she's here in Madrid. Do you think this is some kind of coincidence? Who else could have possibly checked a baby into the hospital under her name?

You must have the wrong Karina, Miguel argued. Or the wrong Yapors. As soon as Karina calls home, this will all be cleared up.

But October passed into November with no word from Karina—no more smiling snapshots from Spanish monuments, no more rambling, hand-scrawled letters about the meaning of life. Just silence, and an increasing dread in the Yapor household that something was seriously wrong. And then, shortly before Christmas, all doubts were settled when a contingent from the Mexican consulate arrived at the Yapors' front door bearing hospital records, a birth certificate, and a grandson.

But if this was Karina's child, what had happened to Karina? Where was she? *Was she even alive?*

Miguel Yapor was desperate for answers but frozen by fear. To him, the most terrifying thing in the world was a policeman in uniform. He'd lived through the Mexican Dirty War of the 1960s, when the police ran roughshod over the country, gunning down hundreds of student protesters in cold blood and routinely beating, robbing, and "disappearing" the citizens they were supposed to protect. Anytime you walked into a police station, for any reason, you had to gulp hard and wonder if it was going to cost your dignity, your teeth, or your freedom.

But after Christmas and New Year's came and went with no sign of their missing daughter, the Yapors couldn't continue to sit and hope.

Miguel rolled into Chihuahua police headquarters in his wheelchair and filed a formal complaint, accusing Sergio and Gloria of rape, kidnapping, and corruption of minors. Karina's mother stood beside him, holding Karina's baby and an official report of child abandonment from the Mexican consulate in Madrid.

In response, Sergio's lawyer erupted in outrage.

Sergio, he told the police, was a selfless and courageous patron of the arts who had spent his own money to develop young musicians, even though he was in the middle of a personal fight against cancer. This smear is despicable! And Sergio won't take it lying down. He was on his way to Chihuahua at that very moment, along with Gloria and Karina, to put this nonsense to rest.

On the appointed day, police and reporters turned out in force at Chihuahua's airport. They watched as one plane after another arrived.

Sergio never appeared. Neither did Gloria or Karina.

This time, law enforcement was quick to spring into action. Mexican police reached out to Interpol, initiating an international search for Gloria, Sergio, and an undetermined number of young women from an unknown number of countries. Gloria was no longer a person of interest; she was now a suspect in a criminal case and a fugitive from international authorities.

The sudden escalation was mind-boggling. Just six months after she'd appeared on national TV—playful, scornful, and defiant—Gloria's smiling face was plastered on WANTED posters across the country, right next to a scowling Sergio. Police were instructed to take the suspects into immediate custody—

But once again, Sergio had vanished without a trace.

In their stifling apartment in Rio de Janeiro, Sergio was putting the second part of the Ronnie Biggs plan into action. Phase 1 was slipping into Brazil. Phase 2 was remaining there forever by parenting a Brazilian baby. Thanks to Sonia and Karla de la Cuesta, Sergio believed he was all set. But what about Gloria?

Easy. Gloria got pregnant, too.

She wouldn't be alone. Sergio's solution to the deportation problem apparently was to father children with every girl in the clan. Sonia was pregnant, and Gloria, and Karla de la Cuesta. When Karla suffered a miscarriage, Sergio impregnated her again, as well as her fifteen-year-old sister, Karola. Sergio lashed out at Karina, who'd recently turned fourteen and was struggling to conceive after giving birth a little more than a year earlier. "Sergio was punishing me," Karina would say, "and having sexual relations with me incessantly."

Soon, Sergio's children began arriving. First, Sonia had a

daughter, whom Sergio named Antonia. Then Karola de la Cuesta had a son, Milton, and her sister, Karla, had a daughter called Valentina. With ten women and three infants plus a fourth baby on the way, Sergio had to rent a second apartment. Gloria was ecstatic and claimed one corner for herself, decorating it as a nursery. In October 1999—one year after the clan went into hiding in Brazil—she gave birth to a daughter, Ana Dalai, named after the Dalai Lama.

As they had with Karina, all the clan women took turns caring for each other's babies. One night in November, Sergio and Gloria were having dinner in the tiny kitchenette when Katia de la Cuesta came in holding baby Ana. According to Karina, Katia was giggling and gesturing toward the silent baby. "Look how cute!" Katia said. "She's sleeping so quietly, it's like she's dead."

Gloria shrieked. As Karina would recount, Sergio grabbed a hysterical Gloria and held her back while Katia, finally realizing something was wrong, dropped to the floor and tried to revive Ana Dalai. Summoned by Gloria's screams, Liliana ran in and joined Katia on the floor over the unresponsive baby.

None of them knew infant CPR or mouth-to-mouth resuscitation. The two girls fumbled desperately, at one point even grabbing a can of Coca-Cola Lite from the fridge and splashing it on the baby's face in hopes of waking her up. Nothing worked. Finally, the girls sat back in defeat. Gloria dissolved into sobs. Sergio tried to quiet her while the rest of the girls gathered silently, looking down at the tiny corpse.

Karina, stunned and horrified, stood in the kitchenette while the older girls discussed what to do next. As Mary Boquitas would later recall, one of the girls said, "We should bring her to the hospital."

Sergio shot that down immediately. "Most of our tourist visas are expired," he said. "So no, obviously we can't call anyone. Besides, there's nothing to be done. Little Ana is already dead."

For the next two days, the dead infant remained in her bassinet. On the third evening, Mary says, Sergio sent Mary and Sonia Ríos out to buy candles. When they returned, Sergio placed the dead infant on one of the beds under a red blanket as the girls gathered and lit their candles.

Mary, say something, Sergio ordered. Mary stammered out a prayer, while Gloria knelt by the side of the bed with her hands clasped. As Mary finished, Gloria said, "Virgin Mary, I deliver her to you." She collapsed on the floor, screaming and covering her mouth with her hands so the neighbors wouldn't hear.

Sergio watched, nervously. Gloria suddenly looked up. *Sergio, she needs a Christian burial.*

Of course, of course, Sergio promised. That quieted Gloria long enough for Sergio to help her to bed, wait for her to sleep, and pull several of the girls aside into another room.

If you believe Mary, Sergio soon returned with a heavy bag knotted at the mouth. He handed it to two of the de la Cuesta sisters and whispered, Bury this in the park by the river.

"I never touched the bag or looked inside," Mary would later swear. "The girls left, and that's the last I heard of it." She said the de la Cuesta sisters told her they were terrified of walking through the streets of Rio with a dead baby in a bag, so as soon as they got near the river, they threw it in and ran back to the apartment.

If you believe Karina Yapor, on the other hand, it was Mary Boquitas who—as usual—took charge of the operation. Karina says Mary went into the kitchen and closed the door, saying she was going to prepare dinner. She ordered everyone else to stay out. Suspicious chopping sounds were heard, then Mary suddenly reappeared carrying a small suitcase. She left the apartment without a word.

While she was gone, the other girls cautiously entered the kitchen. The floor and counters were freshly bleached and mopped. But there was no hint anything had been cooked. And the body of Ana Dalai was gone.

After that, Gloria was a wreck. She wept and refused to eat, moaning to the girls that days before her baby's death, she'd had a nightmare about being punished by God for not baptizing her.

She might be right, Karina thought. "It did seem that God was punishing them," she'd later say.

To this day, the body of Ana Dalai has never been found.

Girls were fleeing, cops were knocking, an infant had died, Gloria was catatonic. Sergio knew he couldn't dodge these disasters forever. He needed a new strategy, one that didn't depend on remaining in hiding from the law. It was tricky, but he came up with a plan that he thought could work. To pull it off, he'd need the help of two allies who had always come through for him in the past:

The Yapors.

Miguel and Teresa were ecstatic to hear Karina's voice on the phone for the first time in nearly a year, but they hardened as soon as Karina began pleading for them to drop the criminal charges against Sergio and Gloria.

We won't even talk about it until you come home, Miguel said. Karina pleaded and cried. Her parents dissolved into tears as well but held their ground, especially because they had a feeling that Sergio was standing right behind Karina, directing everything she said. Karina's brother brought his baby nephew up to the phone, hoping the sound of Francisco Ariel's gurgling would lure Karina home.

"Just tell the police that Gloria and Sergio didn't do anything wrong and I'll fly right home," Karina promised. "The baby isn't even his! The father was my boyfriend in Spain." As much as they feared that this could be the last time they ever heard from Karina, Miguel and Teresa dug in their heels: Until they had Karina in their house, they would not talk about clearing Sergio.

After Karina hung up, Sergio considered the risk. Unlike Karola de la Cuesta, who had climbed out an apartment window while pregnant, Karina had never tried to run away. It would have been so easy for her to reveal everything to the doctors when she was giving birth in Madrid, or simply tell the deportation authorities in Madrid to fly her back to Chihuahua instead of Mexico City. But Karina had apparently become as indoctrinated and obedient as Mary Boquitas.

So ten days before Christmas 1999, less than one month after witnessing the death and disposal of Gloria's baby, Karina boarded a flight for home alongside Marlene Calderón, one of Sergio's most trusted lieutenants. On the plane, the two girls rehearsed the stories Sergio had given them: Karina and Marlene were now studying South American music, and once they added those rhythms to everything they'd learned at the Manuel de Falla Academy, Sergio would be ready to launch their careers and make them rich.

As for the baby . . . *Well*, she was supposed to say, *I was young and made a mistake. I thought the hospital would put him into a good, loving home. Sergio had NOTHING to do with it, in fact he was quite upset with me for sneaking out to date when I should have been focused on my art. I took advantage while he was distracted by his treatment for cancer.*

Karina was then supposed to double down on her parents'

trust: *So if you could just care for him a little bit longer, just till I launch my solo career . . .*

Sergio coached Karina not to say where she was calling from, or even when her plane was landing, nothing that could be used to reveal his location. Karina and Marlene were supposed to fly into Mexico City, then transfer to a local flight to Chihuahua so no one would know where they were arriving from, and then call her parents from the airport. Sergio was going to mask Karina's identity by booking her ticket in Liliana's name and giving her Liliana's passport, but just in time he realized that could get Karina arrested. The last thing he wanted was a frightened young woman being offered a plea deal to give him up.

But the Yapors were done playing by Sergio's rules. They notified the police that Karina was on her way, and all incoming flights had their passenger rosters checked. Soon after the two girls landed, nineteen-year-old Marlene was arrested for kidnapping and led off the plane in handcuffs. The press had also been alerted, and a mob of TV cameras were waiting for Karina when she arrived home with her parents.

Karina stepped out of the car. Instead of covering her head and running inside, she stopped and faced the reporters. By now, she had spent nearly every day of the past few years living side by side with one of the greatest entertainers Mexico had ever known. Karina looked small and frail amid the crush of reporters, but she looked calmly into the cameras and did exactly what Gloria would do:

She lied.

"Mr. Sergio Andrade and Gloria Trevi are wonderful people who have never harmed me in the slightest," Karina stated. "This is all an outrage against two very fine people. I was never raped, I was never kidnapped. I have nothing but respect for Mr. Sergio Andrade."

Despite her attempt to cover for Sergio and Gloria, Karina accidentally gave them away. As soon as investigators discovered that Karina was flying into Chihuahua from Mexico City, they swiftly collected flight manifests for all other airliners arriving in the capital that day. For a long time, they'd suspected Sergio was holed up in Central America, most likely in some remote corner of Guatemala, Panama, or El Salvador. But by tracing Karina's arrival, they knew she must have at least passed through Brazil.

In Rio, investigators discovered Sergio had dropped an even bigger clue to his whereabouts. Karina's deportation from Spain had taught him the dangers of letting a tourist visa expire, so to avoid another catastrophe like that, Sergio had taken pains to renew his and Gloria's documents. He'd listed an old address in Copacabana as their residence, and in an attempt to hide in plain sight, he'd used their full names, thinking that Brazilian police wouldn't make the connection to the more commonly used shorter versions.

And for more than a month, it worked. Until that January morning in 2000, when a sharp-eyed policeman in Rio noticed something a little bit . . . *off* . . . about two women in floppy hats and sunglasses lingering outside a supermarket. He approached them, demanded ID, then followed them back to a darkened apartment—

Where Sergio, at last, emerged from the shadows.

41

THE ACCIDENTAL SNITCH

Karina was horrified to discover that she was the one who had accidentally led police to Sergio and Gloria's hideout in Brazil. Sergio's big gamble of sending Karina home with Marlene Calderón to pacify Karina's parents had blown up in his face. Marlene was arrested and sent to Chihuahua State Prison, while Karina's attempts to defend Sergio only made her sound more like a cult member.

"My parents are pressuring me to testify what they want," she wept. "I feel like a prisoner."

Until Karina's return, no one had thought to connect Sergio with Ronnie Biggs. But once the clan was located in that squalid little apartment in Rio de Janeiro, Sergio's plan seemed unmistakable. Before he was taken into custody, Sergio had fathered children in Brazil with Gloria, Sonia, and two of the de la Cuesta sisters. After Marlene was behind bars, she discovered she was pregnant, too. If Ana Dalai hadn't died and Marlene hadn't been detained, Sergio could have fought his extradition on the basis of five different children.

Brazil, however, was having none of it. Because all of the girls were minors, Brazil swiftly declared them wards of the state of Mexico and sent them home for their own country to deal with. Upon arrival, the two youngest de la Cuesta sisters were allowed to go home with their babies. Their older sister, Katia, was locked up alongside Marlene. When they were brought up for formal charging, the judge took pity and said that because they were young and very possibly the victims of coercion, they could go free right away—if they were willing to come clean and testify against Sergio and Gloria.

Both girls refused. "I never saw any abnormal behavior on the part of Sergio, Gloria, or any member of the group," Katia de la Cuesta insisted, before she and Marlene returned to their cells.

Back in Brazil, only Sergio, Gloria, and Mary Boquitas remained.

Now that Gloria and Sergio were no longer underground and could access their bank accounts, they could afford to hire teams of lawyers in Mexico and Brazil and settle in for a long extradition fight. Brazilian courts denied them bail, which meant the trio would have to wage their battle from behind the walls of a nightmarish federal prison. But even that was better than facing the charges that awaited them back home.

Confidentially, prosecutors in Mexico told me they were okay with the delay. Their case depended on testimony from the clan . . . and at that moment, no one in the clan was talking. But they knew that when it came to mental coercion, time and distance were on their side. The farther away the victims are from their leader, and the more time that passes, the weaker the leader's hold. With Sergio in Brazil and the clan girls in Chihuahua, they were no longer being isolated, punished, starved, beaten, and lectured for hours about the "path of a true artist." For the first time in years, they could think for themselves and see that none of Sergio's promises about fame and wealth had ever come true—for any of them.

Instead, they were impoverished, humiliated, and left caring for Sergio's babies—while Sergio himself remained devoted only to Gloria and Mary Boquitas.

And so, bit by bit, clan secrecy began to crumble. It was the girls who'd left on their own who came forward first to offer testimony. A young beauty pageant winner from Chiapas named Guadalupe Carrasco told prosecutors she'd been recruited by a young woman who promised her a part on Gloria's TV show and then was sexually assaulted by Sergio while the other girls watched. At least seventeen young women were part of the clan, Guadalupe said. Tamara Zúñiga went to police in Chile and described Sergio ripping her clothes off and lashing her with an electrical cord. Gloria's cousin spoke to police in Texas and with Pati Chapoy for TV Azteca.

But the biggest breakthrough was Karina Yapor. In 2001, after months of living at home and seeing a psychologist, Karina finally changed her story and agreed to testify against Sergio, Gloria, and Mary. Her testimony before a fact-finding judge in Chihuahua went on for two full days and detailed years of torture, sexual violence, and mental abuse. Karina also admitted for the first time that Sergio was the father of her baby.

Now, Mexican prosecutors were ready to bring Sergio and Gloria home. They had all the testimony they needed, and their extradition case was strong. Sergio's plea for asylum on the grounds that he was being "politically persecuted" had been denied, and he no longer had any children on Brazilian soil. There was nothing that could stop him from being sent home to face his fate.

And that's when Gloria revealed her miraculous pregnancy.

42

SHUT YOUR MOUTH. WATCH HER EYES.

Whatever Gloria was thinking, she kept it to herself.

Up until the moment I stood outside the door of her jail-house hospital room, Gloria hadn't breathed a word to anyone about how she'd mysteriously gotten pregnant in an all-female ward of a maximum security prison after being incarcerated for two years. Her immaculate conception was as baffling as her endgame: Where was she going with this? What did she hope to gain by refusing to name the father?

Geraldo Magela, her attorney, claimed that Gloria was afraid for her life. The Brazilian corrections system was hiding dark secrets, he suggested, and Gloria wouldn't be safe if she gave even a hint of turning whistleblower. But that didn't make much sense: so many wild rumors were already flying around that nothing Gloria could say would shock anyone anymore.

Including me. I didn't quite believe that Gloria had been waiting all this time for me to show up so she could finally reveal the truth, but at least I could ask tough questions and test her honesty. I'd interviewed a lot of great liars over the years—among them a pair of Mafia bosses, a saintly hometown doctor accused of secretly altering a drug kingpin's fingerprints, and a guerrilla chieftain in Africa who'd stared me dead in the eyes, pressed my hand against his heart, and swore on his mother's soul to be utterly frank with me before unleashing a torrent of absolute bullshit. If I'd learned anything as a journalist from dealing with con artists, it was this: the second you hope for an outcome, you're toast. The only way to keep your mental lie detector in tune is by doubting everything and wishing for nothing. That's true if you receive an investment opportunity from a "deposed Nigerian prince," or an invitation from a music producer promising to turn your tween daughter with zero musical experience into a rock star, or a chance to interview a glamorous international fugitive with a secret everyone was dying to hear. If even a little part of you is hoping the tale you're told is true, your own mind becomes the con artist's accomplice, betraying you by stepping up to unconsciously fill in the gaps in their phony story.

"You don't care if she's guilty, innocent, or nuts," I reminded myself. "You're here to shut your mouth and watch her eyes."

And with that, the guard opened the door and I entered Gloria's world.

We got off to a rough start when I questioned Gloria about her real age. She responded with some nonsense about a birth record mix-up, and her eyes flared when she saw on my face that I didn't buy it.

But we got past that, and before long we were prattling away like a couple of besties in a bar. Gloria was curious about where I'd learned Spanish and poked fun at my Madrid accent ("*Muy soberbio.*" She smiled. "Very snooty").

For my part, I was genuinely intrigued by her writing. It's easy to forget that behind all the showmanship and scandal is a creative artist with serious chops. Gloria left school at age thirteen, just three years after most kids stop believing in

Santa Claus (true fact, look it up), and—on the strength of her own skill and innovation—skyrocketed from a street beggar into a superstar. And no matter how often critics referred to her as the Latest Sergio Andrade Creation, none of it would have happened without those notebooks she'd scrawled full of song lyrics. Behind the scenes, Gloria was figuring out for herself how to craft a hook, build a melody, and weave a story arc into a hit song, and she mastered it better than any other Latin artist of her generation.

Gloria's eyes lit up as soon as I mentioned songwriting. She launched into a re-enactment of all the long nights and many, many drafts it took her to finally get a handle on "Today, I'm Not Going to Scream" ("Hoy No Voy a Gritar"). Reliving that part of her past got her so worked up she couldn't sit still.

"Oh my god, I've been stuck on this thing for a week," she groaned, swinging her legs over the side of her hospital bed and feeling with her feet for the step stool.

"Are you supposed to—?" I asked, glancing at the very pregnant belly of a surprisingly small person.

"Ha!" She laughed and gave me a big wink. It took a beat before I got it. *C'mon, man,* her wink said. *If I did what I was supposed to, I wouldn't be Gloria Trevi.* Or, I thought to myself, in prison.

Gloria toddled over to her second-floor window and cracked the curtains. Down below, the news cameras that had been staking out the hospital 24/7 were still trained on her window. She gave the little crowd of onlookers a wave, sparking a scramble of yells and finger-pointing. Gloria left the curtains parted as she began dragging a steel straight-backed chair out of the corner.

Before I could get up to help her, one of the guards came running, alerted by the faint screech on the hard tile floor.

"*Oi, menina, o que estás fazendo?*" one of the officers asked in Portuguese. "Girl, what are you doing?"

"*Não é nada*," Gloria answered. "I've got it, it's nothing."

The guard took the chair from her anyway. He scanned the room, then selected a nice spot under a beam of afternoon sun.

"How's this?" he asked.

"Perfect," Gloria replied.

The officer held the back of the chair politely while Gloria settled herself. She threw back her hair, then changed her mind and fanned it forward across her chest. Hair, lighting, makeup—perfect.

"Thank you for coming to my aid," she told the guard. He grinned and returned to his post outside the door.

The guard's sudden appearance, however, reminded me that he could return at any second to boot me out of the room. Time to bear down. "You've spent as many years with Sergio Andrade as you have with your own family—" I began.

"Have you met him?" she interrupted.

"I'm trying. The prison has him in lockdown until all of this—" I refrained from pointing at her belly "—is resolved."

"Sergio was a very demanding producer, but they have misinterpreted that brutally," she said, all the conviviality and playfulness draining from her voice. "They have converted him into a kind of hypnotizer. Him into a hypnotizer, and me into some dumb cow. It's all so *false*. Anything I did, I did because I wanted to. That was the price to be great. Ever since I was seven years old I wanted to be great. I knew what I had to do."

"But at thirteen, fourteen years old, is anyone mature enough to make a choice like that? That's the reason—"

Gloria cut me off. "Not just when I was younger," she said. "Once, at a concert in Chihuahua, I was singing 'Los Borregos' ['The Lambs'], and because I was dancing so much, my voice started to give out." Thinking fast, Gloria managed to hide her cracking voice by pointing the mic toward the crowd and having them chant back the chorus. "When I came offstage everyone was shouting 'Bravo! Bravo! You are la máxima!'" Gloria recalled.

Everyone except Sergio.

"He looked at me and shook his head," Gloria recalled. "He said, 'It's shameless, to be the highest-paid female performer in Latin America and have your voice go out during a song about lambs.' I thought he couldn't tell. But he knew."

The next morning, Sergio woke her at dawn and told her to put on sneakers. He took her down to the Chihuahua cathedral, which is surrounded by a public square at least a quarter-mile long.

"Now run," Sergio ordered her.

And Gloria ran—around and around the cathedral, while early morning churchgoers nudged each other and stared as Mexico's biggest star, the uncontrollable wild child, sweated and grimaced as her heavyset manager leaned silently against a wall with his arms folded across his chest. He made her run twenty laps, the equivalent of five miles, before allowing her to stop.

"People were watching me, and they were all whispering 'What an inhuman man, making Gloria Trevi run like that,'" Gloria said. "But I obeyed because I knew it would make me a better artist."

As she finished the story, Gloria dropped back in her chair with a small, expectant smile, as if to say *See? That's how it's done.*

But I was more bewildered than ever. Gloria was in the midst of the fight of her life—the fight *for* her life—and about to go into labor in a prison hospital. If there was ever a time to be self-centered, this was it. Her attorneys told me that Gloria actually had a chance at winning humanitarian asylum and could walk out of prison a free and still-wealthy woman, her baby in her arms—*if* she could persuade the courts she was Sergio's first and longest-suffering victim.

So why was she defending him instead?

"I've talked to Karina Yapor's parents," I said, "and lots of other people who accuse you and Sergio of really shocking abuse."

"It's all false," Gloria said. Her voice trembled and tears came to her eyes. "Not a gram of truth." The scandalous claims, she said, were nothing more than a conspiracy by television-industry enemies and a gold rush by "girls who make book deals, and tell five versions of the same story, and appear on television with long nails and jewelry and new clothes, and can suddenly pay off their houses.

"I'm sorry," Gloria fumed, "but I know that a person who has been abused doesn't go and tell her story in front of the cameras like that, with a lack of shame."

But if she tried to prove that in a Mexican court, Gloria claimed, her life would be in danger. She had left Mexico not as a fugitive, she explained, but as an insider with dangerous information about the entertainment industry. Network executives and their political cronies knew she would expose their corruption, she said, so they had initiated this smear campaign.

"Do you know what would happen to me if I went back to Mexico?" she asked. "Activists are killed in Mexico. That's why I hang on here with my fingernails. If I go back and speak up, I could be found dead in my cell, and what would they say? *She committed suicide.* Who would investigate it? Who would report on it? Nobody, because those are the same people who fear what I have to say."

Gloria, however, never said anything about corruption or conspiracies until after her arrest. And if she were truly in danger, why had she taken five teenagers on the run with her? Possible corruption in the entertainment world also does not explain Sergio's repeated problems with adolescent girls. Well, Gloria said, that's really a matter of context. "In the United States, a minor is a minor, and that's a crime," she offered. "In Mexico, if the minor is over twelve or fourteen, it's not a violation, and you can't say anything."

But no matter how much she pretzeled her logic to defend Sergio in public, I had a feeling something very different was going on behind closed doors. From what I could tell, Gloria was working on a scheme to leave Sergio behind. Somehow, she was poised to succeed where El Maestro had failed: she'd found a way to pull off the Ronnie Biggs escape plot.

How she'd done it was still a mystery. And I better not ask, I was told. Her pregnancy was such a powder keg, Gloria's lawyer said, that if I brought it up, she would kick me right out of the room. I'd seen for myself the way the police tried to raid the prison hospital and force Gloria to surrender some of her amniotic fluid. With her baby due any day, Gloria was extremely on edge.

"If I were you," Geraldo warned, "I'd leave it alone."

When Gloria's pregnancy was first revealed, all eyes were immediately on Fernandinho Beira Mar, Brazil's biggest drug trafficker and a fervent womanizer. Fernandinho had been captured in a raid right around the time Gloria was apprehended, and both were in the same prison in Brasilia. They were in separate, gender-specific cellblocks, but for the drug lord that was laughable. Fernandinho was fabulously wealthy and rumored to pay such lavish bribes that the guards ran errands for him and allowed him to roam where he pleased. If Gloria had agreed, he could have arranged an overnight anytime he pleased. But the theories surrounding Gloria's mysterious prison pregnancy didn't stop there.

The police launched an investigation and returned with another possibility: they insisted that Gloria had impregnated herself with the sperm of Marcelo Borelli, a ruthless Brazilian gangster. According to the police report, Gloria chose Borelli because he was marked for death, sure to be shanked in prison for having tortured and raped a rival's three-year-old daughter. With Borelli out of the way, Gloria's child would get all the benefits of a Brazilian father with none of the drawbacks: Gloria would never have to worry about an ex-con turning up as a free man and pressing a claim on the family fortune.

According to investigators, Borelli would masturbate into plastic sandwich bags; seal them; then submerge the bags in glasses of warm milk and pass them along to prison guards who were in on the plot. (The milk was supposed to preserve the semen by keeping it roughly at body temperature.) Gloria would then inseminate herself with a syringe constructed from a ballpoint pen. When an enterprising journalist sought to debunk this account by interviewing the gangster in a prisoner visitation room, he was astonished when Borelli confirmed it. Borelli told *ISTOÉ*, a respected Brazilian newsmagazine, that he'd sent Trevi at least five bags of sperm.

"Gloria has an interest in remaining in Brazil and not being deported to Mexico," concluded Francisco de Assiz Guimaraes, the chief investigator. "A Brazilian child would help her."

Gloria's lawyers went ballistic. They denied the gangster sperm story and insisted that prison guards raped Gloria and then hoped to cover it up by killing her and Borelli. As proof, they noted that Borelli was beaten nearly to death by his fellow prisoners one night when his cell was inexplicably left unlocked. The day Borelli returned from the hospital, a burning mattress was stuffed inside his cell, starting a fire that severely burned him and, according to Trevi's lawyers, filled the nearby women's cells with choking smoke.

"There are people in that prison who have something to hide," Geraldo Magela thundered. "They don't care if they have to burn the prison down to hide it."

Even the Brazilian government admits that someone screwed up, badly. "There was obviously a failure in police procedures, and now it will be much more complicated to extradite her," said Djalma Nascimento Jr., a Justice Ministry spokesman. "The child will be a Brazilian citizen and therefore cannot be extradited. And it is difficult to imagine extraditing the parent without her child."

When I had arrived at Gloria's door, I had half expected the interview to be a waste of time. Gloria was a public relations genius. She could wrap the toughest reporters around her finger and make every single person in a 40,000-seat arena think she was singing directly to them. I was pretty sure I'd be up against one of two Glorias: either stone-cold silent or shamelessly lying.

But now, after two hours of listening to her talk, I realized I'd met a third Gloria: the one who had lived so long with Sergio that she no longer realized how strange and cruel he really was. There's a famous quote from *The Usual Suspects*: "The greatest trick the devil ever pulled was convincing the world he did not exist." But maybe the devil's greatest trick is convincing himself he's not the devil.

The more time I spent with her, the more I felt that Gloria's lawyers had a case. Gloria really was the first of Sergio's disciples, so probably the most deeply conditioned. Sergio had years to root around inside Gloria's head, tinkering like a software codewriter as he reprogrammed her thinking to accept everything he did as an act of the one true god: *El gran maestro*, Sergio Andrade. Was she even capable of telling the difference between acceptable discipline and pure cruelty anymore? And that was the heart of Geraldo Magela's argument: Gloria wasn't really responsible for what went on inside the clan. Her mind was so messed up, she didn't know any better. Yes, Gloria was smart enough to keep her mouth shut about rape, torture, and beatings, but behind her eyes, I wondered if she'd long ago forgotten what evil really is.

This whole reverie felt a little too pro-Gloria. I snapped myself out of it by plunging into the Forbidden Zone. "Who is the father of your child?" I asked.

Gloria didn't blow up. She didn't seem upset or rattled. She gazed at me silently and a little sadly.

"A lot of people are getting into a lot of trouble over this," I insisted. "If they're innocent, shouldn't you say so?"

Gloria leaned forward and put her hand on my arm. Her voice was a husky, confidential whisper. "Sometimes God writes straightforward in twisted lines," she said. Her eyes welled. She smiled as she wiped away her tears. "This baby I am expecting is Scripture directly from heaven. Do you understand?"

Nope. I didn't have a clue but nodded anyway, her hand still on my arm.

"That is why I'm naming my baby Ángel Gabriel," Gloria said, caressing her belly with her other hand. "So God will give him wings to fly away from all these troubles."

To this day, I have no idea what I said in response, although I have a vague memory of muttering something supportive and reassuring. I mean, c'mon! The woman is about to give birth behind bars! All alone, without her beloved mother by her side or even the baby's father, whoever that was. You'd be a monster not to feel some compassion, right?

It was getting dark, and Gloria—my new friend I was seeing through new eyes—was feeling tired.

"Before you go, can you do me a favor?" she asked. "I've written a new song and I have no one to play it to. Would you mind telling me what you think?"

Would I mind, in other words, getting a private serenade of an original work by one of Latin America's greatest stars? Gloria gestured toward a guitar in the corner near her bed. I fetched it and she began to strum, softly and expertly. She started to sing, her voice low and surprisingly beautiful, nothing like the banshee yowl on most of her records.

I want to take the mountains from your shoulders, she sang.

> *And give you rest.*
> *Because there's no one like you,*
> *There's no one . . . like you.*

Applause broke out behind us. The two police officers had pulled open the door and let pregnant prison moms gather from other rooms. Gloria's eyes filled with tears again.

"From my heart to all of yours," she said.

The moms had to return to their rooms so I left with them. Gloria pressed her fingers to her lips and blew us all a kiss goodbye.

43

BREAKING INTO PRISON. AGAIN.

There's a heist film about stage magicians called *Now You See Me* that opens like this:

Come in close.
Closer.
Because the more you think you see—
The easier it will be to fool you.

That's how I felt as the spell began to wear off after I left Gloria's room. When I'd arrived that morning, I had no doubt she was guilty. I'd spent the past year researching her case, learning everything I could from everyone I could find. I'd heard so many horrifying stories from so many believable victims and firsthand witnesses that by the time I got to the prison, I was convinced of two things: Gloria had a lot to answer for, and there was no way she could talk her way out of it.

Three hours later, I was being escorted by two guards back toward the prison gate and thinking, *That poor woman! If people could only see what she's really like and hear her side of the story . . .*

Wait, what? My own words sounded so strange inside my

head that they jerked me back to reality. So, what was I saying here—that I was prepared to push aside all the witness statements and criminal complaints I'd gathered for the past year because of—what, exactly? What news had I uncovered? What exonerating information had Gloria shared?

Zero.

Gloria had sung Sergio's praises and said something about angels, and in between had trash-talked a bunch of defenseless teenagers. That was it. And on the strength of that alone, I was suddenly questioning hard facts and my own judgment? What had just happened?

While all this was running through my mind, I was buzzed out through three sets of metal doors and found myself on an empty street on the outskirts of Brasilia. I stood there, lost in thought, as it all began to make sense: *Wow. So that's how it's done.* That's how you get millions of strangers to think they know you personally. That's how you get a lone fan high up in the nosebleed section of a 20,000-seat auditorium to feel like that love song you're crooning is meant for him. And that's how you pull off not one but two astonishing switcheroos.

One thing I'd always wondered about Gloria was how, in a stunningly short amount of time, she'd transformed from a panhandler begging for change on the street into a multimillionaire pop star. You can't chalk it up strictly to her talent, charm, access, or beauty because Latin America is bursting with finer singers, sharper songwriters, better-known names, and equally lovely performers. Yet Gloria blew past them all, rising above thousands and thousands of rivals to reign at the top for years. How had she pulled it off? To me, her astonishing rise was as baffling as whatever reinvention she was trying to pull off now in Brazil with this bizarre secretive pregnancy.

But out there on the sidewalk, it all started to click into place.

Gloria's greatest talent wasn't convincing me she was innocent. It was convincing herself. Sitting across from her, I wasn't watching a performance; I was watching an outpouring of anguish from someone who believed she deserved all the good things that came her way and none of the bad. She reminded me of the piercing insight a reporter once had about American politics: after deep diving into the psychology of all the candidates for president in one election cycle, he realized that it takes such a monstrously oversized ego to believe you're qualified to become the most powerful person on earth that anyone who runs for that office probably shouldn't be allowed to hold it.

Same with Gloria. Her one great super talent was a burning belief in herself, her own worthiness. She could lie to your face with self-righteous tears on her cheeks, and put her bare feet up on your desk, and go onstage in her panties years before anyone else dared to follow, and share her deeply personal songs and cringingly childlike drawings and argue with her grandmother in public . . .

Because she doesn't care what you think of her.

Gloria is truly, deeply, madly in love with Gloria, and she'll fight to the death for the one she adores most. That kind of self-worship is both enormously empowering and irresistibly attractive. It armors Gloria against any humiliation, letting her act out like a maniac on national TV and run punishment laps in front of Sunday-morning churchgoers, while at the same time granting her an absolutely magnetic self-confidence. It draws you closer, and when you see her quirks and silliness and the tattered boots she's wearing that she borrowed from a backup singer, you feel like she's dropping her guard and letting you in. You become a fan because you think you're experiencing the real Gloria, the raw Gloria.

You've gotten so close, you're easy to fool.

Two days after our interview, on February 18, 2002, Gloria gave birth to a son. By the following morning, Brazilian police had solved the mystery of her pregnancy once and for all. It turns out prison guards actually were involved. By seizing DNA material from the delivery room, investigators were able to prove, without a doubt, that the father of Gloria's child wasn't the drug lord, the gang leader, or any of the prison staff.

It was Sergio Andrade.

Working backward from these genetic tests, investigators reviewed security cameras and discovered that Gloria and Sergio had repeatedly been given access to an attorney-client privilege room without any attorneys to get in the way. Prison staffers had been bribed to look aside, essentially giving Sergio and Gloria their own No-Tell Motel in the heart of a maximum-security penitentiary.

The news hit like a bombshell. Technically, this now meant that Sergio and Gloria were *both* the parents of a Brazilian child, giving them a legal loophole to avoid extradition for criminal trial in Mexico. But if they thought that Ángel Gabriel would turn them into the next Ronnie Biggs, freeing them from prison and turning them into popular heroes, they were in for a letdown.

Unlike the Great Train Robber—and the Lantern and Pretty Mary before him—Gloria and Sergio had lost the battle of public opinion before it began. They weren't scrappy underdogs fighting for freedom with nothing but wits and courage. They were rich celebrities with rich people's lawyers. They weren't crushed by the system; they *were* the system, and they'd used it to take advantage of poor young women and gullible parents. Brazilians had watched this drama unfold for nearly two years, and they'd seen the way their fellow Brazilians who worked in the prisons had been scapegoated and manipulated.

Overnight, Gloria's public image plummeted. In the Brazilian press, she was no longer a brave victim fighting for her unborn baby. Now she was just another privileged pain in the ass—and the sooner she became Mexico's problem again, the better.

The Brazilian courts agreed. Not in so many words, but certainly in sentiment. Because of the Ronnie Biggs affair, the Brazilian government had tightened up its extradition policy. A new law was passed which declared that the parent of a Brazilian child could still be spared extradition—*but only at the mercy of the court*. And it didn't take a big legal brain like Geraldo Magela to realize that when it came to the mercy of the court, Gloria and Sergio were in big trouble.

Gloria didn't see it that way. Rather than accepting the hard DNA evidence, Gloria continued to fight back, even going so far as to double down on her prison-rape insinuations. She was the victim of human-rights abuse, Gloria claimed, and so was her infant son, who was forced to live with her in a filthy cell. She vowed she would never surrender in her battle for asylum because now she was fighting for her son as well. But Brazilian human-rights advocates weren't rallying to her cause, with one even suggesting Gloria was lucky that Brazilian prosecutors weren't charging her with abuse of a corpse or manslaughter for the death of Ana Dalai.

Mary Boquitas, on the other hand, was settling in peacefully to prison life. Years of acting as a drill sergeant for Sergio's teenage clan girls had turned her into a fitness instructor who knew how to command a room, so she began teaching dance and aerobics to her fellow prisoners. Her classes were so popular, they had to be switched to an outdoor space to accommodate the demand.

Sergio remained as silent as always. Until one day in April 2002, when a strange envelope appeared in my mailbox.

"Don't take this as a lack of modesty, but I consider myself one of the most talented musicians, composers, and producers in many years," Sergio Andrade wrote to me in a hand-printed letter from prison. "And that's something indisputable even among my enemies."

Sergio was locked away in virtual isolation in a small cell in the dreaded Papuda Correctional Facility, deep in the Brazilian interior, where he'd been ever since he was identified as the true father of Gloria's jailhouse baby. Papuda is so cut off from the rest of the world that when the cell door slams shut behind you, you can expect very few visitors to make the grueling trek to see you.

I'd tried to get in there several times to interview Sergio, but my request to the prison for journalist access was always denied. The only other option was to be put on the list of family members or legal counsel, but for very good reasons, Sergio's attorneys weren't going to lie on my behalf. But Sergio had a plan. "Wait for a phone call from a woman named Silvia," he told me in his letter.

Who the heck is Silvia? I wondered.

"I'm Sergio's fiancée," a merry voice told me over the phone a few days later. Silvia Beeg was a legal assistant who'd worked for one of Sergio's attorneys. Before she'd met Sergio in person, she was intrigued by phone calls she said she kept receiving from some of the clan girls, begging her to deliver messages of support to Sergio.

"Every day in the newspaper I'm reading statements from these little girls back in Mexico accusing him of the most terrible things. They're saying he beat them, starved them, forced them to eat shit off the floor—well, not shit, just his scraps and garbage. And then these same girls are calling me on the phone, crying, saying they can't live without him. I saw Liliana crying for Sergio, Karina crying for Sergio, Karla de la Cuesta crying for Sergio . . .

"Well, that naturally excited my woman's curiosity," Silvia continued. "I had to ask myself, What kind of man is this?"

During one of her jailhouse visits to get Sergio's signature on documents, Sergio told Silvia he'd fallen in love with her. Silvia immediately returned to the office, quit her job, and ever since has been Sergio's unofficial—and unpaid—personal assistant, living off her dwindling savings while running his errands. Because Silvia was now Sergio's fiancée, she said, she was also able to add an additional family name to the visitation rolls: me.

This felt like a really bad idea. Sergio was despised by the Brazilian justice department and under a microscope by the prison administration. Even if my name didn't send up any red flags, I was pretty sure no one would mistake me for the blood relative of a Brazilian paralegal or a Mexican pop mogul. That assessment was correct, Geraldo Magela agreed after I made my way back to Brasilia.

"*Maluco!*" he snorted. "You're nuts! You might be spending more time with Sergio than you bargained for with this scheme," he added, I hoped in jest. If I wanted to try, it was up to me, but he was staying out of this one.

Silvia drove me to the prison and guided me to the visitor check-in window, where she was greeted like an old friend. Silvia seemed so good-hearted that I felt a pang of guilt, wondering if I should let her know that there was already a fourth Mrs. Sergio Andrade in the form of a Mexican teenager currently raising one of Sergio's multiple newborns. I decided to wait and confront Sergio first. Meanwhile, Silvia had charmed the guards so thoroughly that they barely gave me a glance, and within minutes I was buzzed in, patted down, and shown to a meeting room.

"Ey, Chris!" a jubilant voice cried out as the door swung open.

I tried to reply, but no words came. I'd seen tons of photos of Sergio and heard so much about his power and anger, his domination and titanic presence, but nothing could prepare me for—

This? This is the guy everyone is afraid of? Standing between two glowering guards was a tiny, squishy-looking man who barely reached their chests. Sergio was no taller than the shortest of his clan girls, with a body so soft and bloated it seemed boneless. His teeth, bared in flashes as he spoke to the guards, looked jagged and dirty, and his jowly face bristled with stubble. With his thick, unruly hair, he reminded me of a stuffed werewolf toy I had as a kid.

"Sergio!" I finally mustered, reminding myself to get with the program and play along with the long-lost-cousins bit. "Good to see you."

For an extra touch, I stepped forward to hug him, but Sergio raised his arms apologetically: handcuffs. Still shackled, he took a seat while the guards stood post on either side of the door.

"I still have not figured out exactly what, why, and how all this has happened to me," Sergio began, launching right in without any small talk. "Yes, I knew there would be trouble. But I never thought it would be anything like this."

He dropped his eyes mournfully to the floor, then gazed up toward the window to the grim view beyond: a cement courtyard, a razor-wire fence, a gloomy gray sky. "No," he murmured, so quietly I could barely hear him. "Not even the half of this."

Maybe if I hadn't already seen a better version of this act from Gloria I might have wondered how much was real, but as it was, I didn't have time to wonder about his true feelings. I hadn't expected the guards to remain in the room with us, so I had a feeling that as soon as I began taking notes, they'd get suspicious and alert the warden. That might only leave me a tight window, so I got right to it.

"Sergio, you've been having sex with underage women for years," I said, as I slipped my notebook and pen out of my back pocket. "You impregnated"—I paused, realizing I'd lost track of all the clan women and their babies—"at least six teenage girls. What did you think was going to happen?"

I flipped open my notebook and got ready to write, but Sergio didn't say a word. When I glanced up, he was grinning.

"What man would resist?" he said, spreading his manacled hands like a martyred saint. "So many beautiful, talented young women who followed me wherever I went—can anyone blame me if accidents occurred? Believe me, I was trying to get away from the girls, but they followed me wherever I went."

"Followed you? You're a grown man " I began, but Sergio cut me off, lurching forward to the edge of his seat.

"The very notion that Sergio Andrade had ever raped or corrupted a minor is absolutely absurd and surreal," he blurted, with a wounded self-righteousness that ignored the fact that a second earlier he'd been leering like a frat boy. As I opened my mouth to challenge him, Sergio raised his voice and kept going, launching into a feverish monologue about how greedy stage parents were always taking advantage of his soft heart by shoving their daughters at him, maybe even lying about their age—how was he supposed to know, after all?—and of course, that just played into the hands of his enemies, not his enemies actually but more accurately his brother's—

I wrote rapidly to keep up, at the same time wondering what

kind of person cycles in less than five minutes from depression, to lechery, to defiance. Sergio stared at me, his eyes flashing and nearly unblinking, as he explained that all his troubles were really on account of his brother, Lalo, who'd stirred up a hornet's nest when he tried to torpedo the presidential candidacy of Vicente Fox. Lalo's scheme had failed and now Sergio was in the crosshairs of a vengeful Mexican president who was determined to ruin Lalo and everyone around him.

"I have proof," Sergio claimed. "I have letters, documents, photographs. I can prove what I'm saying is true! Don't let me be forgotten. I know the dimension of the people who have put us in this mess, the way they are, the power they handle. You know the political system there, the 'suicides' that occur in jail . . ."

Sergio abruptly paused, the sudden silence coming as a shock after twenty-some nonstop minutes of his voice filling the room like a car alarm. Sergio swiveled toward the guards and pointed to his belly. "*Chefe, posso?*" he said. "Boss, may I?"

The guard nodded. Sergio's hand disappeared beneath his prison denim shirt, digging around in the waistband of his jeans, and re-emerged with a thick pamphlet. I never really expected Sergio to produce all this proof he'd been talking about, let alone from inside his pants, but as he handed me the documents I realized my first instinct was right. This wasn't evidence of a government conspiracy. It was a collection of Sergio's erotic stories and poems.

I flipped through the pages, jumping from a poem called "I Am God" to a story titled "Private Caligula," which opened with "The following morning, they got up late. The girls who'd lost the striptease contest the night before got up a little earlier." Nearly all of the poems were dedicated to Sergio's clan and the babies he'd had with them.

Sergio was talking again, as urgently and breathlessly as before, this time about the inspiration for his poems, and his role as an artist behind bars to speak his truth, and and and . . .

Can Sergio tell from my face, I wondered, *how insane this all sounds?* Was he so full of himself that he didn't realize how strange it was for a middle-aged man to dedicate love poems to adolescent girls he'd lured from their parents and secretly impregnated in a foreign country? Was he so egotistical that he couldn't resist sharing these smutty reveries with someone—*even a reporter*?

I opened my mouth to warn him, then froze. Was it my place to warn him this booklet could be a death sentence? Because with extradition looming, Sergio could soon be on his way to Chihuahua's notoriously violent Aquiles Serdán prison, right in the hometown of many of the girls he was accused of abusing. It's a code of honor among convicts that children and vulnerable women are off-limits, so if word got out that Sergio had beaten and raped local teenagers, it wouldn't be long before his fellow inmates took jailhouse justice into their own hands.

But Sergio was envisioning a very different future for himself. Brazil, he said, would be crazy to let him go. After all, he's Mr. Midas! The genius with the golden touch who could turn poor, struggling performers into superstars. "I can't wait to see what kind of talent I can discover in the slums of Brazil," Sergio said, riding the edge of his chair, shaping the air with his cuffed hands to sculpt his points. "I can't wait to see how much joy we can bring into people's lives here!"

Behind him, the guards were shifting impatiently. Sergio had been going strong for nearly three hours, monologuing so insistently that I'd barely managed to squeeze in a handful of questions. I didn't mind, though, because watching the show was better than digging for answers. Just like Gloria, Sergio knew how to use his strengths when he was backed into a corner, and his ploy for me was the same as his legal defense:

Keep talking until something finally sticks.

The longer he delayed extradition, the better his chances that the furor in Mexico would fade and the Brazilian courts would decide to wash their hands of the mess and let him walk. Behind Sergio's bragging and bluster, he was deploying a strategy that just might work.

"I have to wait until passions cool down," he said, "and people can listen to me with calm hearts and open minds."

44

ALINE, UNSINKABLE

"Did Gloria mention the spankings?" Aline asks me.

"No."

"I didn't think so," Aline says. "I don't think she'll ever talk about it. To anyone."

When Aline and I met in the spring of 2003, Gloria was still in prison while Aline had become the twenty-seven-year-old host of a TV Azteca variety show. It was a massive evolution from her time as a frightened teenager sipping hot milk in her mother's kitchen after fleeing her middle-aged husband in the middle of the night, and I was impressed to see how well she handled it. Aline and I sat on a shady bench behind her soundstage, where moments earlier I'd watched as she conducted her show with bubbling joy, hugging her castmates and laughing so happily that she seemed to be having the time of her life. Aline was the same off-camera, too. She looks you in the eyes, listens carefully, and encourages your questions with a warm smile—

Which melts as soon as I ask about Adolfo Prieto Street.

Aline drops her eyes. She pauses a long time. When she

eventually answers, she keeps her eyes fixed on the ground, as if scenes from her past were flickering across the black asphalt.

"I trusted Gloria," Aline says quietly. "I thought she was my friend. She was big back then, as big as Shakira. And here she was, a superstar—the biggest star in the country!—spending time with a goofy little thirteen-year-old like me."

"And Sergio?" I ask. "Were you attracted to him in the beginning?"

"Not at all!" Aline says. "He was thirty-three, fat, and ugly, and I was thirteen. When I first met him, I thought he was rude, and unbearable, and pretentious. Attracted to him? Never!"

"So what happened? What changed?"

"I started to like him. I thought he was intelligent, fun, interesting, talented, sensitive. Sometimes he would talk to me about his pain as if he were a little child, very softly, and I would think, Oh, poor man, and feel sorry for him. He understands people very well and knows exactly how to make each person like him or fear him . . ."

Aline saw him do it over and over, but only with girls. Sergio did everything possible to avoid other men. "Very few men ever came into the studio, and when they did, we were forbidden to talk to them. Not even to say 'Good morning.' If any man came close to me, I had to step away and conceal myself. We obeyed him because we were afraid."

"Was it the same with the other girls?"

"As time went by, I grew and matured a little more. I think I was one of the rebels of the group. When he was hitting me, I always said, Why, Sergio? Why are you doing this? The others just curled up and said nothing."

"Can you explain something to me—" I begin, and instantly I see Aline tense up. She knows what's coming and isn't happy about it. "Can you explain why you stayed so long?" I ask.

Aline searches my face. Many times she's been asked this question, by her mother and judges and reporters, but no matter how many ways she tries to answer, she can always see in their eyes that this is the moment when they stop listening and start judging.

Aline resigns herself to try again. "Fear," she tells me. "Every day I wanted to leave, but I didn't have the courage to do it."

Aline knows how dubious this sounds. Back then, it wasn't as if she relied on Sergio for food or shelter; she wasn't in a domestic dependence situation with nowhere else to go and children to care for. Aline had a loving mother waiting by the phone to come get her anytime she wanted. True, Aline was starry-eyed but she wasn't blind; she'd hoped that Sergio would make her famous, but all she had to do was look around to realize that out of all the girls who'd come through his "star school," Gloria was the only one who'd ever made it big—and that was a long time before Aline showed up. Not even Mary Boquitas, the ultimate ride-or-die second-in-command, was ever rewarded for her years of service with anything more than a tambourine in Gloria's shadow.

So if Aline was free to go—and if Sergio really did begin whipping, starving, and humiliating her at age thirteen—why on earth did she marry him at fifteen? After Aline's mother locked her in the house and hid the key, why did Aline escape and return to a man who kept her a naked prisoner in his hotel bathroom?

"Fear," Aline said again. But digging into it this time, it started to make sense.

Aline was afraid of Sergio—but on a deeper level, she was more afraid of a life without him. Aline can't speak for the other girls; she can't say for sure what anxieties each of them might have had that Sergio could exploit. But in her case, it was Aline's terror of being left alone. Sergio showed up while

Aline was still processing her father's sudden death. That accident not only ripped away her father but her mother as well, because now Jossie had to leave Aline alone while she worked to support the two of them.

That's why once Sergio, in his own perverse way, became the daddy figure in her life, she was too paralyzed by emotional dependence to pull herself free. Her mind may have been yelling Run!—but her emotional core was whispering *Can you deal with the pain of losing your father again?*

Sergio was cruel. He was slovenly and demeaning and terrifyingly unpredictable—but he was there. Sergio both inflamed and comforted Aline's most destructive fears—the ones she could never run away from because they came from within.

"Was it like that for the girls you helped recruit?"

Aline swallows, hard. Tears spring to her eyes, and she looks away. For a long time we sit in silence, watching young actors and TV staffers hurry past on the sunny TV Azteca lot, laughing and chatting as they head for the outdoor cantina.

"Yes," Aline says, her voice a whisper. "Yes, and I feel horrible. I did the same thing to other girls that Gloria did to me. I think—"

She falters, tears trickling down her cheeks, and I suddenly realize that in all the months I've been researching this saga, I'm seeing something for the first time:

Remorse.

I spent hours talking to Gloria and Sergio, but never once did they ever express anything except scorn and disregard for all the teenagers who'd depended on them, who'd lived in poverty and secrecy and homesickness for years because of their trust in Sergio and Gloria, and were now dealing with humiliation, incarceration, and single motherhood. Sergio and Gloria both had a lot to say about all the evil people who were out to get them—everyone from Karina Yapor's crippled father to mysterious dark forces in the Mexican government—but I can't recall any time when they expressed even a pang of sympathy for anyone besides themselves.

Aline is coming to terms with that as well. Even when Gloria was an adult woman in her thirties, she was still dressing up and acting like the clan girls who were half her age, literally wearing their clothes. Gloria's Naughty Teenager cosplay played great with the public and fooled the girls around her as well, because despite everything Aline had been through, she still felt an ache of loss for the sister she thought she had.

"When I look back, I don't think Gloria ever really liked me at all. If she cared about anyone except Sergio, she would have saved me."

45

THE ARMANDO FACTOR

Suddenly, just before Ángel Gabriel's first Christmas in prison, the united front of Gloria, Sergio, and Mary Boquitas cracked.

After nearly three full years of vowing that she'd fight to the death to stay in Brazil on behalf of her infant son, Gloria abruptly reversed course and agreed to return voluntarily to Mexico. On December 21, 2003, she and Ángel Gabriel were marched onto a flight to Chihuahua, followed soon after by Mary Boquitas. Because they were such a flight risk, both were denied bail and locked up. Ángel Gabriel went home with Gloria's mother.

Sergio Andrade remained behind, alone.

Speculation swirled about what—or more precisely, "who"—had changed Gloria's mind. Some thought motherhood had rewired Gloria's heart, with her infant son replacing Sergio as the most important man in her life. For the first time since she was thirteen years old, Gloria had gone multiple months without El Maestro by her side. Prison authorities had clamped down and made sure Sergio had absolutely no access to Gloria's cellblock. Maybe separation had finally broken Sergio's grip on her.

Gloria, however, hinted at another cause. Soon after she arrived in Chihuahua, a local journalist scored the interview of a lifetime. A reporter on the cops beat for Mexico's *El Diario* was in the prison's family visitation room when Gloria appeared. During the brief lull before Gloria's mom arrived, the reporter was able to get Gloria alone.

"In Brazil, I was a weaker Gloria," the singer said. "My eyes are not the same anymore. And why? Because God has given me proof of his love."

The reporter ignored the divine-intervention feint and bore down on the real story. "You say you've grown," she asked. "So how do you now feel about Sergio Andrade?"

Gloria paused. "What I feel," she said, "is what I'd feel for anyone in his situation."

"*Anyone?* You've said he's the one person you truly love. And now you're saying he's the same as anyone else?"

"Look," Gloria replied. "For starters, Sergio is in Brazil. He's not here. He's living his life. He has his fiancée, he has his wife, I don't know who he's going to stay with, I don't know if he's going to break up with his wife or fiancée, or what he's going to do. I've got no idea. I haven't spoken to him."

This was a whiplash change. For half her life, Gloria had been content to play second, third, or fourth fiddle behind Sergio's girlfriends, wives, and teenage targets. She'd been summoned from the basement for sex on demand while Sergio was married to Mary Boquitas, and she'd nursed Sergio's infant daughter while he was impregnating other young women in the room next door. Despite all that, Gloria had always defended El Maestro as the helpless victim of both scheming women and his own passionate heart.

Until now.

Of course, it's no surprise that even a disciple like Gloria would feel her devotion to Sergio draining fast while she was caring for a newborn in a cement cell and he was off romancing yet another woman. And it wasn't like Silvia was keeping her love affair a secret. In her campaign to free Sergio, she'd tried to humanize him by staging a little media blitz. "He's so incredibly romantic," Silvia gushed in one interview. "He has the most sensual, magical hands, and when he speaks about love, he knows what he's talking about."

To me, she'd said: "He has such a sense of humor! Do you know what he wanted to call his book? Either *The Sultan of Copacabana*, or *How to Make Women Your Slaves, from an Expert*." Correctly reading my appalled silence, she hurried to explain. "See, he really has a Brazilian sense of humor and a great head for marketing!"

Silvia erupted with laughter, then quieted. "But I don't think that plays very well in Mexico. That has always been Sergio's problem—he's too brilliant for many people to understand."

But as much as Silvia and Sergio might have gotten under Gloria's skin, they may have played only a small part in her sudden change of heart. Because behind the scenes, an invisible someone else was in the process of rocking Gloria's world.

While Gloria was locked up in Brazil, a lawyer named Armando Gómez who lived in her hometown reached out to her mother, Gloria Ruiz. Armando asked if there was any legal work he could do to help.

Not now, Gloria Ruiz replied. Not while she's in Brazil. The big challenge we're facing is getting ready cash while she's in prison.

Well, maybe they could help each other out, Armando said (or words to that effect). Does Gloria have any songs she'd be willing to share, for whatever price Gloria Ruiz felt was fair? Because did he mention he was a singer, too?

They quickly struck a rights deal for two of Gloria's songs. It's unclear whether Armando happened to mention that besides Lawyer and Crooner, he had two additional titles: Money Smuggler and Wanted Fugitive.

A few years earlier, Armando was caught trying to cross from Texas into Mexico with nearly half a million dollars stashed in his car and was arrested on charges of money smuggling. He was released on bond and quickly skedaddled back to Mexico, relinquishing the seized cash and never returning to the U.S. for trial.

But despite an arrest warrant hanging over his head, Armando quickly progressed from a caring-neighbor-and-aspiring-singer to Gloria's attorney of record in Mexico. And once he came onboard, things began to move fast. Gloria abruptly agreed to return to Chihuahua, and soon an investigating judge was appointed to bring Gloria and Mary to trial. Karina and Aline gave sworn statements, as did their parents and other clan girls, but Armando was confident.

"Don't worry," he promised Gloria during a jailhouse visit. "I'm not leaving here without you."

He kept his word. Before the first witness was called, the judge announced he had something to say. He'd reviewed the three-hundred-page case file, he said, plus the mountains of horrific accounts from the clan girls, the firsthand testimony of their parents, the description of the near-fatal abandonment of Karina's baby in Madrid, the depositions of teenagers impregnated by Sergio while Gloria and Mary were their caretakers, the lies Gloria had told on national TV, the consciousness of guilt displayed by months on the run and years battling extradition—he'd read all that, the judge said, and he'd come to a conclusion:

Not enough evidence for trial. Case dismissed.

Gloria and Mary Boquitas were free to go.

Sergio must have been ecstatic.

He'd exhausted all his appeals in Brazil and was finally sent back to Mexico, but now his prospects were looking better. After all, he faced the same charges as Gloria, on the same evidence, from the same witnesses, before the same judge, so he ought to get the same swift exoneration. But there was one difference: Sergio wasn't represented by an attorney who'd fallen in love with him and had a history of moving huge amounts of illicit cash. Sergio was stunned to learn that although there wasn't enough evidence against Gloria for her to be put on trial, apparently there was plenty against him, even though he and Gloria were often in the same room at the same time with the same young women who were making the same accusations.

Sergio's trial was short and mostly invisible. It was unclear how many of the clan girls were willing to testify, and rather than air their accounts in open court, the judge questioned them privately. The entire proceeding was over in less than a week, and the verdict came fast: Sergio was found guilty of rape, kidnapping, and corruption of minors and sentenced to eight years in prison.

Considering the charges it was a sweetheart sentence, but it only got sweeter. The judge offered Sergio a deal—the kind of deal, one might speculate, that a wealthy man would get in a country where the judiciary "only works for the privileged few," as Mexican president Andrés Manuel López Obrador himself has said, and judges are appointed by powerful politicians—powerful politicians much like Sergio's big brother. Sergio was given a choice: he could serve his time behind bars like all the other rapists and kidnappers . . .

Or he could buy his freedom by paying his principal accuser, Karina Yapor, about $100,000. Sergio wrote a check, walked out of prison, and did what he has always done:

He disappeared.

46

MISS WICKED, UNCHAINED

Not Gloria, though. No way was she dropping out of sight.

Soon after Gloria's problems finally ended, Luis Medina's began. "My phone started ringing nonstop," said Luis, who at the time was just a few days out from staging the Latin Music Fan Awards in Los Angeles. "Hundreds of people were calling and asking: 'Is Gloria going to be there? Oh my God, I can't wait to see her. Is she going to sing?'"

Luis hated to tell them it was impossible. The awards are decided by popular vote, and Gloria wasn't on the ballot for obvious reasons: she hadn't recorded in years, and her only recent appearance on a Top 10 list was a police Most Wanted poster. But Luis's phone kept blowing up, and the last thing any awards director wants to do is kick off his big night by pissing off some very vocal fans.

His solution?

Simple. Make something up.

Luis announced that Gloria would receive the first-ever "Soul of the People" award (whatever that's supposed to mean). It felt a little icky to invent something just to satisfy a bunch of superfans of a woman who'd been accused of abusing other women, but by the time the awards night rolled around, Luis was glad he had. Excitement about a Gloria appearance raged with the intensity of a religious visitation: after a half decade of being entombed behind bars, the girl-power goddess was finally re-emerging. So many gawkers were expected that Luis had to double his street security and *triple* the space for satellite news trucks.

Naturally, Gloria's Second Coming wouldn't be complete without a few Gloria-style hiccups: as soon as Gloria and Armando arrived at Los Angeles Airport, police swooped in and arrested him on his outstanding warrant for money smuggling. Armando was extradited to Texas, where he would serve four months in prison.

But not even the jailing of her new fiancé could ruin Gloria's night. During her time in Chihuahua prison, she persuaded the warden to convert an unused sewing room into a sound studio. Gloria got busy writing and recording, and by her release she had an album's worth of songs. To prove to Luis Medina that she was ready to perform at the Latin Music Fan Awards, she played him a few cuts. "I was blown back in my chair," Luis gushed.

So was everyone else. Once onstage in L.A., Gloria dazzled. Even though she hadn't sung a note in public for nearly a decade, Gloria had the gowned and tuxedo-ed audience roaring and dancing in the aisles. Watching from the wings, Luis Medina had a sudden flash of insight.

"Latinos like a rebel," he said. "But we love a martyr."

Gloria drew a different conclusion.

Fancy prizes are fine, but they don't sell albums or fill arenas. As she stood on that stage in Los Angeles, Gloria realized she didn't need another Mr. Midas to stage a comeback, or even her old fans. After all, the awards ceremony was in America, not Mexico. It was Latin music fans from *north* of the border who were clamoring to see her.

"Most people thought her only strength was in her home country, but Gloria has a different game plan," I was told by Paula Kaminsky, a vice president of marketing for BMG U.S. Latin records. "First, many of her old fans are now new Americans. She appealed to the rebels, the bolder kids, and they're the ones who came over here and brought their tastes with them."

She might have a lot of image repair and fence building to do back home, where the brutality of her scandals hit closer to the heart, but America is one place where a little notoriety never hurts. And after five years of front-page allegations about torture, sex abuse, a missing infant, and a Harry Houdini–like jailhouse pregnancy, Gloria was much better known in the United States than any other time in her career.

"Curiosity is going to draw a lot of first-time buyers," Paula Kaminsky added. "But when they find out how talented she is, they're going to be hungry for more."

Gloria quickly signed with a record label, a TV studio, and an agency specializing in massive concert tours. She bought a gorgeous waterfront home in Miami, hired a personal trainer and stylist, and planned a wedding as soon as her handsome lawyer fiancé got out of jail. "If Gloria used to be an idol," predicted Juan Osorio, the legendary Mexican TV magnate, "she will now become a phenomenon."

Gloria was looking forward to a future even brighter than her teenage dreams—and leaving behind more than a dozen young women with nightmares that could last a lifetime.

Like . . .

Marlene Calderón, who was returning home after giving birth to Sergio's son in a Chihuahua prison.

Karina Yapor, who was getting to know the son she'd abandoned in Spain.

Katia de la Cuesta, who was leaving prison and reuniting with her sister, Karola, who was raising Sergio's baby son, Milton; and her other sister Karla, who was raising Sergio's daughter Valentina.

Sonia Ríos, who was raising Sergio's infant daughter.

Liliana Regueiro, who was home in Argentina and dealing with the trauma of Ana Dalai's disappearance.

Tamara Zúñiga, who was undergoing therapy in Chile.

Delia Gonzalez, who claimed Gloria had begged her not to testify against her, was back with her parents in Mexico City.

Brandy Ruiz, who was talking to police in Texas.

And Wendy Castelo, who was trying to find work as a teenage single mom while raising Sergio's daughter, Maria Mel.

As for Sergio: he was reportedly finding his way back into the business—

By opening a music school for children.

47

JANE DOE 1 AND JANE DOE 2

My radar went to red alert before I was halfway through the email. It arrived on August 21, 2024, and began like this:

> Dear Chris,
> I hope this message finds you well.
> I am writing to inquire if you have followed up on the Gloria Trevi case or would be interested in doing so . . .

I hadn't written a word about Gloria in twenty years. So why, out of the blue, was some stranger contacting me after all this time about picking up her story again? I could make a pretty good guess.

On December 31, 2022, with hours to spare, two women filed a lawsuit in Los Angeles just before the expiration of a three-year "Lookback Window" for child sexual abuse. Lookback Windows are special statutes created to fix a broken system. Most states have a rule that says if you were sexually abused as a child, you must speak up within two, six, or ten years (depending on the state). If you were molested in

Georgia on your sixth birthday, for instance, and you told your parents the day after you turned eight, then too bad: you missed your chance to hold your predator accountable in a civil case. Likewise in Georgia, if you're one day older than twenty-three, no matter when the abuse happened, you can no longer sue your abuser.

For predators, these laws are fantastic. Their victims are typically groomed to obey and keep quiet, so it can take a long time for them to process the trauma and even realize they've been abused. They may need years more to get past the shame and confusion and stop blaming themselves—and by then, the statute of limitations has long expired. If you'd care to guess at what age most child abuse victims come forward, you'd be wrong. It's not within ten, twenty, or even thirty years.

On average, they're fifty-two years old.

Fortunately, the #MeToo movement and investigations into the epidemic of molestation by Catholic priests has inched some states closer to ending these predator-friendly statutes. In 2019, California took a step by suspending the statute of limitations for three years: any victim who'd been too late to report their abuse could now have another chance.

And so, in the closing hours of New Year's Eve, *Doe v. Doe* was filed in Los Angeles. No names were used, but the description left no doubt who was involved. The purported victims were "a 15-year-old child" and "a 13-year-old child" who said they'd been targeted by "a famous producer" and "a famous and popular pop star, and one of the most highly compensated female artists in Latin America" and coerced into "sexual contact with them over a course of years."

Sergio, however, didn't live long enough to face his accusers. By the time attorneys were dispatched to serve Sergio with the lawsuit, he was dead.

Or so he'd have us believe. News outlets in Mexico had

begun receiving anonymous reports saying Sergio had died while undergoing a surgical procedure in Spain. True enough, official documents verified Sergio had arrived in the country and checked into a private hospital—but where was his body? The California judge presiding over the lawsuit wasn't buying it. "It's clear the parties are making substantial efforts to locate and serve Mr. Andrade Sanchez, who may be in Mexico or may be in Spain," said Judge Jared Moses of Pasadena, as he issued a request for Mexico's Ministry of Foreign Affairs to hunt down its fugitive son. "He mysteriously appeared in some medical facility in Madrid, and then seemingly disappeared after that."

For Gloria, this finger of blame from the past had to be a shock. In the twenty years since she first stepped out of prison and on to the stage of the Latin Music Fan Awards, she's been an absolute juggernaut. She's sold a staggering 25 million albums, racked up 6 million social media followers, and packs so many concert halls that in 2022 she ranked #5 in the world among touring artists, right behind Madonna and Tina Fey. In 2025, she was honored with the Hispanic Heritage Legend Award, joining an elite class of past recipients including U.S. Supreme Court Justice Sonia Sotomayor, Gloria Estefan, and Martin Sheen.

Not that her new life was all platinum records and applause. Gloria's post-prison era still featured some of the bizarre escapades that have always seemed to swirl around her. In 2010, Gloria's mother was due for a tax hearing in Mexico but never appeared, popping up instead in Texas. Before she could be extradited, she vanished again. However, an alert runway worker in Panama recognized her from an Interpol alert as she was exiting a private plane. Gloria Ruiz was apprehended, but after being flown back to Mexico, she clammed up and refused to say anything about the $2 million she was accused of concealing. She spent seven months in federal prison before Gloria finally managed to get her freed on bail.

A few months later, it was Gloria's husband's turn to disappear. On October 6, 2011, Gloria and Armando were having dinner with friends in Monterrey. After Gloria went home, Armando stayed out for a last drink—and wasn't seen again. Gloria got word that a band of armed men had snatched Armando off the street and hustled him into a darkened car. Gloria reportedly received a threatening demand for ransom and paid it.

Three days later, Armando was safely returned. In a weird twist, one of the kidnappers was later revealed to be a former pro soccer player, a beloved goalkeeper who'd fallen on hard times and is now doing seventy-five years in prison. Whether Armando had some previous connections to the criminals, and why they snatched him instead of his much more famous wife, was never revealed. But a few years later, Armando's family was targeted again: his thirty-eight-year-old brother, Gerardo, was gunned down on the streets of Mission, Texas. One of the suspects, a convicted drug dealer, was arrested, while the other fled to Mexico and was never apprehended.

Through it all, Gloria was undaunted. Unlike her mentor, she wasn't going to hide this time. She was going to hit back—and hard.

Before the *Jane Doe* lawsuit was even filed, Gloria was already locked in a bitter defamation fight with her old nemesis, Pati Chapoy. Pati had made some unflattering comments about Gloria and Armando on a radio broadcast in Mexico, but because the signal had accidentally strayed into U.S. airspace and could be picked up by a few borderlands listeners in Texas, Gloria was going after Pati in America with such determination that the case was traveling all the way to the U.S. Supreme Court.

Gloria refused to back off, even though the lawsuit threatened to inform her new fans about a past they might not have known. "I think she did the damage to herself," Pati would say. "Five crimes were reported. Five crimes of rape, child trafficking, kidnapping, corruption of minors, forced labor. That's what I documented."

Gloria was just as forceful against the two Jane Does. "Being a victim of physical and sexual abuse is one of the worst things that can happen to a human being. I say it, and I know it, because I am a survivor. And my thoughts go out to anyone who, like me, has ever been the victim of any kind of abuse," Gloria wrote on Instagram. "But I will not remain silent while I am unfairly accused of crimes I did not commit. These false accusations, which were first made against me more than 25 years ago, have been tried in various courts and, in all instances, I have been completely and totally acquitted."

She hired celebrity attorney Camille M. Vasquez, who rose to fame with such a punishing cross-examination of Johnny Depp's ex-wife, Amber Heard, that it secured victory for Depp in his defamation lawsuit. Camille's roster of A-list clients also includes Ben Affleck, Jennifer Lopez, and Leonardo DiCaprio.

But even for a battle-hardened litigator like her, something about Gloria's case seemed to stick in her throat—if only for a moment. During a Spanish-language interview, Camille is crisp and vigorous in her defense of Gloria until the reporter asks this question:

"What do you think is behind this lawsuit?"

Camille seems to freeze, lost in thought. Then, as if speaking to herself, she can be heard murmuring in English, "That's a tricky question."

Not for her male partner, though. Overlooking any qualms about potentially badmouthing two women who may truly have been harmed, Camille's fellow attorney instantly comes to her rescue. "We think they want money," he says in Spanish. "And also, perhaps, a conspiracy to defame Gloria. She has enemies."

And in court, they came out blazing. Gloria's attorneys hit the two Jane Does with a stunning cross-complaint, claiming that if anyone was guilty of a cover-up, it was the girls. After all, these two young women admitted they were in the room when Sergio was abusing people. And one of those people was Gloria. And neither of the Jane Does did anything to stop it. So aren't they liable because they helped Sergio "perpetuate the abuse"?

The thirteen-year-old and the fifteen-year-old, in other words, should have somehow stepped up and shielded the wealthy adult celebrity from her own manager. "Ms. Trevi was his true star—and, thus, the girl he most needed and wanted to dominate and control," her lawsuit states. "Instead of living the lifestyle of the rich and famous that one might expect of the 'Mexican Madonna,' Ms. Trevi, in private, was often dressed in old rags, sometimes forced to sleep naked for days on a cold bathroom floor." This poor, sad Cinderella version doesn't bear much resemblance to the Gloria I met in Brazil. She was a multimillionaire in her mid-thirties at the time who refused to call herself a victim of anything except the justice system and expressed nothing but praise for the man whose child she was carrying for the second time and scorn for the girls she was now saying should have protected her. Back then, Gloria didn't say, "Yes, those poor girls were beaten and abused just like I was." Instead, she called them all greedy liars.

I wanted to hear directly from Gloria what she had to say about this, but my attempts to reach her through her publicists went unanswered. Still, Gloria would always find a way to be heard. She recently launched a TV series called *Ellas Soy Yo*—

"I Am Them." In it, she depicts herself as Victim #1 of Sergio's abuse, exactly as her lawyers in Brazil had hoped she would many years ago. Watching the show is like seeing Gloria's legal argument acted out in living color, with each episode clawing back all those decades of praise she lavished on Sergio and recasting herself not as his longtime lover, business partner, and media representative but as just another bewildered clan member.

"Once these young girls and women had been drawn into his sphere by dreams of stardom, he subjected them to total control and sadistic abuse—mental, financial, physical, and sexual. Ms. Trevi was one of those young women," the show declared.

But one of those young women wasn't having it. Another voice emerged from Sergio and Gloria's past, and this one didn't want their money or an apology. It wanted the truth. A fiery young woman began demanding a human-rights investigation into whether there had been any fishiness behind the scenes in that Chihuahua courtroom. She was an attorney, sharp as a whip and every bit as ferocious as Gloria's legal team. One of her first moves was an audacious stroke: she petitioned Mexico's business license bureau to ban Gloria Trevi from performing as . . . Gloria Trevi. "This is a brand that's been linked to serious human-rights violations, and as such should be prohibited from profiting commercially," the young attorney argued. Any label that "promotes illegal or immoral activity" is prohibited. You can't name your hat company "Meth Heads," right? So shouldn't the same rule apply to the Trevi-Andrade clan? Her petition was denied, but the lawyer had served notice that she was coming after Gloria with every legal weapon she could find.

And her name?

Karla de la Cuesta.

48

"EVERYTHING COMES TO LIGHT"

Yes, *that* Karla de la Cuesta. The Sergio loyalist who was so devoted that she bore him a daughter, recruited her own sisters for his clan, and went to prison rather than reveal his secrets.

But after she was freed, Karla began a remarkable transformation. She returned home to live with her parents, who helped care for Karla's baby while Karla put herself back through school. As a teenage dropout who'd lived for years in the isolation of the clan bubble, Karla's basic education and knowledge of the world were woefully deficient. She had a quick mind, however, and a hunger to discover everything she'd missed out on in hiding, and in a remarkably short time she caught up enough to begin university studies. Karla went on to law school and became a human-rights attorney, driven by a desire to protect other young women from the abuse she had suffered. Despite her success at leaving her past behind, she was nagged by one guilty secret: no one had ever heard the truth about the Trevi-Andrade clan. And as long as it remained hidden, more girls were in danger of it happening again.

Karla wasn't going to rely just on her own memory to set the record straight. She went back to eleven former clan members, including two of her sisters, and compiled their first-person accounts into a book called *Todo a la Luz* ("Everything Comes to Light"). Gloria's attorneys tried to block its publication, but Karla fought back and won. Now, she's using the book as evidence in her campaign to demand accountability from the Mexican legal system about whether Sergio and Gloria had gotten special treatment. Karla's next move was to demand the release of witness testimony from Sergio's trial, much of which had been given privately and never publicly revealed. She had to battle the courts for more than a year before she finally gained access to the records. She began to read—and felt sickened and enraged.

"How is this possible?" she says. She had no idea that while she'd remained silent in defense of Sergio, many other girls had been brave enough to tell the truth. Their stories were shocking and horrific, but more importantly, *they were consistent*. "They described all the brutality they'd suffered, one after the other, and the details in many cases matched exactly," Karla says. Yet somehow, a judge listened to all these atrocities and decided Sergio deserved only a slap on the wrist and for Gloria, no punishment at all.

Well, Karla decided, maybe a human-rights court will feel otherwise. She is now spearheading a campaign for an international tribunal to step in and do what the Mexican courts wouldn't by bringing all the sexual-abuse allegations to light and forcing Gloria and Mary Boquitas to finally take the stand and testify.

"I'm through being quiet. It's time for me to speak up, and I'm ready," Karla has said. "We're talking about a case that created enormous pain for dozens of families yet has been handled so superficially, so frivolously, that it seems more like a show business joke than an enormous scandal."

Recently, Karla got some unexpected support when the Supreme Court of Justice of Mexico ruled in favor of Sasha Sokol, a former teen sensation who accused her ex-producer of sexually abusing her when Sasha was fourteen and he was thirty-nine. According to Sasha, she was a member of the children's music group Timbiriche when she was groomed by its producer, Luis de Llano. For decades, Sasha was too ashamed to tell anyone what had happened until, astonishingly, de Llano decided to address some old rumors and blamed Sasha for breaking *his* heart. "Yes, I had an affair with Sasha," he said on a video podcast. "I fell in love, and she sent me to hell. It makes me very sad that instead of talking about Sasha for what she is now, we have to talk about 'poor little girl.' It's not true."

Sasha refused to let him whitewash his behavior. She sued de Llano for child sexual abuse and demanded not only a public apology and financial compensation, but a criminal investigation. Mexico's highest court found de Llano liable for moral turpitude, and while it was not in a position to order criminal charges, its decision was hailed as a major blow against predators who'd managed to escape accountability.

"This sentence transcends by far my personal case and opens the way to civil lawsuits for other victims," Sasha declared, because a precedent had now been set that allowed victims to come forward without a statute of limitations. "At fourteen years old, I didn't have the tools to understand what was happening, let alone defend myself. Establishing the truth is the starting point for healing."

I had to believe that for Gloria, Karla and Sasha were a gathering storm of danger.

A very vocal adversary was coming after her right when Sean Combs was on trial and the Jeffrey Epstein file was front-page news. Some online commentators were already comparing Gloria to Ghislaine Maxwell, who'd gone to prison for acting as Jeffrey Epstein's confidante and recruiter. And like Ghislaine, Gloria was left alone to take the heat because Sergio remained underground—possibly literally. That's why my suspicions were on high alert as soon as that strange email arrived in my inbox. When I was a foreign correspondent for the Associated Press, my bureau chief always warned me to be suspicious of anyone volunteering information "just to help"—or that reddest of red flags: to "collaborate."

"Reporters on deadline are sitting ducks," she'd say. "You've got to file a thousand words in the next thirty minutes, you need some quotes and a source who can explain things, and you've got a boss like me breathing down your neck. You're desperate. So if some 'expert' suddenly gives you a call, watch out. Whoever they're trying to help, it's not you."

My mystery messenger claimed to be "a doctoral student in international relations" named Armando who specialized in "critical humanitarian studies, including the rescue industry as a significant issue in the fight against trafficking." And what was Armando offering?

> If you are interested in learning more about the case or would like to collaborate on any related work, I am more than willing to assist and contribute.

Because if I wasn't careful, he cautioned, I was in danger of being hoodwinked. "My intention is not to assign blame," he stressed, before doing just that. "There is a significant 'rescue industry' in Mexico and the United States that exploits trafficking victims. This industry is often led by extreme right-wing and evangelical groups, who, under the guise of religion, strip victims of their identity and exploit their stories for financial and political gain."

That's what's really going on with this lawsuit, he explained. These so-called rescuers are just as bad as the abusers; they're messing with the heads of these women and tricking them into attacking their true friends. "Many of the victims initially acknowledged her as another victim and maintained close relationships with her for years. However, they have recently changed their stance and are now attacking her," he concludes.

Like all conspiracy theories, this one lacked one key component: a motive. So why, exactly, would these alt-right weirdos and church folks decide that a smart way to push their secret agenda (whatever that was) would be to revive accusations from the past century and brainwash young women into attacking a pop star and a now-reclusive ex-convict? If Gloria truly is innocent, what was their endgame?

My volunteer expert didn't say. But a little research offered a bit of clarity: his LinkedIn page contained references to Camille M. Vasquez and her law firm. Was he actually working for Gloria's lawyers to torpedo her accusers in the press? Or was he just a fan meddling in stuff that was none of his business? Either way, it was enough for anyone to steer clear.

But where this guy saw dark forces behind the lawsuit, Gloria spotted at least one silver lining. Soon after she first heard about the lawsuit by her former clan members, she began writing a new song called "Medusa." According to the myth, Medusa was a priestess who was raped by Poseidon in Athena's temple. Athena blamed Medusa for the defilement of her sanctum and punished her by transforming her into a monster with a head full of snakes.

"We have all experienced having your story told the wrong way, being made to look like the bad guy," Gloria explained in an interview. "I was unfairly punished, but that has made me more powerful." Not just stronger—more like an unconquerable force that's nearly impossible to defeat.

Or as Gloria puts it:

"I am Medusa."

ACKNOWLEDGMENTS

Let's not forget . . .

Many people wanted this story to go away. Right from the start they had the power to protect these girls but decided to protect themselves instead, playing dumb while it was happening and remaining silent during the one brief chance for justice. Still, some did speak to me in private, and for those critical contributions, I have to say I'm grateful. My deepest respect, though, goes to the clan girls and their families. They had the most to fear and came forward nevertheless.

Without the courage of Aline Hernández, this story may never have come to light. Astonishingly, following in her footsteps is Karla de la Cuesta. Her transformation from Sergio's brainwashed stooge into a fiery legal advocate is mind-boggling, and even more remarkable when you consider she had no reason to wade back into this fight. Karla could have taken her law degree and slid quietly into a high-paying, low-profile job with no risk of embarrassment or retribution. Instead, she's revealed embarrassing details of her own involvement in the clan and now devotes herself to protecting other young women from the hell she endured. Thanks to her contributions, I discovered secrets that had been hidden for decades.

Personally, I wasn't sure I could handle this project myself. Knotting together so many years' worth of twists, timelines, and bizarre backstories was just *too much*—and that's when my daughter, Sophie McDougall, came to the rescue. Sophie had already proven her chops as a sharp and intuitive writer, and she adapted those skills for editing. She became both my higher consciousness and human external hard drive, copy-editing all 97,375 words of this manuscript and not only molding my storytelling but keeping track of the spiraling narratives. If that sounds like a crazy hard job, you're correct. It's a bear, and she did it beautifully. My only regret is that we didn't publish her side comments. We need more books with "*OMG, gross!*" and "*I love this!!*" running down the margins.

But the first to take a mighty big chance on this story was Dean Robinson when he hired me to track Gloria for *The New York Times Magazine*. Giving me a crack at that assignment was a tremendous favor, and I hope I've paid you back by shielding you till now from the knowledge of how close I came to blowing it. Luckily, Gabe the Imaginary Passport Officer materialized just in time to save our bacon before vanishing back into the mists of legend, while Craig and Elise Boyan took my desperate call from JFK and gave me a sofa for the night (once again) so I could stay on the hunt. Jodi Kantor of *The New York Times* later picked up where Dean left off, kindly bringing me back on board a few years later to chronicle Gloria's post-prison comeback.

Edward Kastenmeier, it's time for us to blow out some candles. This book marks our fifth and twentieth anniversaries: the fifth book we've done together, and twenty years nearly to the month since the first contract we signed. I still remember every detail of the first time we met, because I couldn't believe such an influential editor at Knopf Doubleday was so gracious and friendly. We've had a lot of adventures together, from shooting a burro race video in Peach Bottom, PA, to leading a fun run through Central Park, and my debt to you is immense. But we couldn't have done it on our own. Without my tough-love mentor at Inkwell Management, Richard Pine, I'm sure I would have mucked up this marriage a long time ago. Thanks as well to Eliza Rothstein, and Alexis Hurley, and everyone else at Inkwell who takes such good care of me.

Every book I've written begins and ends with the same thought: I hope it's something that Mika and Maya and Sophie, the loves of my life, will be proud of.

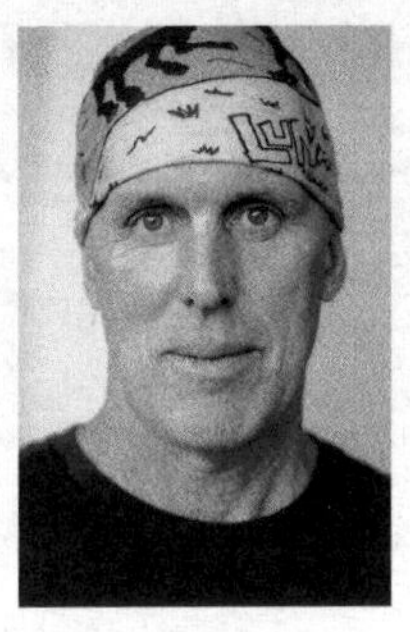

ABOUT THE AUTHOR

Christopher McDougall covered wars in Rwanda and Angola as a foreign correspondent before writing his blockbuster bestseller *Born to Run*. His fascination with human potential led to his adventure books *Running with Sherman* and *Natural Born Heroes*, as well as to an exploration of darker behavior in his first true-crime book, *Starstruck*. He's currently at work on a new project based in the shore breaks of Hawaii.

chrismcdougall.com

ALSO BY

Christopher McDougall

NATURAL BORN HEROES

Mastering the Lost Secrets of Strength amd Endurance

Christopher McDougall's journey begins with a story of remarkable athletic prowess: In the treacherous mountains of Crete, a motley band of World War II Resistance fighters—an artist, a shepherd, and a poet—abducted a German commander from the heart of the Axis occupation. To understand how, McDougall retraces their steps across the island that birthed Herakles and Odysseus, and discovers ancient techniques for endurance, sustenance, and natural movement that have been preserved in unique communities around the world. His search takes us scrambling over rooftops with a parkour crew in London, foraging for greens with a ballerina in Brooklyn, tossing heavy pieces of driftwood on a Brazilian beach with the creator of MovNat—and, finally, to our own backyards. *Natural Born Heroes* will inspire readers to unleash the extraordinary potential of the human body and climb, swim, skip, throw, and jump their way to heroic feats.

Sports/Adventure

ALSO AVAILABLE

Born to Run
Running with Sherman
AND OTHERS

VINTAGE BOOKS
Available wherever books are sold.
vintagebooks.com